THE TILTED PLAYING FIELD

THE TILTED PLAYING FIELD

Is Criminal Justice Unfair?

H. Richard Uviller

YALE UNIVERSITY PRESS   NEW HAVEN AND LONDON

Published with assistance from the
Kingsley Trust Association Publication Fund
established by the Scroll and Key Society of Yale College.

Designed by Rebecca Gibb. Set in Adobe Garamond and Univers types by Keystone
Typesetting, Inc., Orwigsburg, Pennsylvania. Printed in the United States of America.

Library of Congress Cataloging-in-Publication Data
Uviller, H. Richard.
The tilted playing field : is criminal justice unfair? /
H. Richard Uviller.
      p.   cm.
Includes index.
ISBN 0-300-07584-7 (cloth : alk. paper)
1. Discrimination in criminal justice administration—United
States.   2. Criminal justice, Administration of—Moral and ethical
aspects—United States.   I. Title.
HV9950.U85   1999
364'.089'00973—dc21   98-46459

A catalogue record for this book is available from the British Library.

The paper in this book meets the guidelines for permanence and durability of the
Committee on Production Guidelines for Book Longevity of the Council on Library
Resources.

10 9 8 7 6 5 4 3 2 1

To my esteemed colleagues on the Columbia University law faculty, and especially to my close friends among them. For almost thirty years I have felt privileged to be in this company. They have taught me to appreciate the rare beauty of a good idea, well expressed.

CONTENTS

Acknowledgments ix

Introduction: Metaphorically Speaking 1

1. Level Playing Fields and the Idea of Fairness 7

2. Discretion and the Advantage of Initiation: Choosing a Target,

Bringing a Charge 32

3. Access to Information, First- and Secondhand:

You Are What You Know 73

4. Voucher and the Virtue of Office: The White-Hat Factor 113

5. Burdens and Presumptions: Rescue from the Quandary of Perhaps 141

6. The Blessing of Bankroll: Financial Disparity and the Riddle of Bail 162

7. Excluding Adverse Evidence: Truth or Justice? 189

8. Appealability and the Ordeal of Jeopardy: Capitalization of Error 216

9. Truth Telling and the Limits of Ethical License:

Counsel's Tolerable Deceptions 236

10. Jury Irrationality and Its Insulation:

Arousing the Unimpeachable Impulse 255

11. Summary: The Fair Tilt 279

Conclusion, if any 305

Index 309

ACKNOWLEDGMENTS

I AM DEEPLY INDEBTED to my excellent and learned colleagues Debra Livingston and Jerry Lynch for the extremely helpful criticism they offered on a draft I thought was in pretty good shape. My thanks, too, to Mary Davis and Harlan Levy for their contributions. I was blessed with a student research assistant, Liz Small, whose diligent, resourceful, and intelligent work added much to the legal authenticity of the book. Let me also express appreciation to my good-humored style editor (in this and my prior book, *Virtual Justice*), Dan Heaton, who has gently persuaded me to clean up my syntax on more occasions than I care to admit. But over and beyond all else, my gratitude goes to my beloved wife, Rena, for her unstinting support, her love and confidence, and for more than a few insights into how things really work in this peculiar world of criminal justice.

THE TILTED PLAYING FIELD

INTRODUCTION

Metaphorically Speaking

THE PROCESS WE HAVE DEVISED for accusing and trying our suspected criminals attracts enormous public attention. Why this rather dull, sordid business has become daily top-story newsfare and an inexhaustible resource for print and pixel fiction is not immediately apparent. When I first heard that a television channel planned to broadcast continuous live coverage of trials "gavel to gavel," I saw boredom rolling in like a San Francisco fog. Having had some firsthand experience with the tedium of criminal trials in real time, I couldn't imagine a rapt audience. "Like watching paint dry," is the way a trial judge I know puts it. Yet there it is: *Court TV* still offers its unleavened daily diet of courtroom fare. Not to be outdone, the evening news takes advantage of the new tolerance of cameras in courtrooms to beam us snippets of this trial or that almost every day, and the fiction mill grinds on.

The phenomenon cries for a metaphor to describe it. What is actually going on—at least what can be seen by dropping in at your local courthouse—can hardly explain the popular obsession with the criminal trial. Calling it "law in action" (which it is, after all) offers no clue to its drawing power. Law is "in action" in too many other ways that attract no public attention whatever. The workings of the administrative structure that rules so much of our everyday life in this highly regulated state, for example, has no noticeable appeal, except perhaps as a cure for insomnia. Corporate mergers and acquisitions, with their complex financial, tax, and antitrust aspects, fascinate legions of lawyers—and few others. True, underlying every criminal trial is a crime story, and crime stories are endlessly engrossing. But crime stories, real and fictional, can be told—and are told—as *crime* stories, not as *trial* stories. From a literary standpoint, the trial is actually a rather awkward way to tell the story of the crime behind it. But the trial provides its own story, has its own plot, characters, suspense, and resolution quite independent of the events with which it is concerned. And it is the popularity of the trial story, as such, that interests me here.

The metaphor that most readily suggests itself is theater. *Drama* is the word most commonly associated with courtrooms. The trial is undeniably staged, in a literal sense. The set—familiar, solemn, ceremonious as a church—is constructed for performance "in the round" to an audience: the public and their delegates, the jury. The judge, the lawyers, even the witnesses appear to be playing roles, acting their parts in the unfolding story. And, most important, the play has a plot. The plot is always the same: justice. Justice done or justice denied. But it is a great plot.

Ever since the demise of the medieval morality play, ever since the invention of the humanistic society, we have craved some highly structured enactment of the great conflict between good and evil, a secular presentation of the ancient Christian struggle between the forces of light and darkness. Here battle is done in the name of virtue and social order against the unbridled beast in us all. Here we can witness the triumph of communitarian values over greed, lust, brutality, and corruption. Or, occasionally, the vindication of the innocent caught in the toils of calumny and false witnessing. This is high drama—and with a particularly urgent message. If the criminal trial does not assure the preservation of a virtuous community, at least it constitutes the reassertion of its basic tenets of respect for the persons and property of others. If its proclaimed moral message is not subtly nuanced, at least it is often and earnestly voiced.

There's no getting away from it: the American criminal trial is theater. And as such, it converts easily to fiction while serving admirably as a broadcast medium for its own storyline. And with the excitement generated by theatrical representations, we should be grateful that the old gray and twisted trunk turns out to be so fruitful. We certainly cannot reject altogether the dramatic virtues of the criminal justice system nor the enlightenment of the theatrical metaphor.

Yet attractive as it is, the theatrical metaphor does not completely cover the way we think of the courtroom confrontation or explain our enduring fascination. What's missing is the central feature of our adversary process: that our system of adjudication *is* confrontation. Not only confrontation in the way that characters or themes conflict in theater, but the clash of adversaries each seeking victory—a test of skill, agility, strength, one-on-one. Real stakes, the ultimate outcome unknown. So the sports metaphor is inescapable. Sometimes the imagery shades into its darker counterpart: battle. After all, someone nearly always "wins" at a trial, and news reporters like to inform us along the way that one side or another has "scored points" or "won the day." Though who represents good and who evil is not always clear, and differing views of the matter may divide the viewing public and perhaps the jury, it is clear throughout that the trial is a polarized conflict. In criminal cases in particular, there are only two sides and they are, in virtually all things (save the process itself), opposed. This is a "match" if ever we saw one.

One commentator, Professor Barbara Babcock, came right out and adopted the sports metaphor to make her point. "In the following pages," she wrote, "I use the metaphor of the sporting event as an analytical tool. I do not embark on this course unadvisedly or lightly, nor in derogation of criminal trials as deadly serious business, but in the belief that the concepts of fair play in sports and due process in criminal trials are in fact united. We have taken the notion of fair play from its native habitat in the world of games and sports and applied it directly to our legal procedures."

Our sports ethic demands that a contest be "fair." Of course, free of the metaphorical shackles, the law itself requires that a trial be "fair." Due process, a constitutional imperative, may be paraphrased as "a fair trial." Nor is the concept a dead letter. Only recently, the United States Supreme Court, striking down a conviction for first-degree murder, ruled that the law of Oklahoma, by allowing a person to be put to trial though he was more likely than not mentally incompetent, violated "fundamental fairness" and hence, due process. As you can imagine, considerable judicial ink has been spilled on the meaning of that term—all without much reference to what would be "fair" on an athletic field. Yet fairness is largely in the perception of it, and Barbara Babcock is right: the sports metaphor has, to a significant extent, affected how we feel about the fairness of the criminal trial.

For one thing, contestants in a sporting event should be evenly matched. We like a close outcome, and if one track athlete can run circles around her adversaries, we think the meet was "unfair." In some matchings, like horseracing, we handicap the stronger animal to put the outcome of the race in doubt. A "fair fight" is the sports ideal, a contest between combatants neither of whom enjoys an undue advantage over the other.

In the same way, some commentators seem to think the fairness of a criminal trial can be improved by balancing the comparative advantages of the parties. Thus Supreme Court Justice William Brennan, in a speech he gave in 1963, said, "Justice is indeed served when prosecution and defense are fairly evenly matched." Along these lines, some years ago, the Supreme Court decreed that since the prosecution is represented by a lawyer in court at all stages of every case no matter how trivial, defendants are entitled to no less. And in several jurisdictions today, the access defendants enjoy to the prosecution's files is balanced by requiring them to yield to prosecution discovery. What's sauce for the goose . . .

In 1960 a scholar named Abraham Goldstein published an article that has become the point of reference for this conception of fairness. "The Balance of Advantage," he called it, and he calculated that the prosecution was the favored party. More recently, other academic commentators have taken a reading and concluded that, despite the great expansion of defendants' rights during the sixties and seventies, the balance still tipped in favor of the prosecution. How can we have due process, they demanded, unless we can construct a level playing field? Bringing the oft-cited Goldstein thesis up to date, Professor Bennett Gershman in 1992 compiled a long list demonstrating what he called "the vast accretion of prosecutorial power" over the previous twenty years. "This transformation," he concluded, "has resulted in a radical skewing of the balance of advantage in the criminal justice system in favor of the state."

I think these writers express the concerns of many Americans when they look at our system of criminal justice and ask, "Is it fair?" Of course, in the general populace we can probably find more than a few who would dispute Gershman's bottom line. But the source of discontent is the same, a perception that the respective empowerment of the parties is "skewed," that the playing field is tilted.

The more sophisticated among scholars and practitioners dismiss the idea that justice requires an equal distribution of power between adversaries, preferring to consider the success of our criminal justice system either in terms of the truth of the verdicts produced, sensitivity to abuse of authority, or civic approval ratings. And we will, of course, take this enlightened path as we consider the meaning of fairness in the world of criminal law enforcement and the vindication of the innocent. We will abandon common parlance in due course and discover that the balance we seek is a far more subtle construct than a simple level field, which can be obtained by trimming or matching the perceived edge enjoyed by one contestant or the other at a sporting event.

My plan is to take up and consider several basic claims that one side or the other enjoys an advantage in the investigation or trial of a criminal case. Disparities, where found, will then be measured and weighed to determine their congruence with a communal sense of fairness in public law. Various authors have constructed catalogues of this sort, and I have probably failed to do full justice to their cherished lists. I have, rather, taken a few of the basic claims of both sides by which the idea can be fairly captured and analyzed—and added a few of my own devising. But it is decidedly not my object to go over their calculations, to tote up anew the advantages and disadvantages. Fear not, I am not headed to the boring conclusion that the playing field is indeed tilted one way or the other in this respect or that.

It is, rather, my thesis that the whole idea that fairness in a criminal trial depends upon a literal balance of advantage is an unfortunate metaphorical transposition, and that we should have a closer look at what we mean by a fair trial within our adversary model.

1

LEVEL PLAYING FIELDS AND THE IDEA OF FAIRNESS

THE CHIEF GRIEVANCE HARBORED by most folk, I suspect, is that somehow they did not get their due. Even among my friends and colleagues—privileged by any standard—many feel underappreciated, perhaps ignored, by the fates and their peers. And so many people from all classes of society describe themselves, in one way or another, as victims of "the system," a system that rewards the insider, the hustler, and the charlatan (always somebody else, of course) while it rejects—if, indeed, it does not actually oppress—the worthy, the diligent, and the virtuous. The attitude is, we hear, the bitter dregs of unrealistic expectations, the legacy of liberalism. We have been taught by our political philosophy (as well as our mothers) that we are each just as good as everyone else and hence entitled to the same good life as the most fortunate among us.

Maybe we do suffer in the grim shadow of the egalitarian myth. And the law must surely bear some responsibility for spreading it. "Equal Justice Under Law" is chiseled on courthouse pediments and on the consciousness of all Americans. But to many, it is a cruel hoax. The grievance of disappointed expectation nourishes the belief that, far from enhancing the dignity of individual sovereignty, our liberal democracy today imposes—or fails to relieve—diverse unfair deprivations.

Political cynicism (only one of the pernicious by-products of the grievance construct) is turned by many sufferers on the delivery of criminal justice. "It's like everything else, you only get what you pay for," runs one popular homily. "Are you kidding? Racism is endemic. Just look at the disproportion of blacks in prisons." "Judges? Politicians in robes." "Don't be naive, you think the Supreme Court doesn't read the newspapers?" "We're in serious trouble if we have to put our confidence in the credibility of a cop." "Trials? Games lawyers play. Games of mutual deceit masked by contrived shows of sincerity." There's some truth in all these charming bromides. But the theme—usually sung by those who have had little personal experience in the justice system—is clear: law is just another social institution that is basically unfair.

In spite of its popularity, the attitude rubs against the social grain. All of us, cynics along with the rest, want very much to believe that courtroom justice—unlike life in general—is fair. The corruption of the ideal of fairness is particularly loathsome when it is evident in the processes of law, and especially the most visible, urgent business of criminal trials. There's not much left to believe in, but we desperately want to put our faith in the fairness of our system of criminal adjudication. Courts are the last flower of government to claim our optimism. And the sharply projected criminal trial is inevitably the last testing of our liberal democratic credo.

But what do we mean by *fair* in this context?

There are essentially two ways the law—or perhaps any one of us—looks at fairness: fairness born of the symmetry of the dialectic process and fairness born of experience and contemplation of the eternal verities. In the first, the idea is that the law should do no more than provide a forum, a referee, and an orderly process of contention. What is fair is what emerges from the free interaction of the competing interests of the parties in a neutral arena. This conception of fairness is reinforced by the sports metaphor. It appeals to a common cultural heritage of sportsmanship. And it is hardly the only manifestation of our process-oriented understanding of fairness. Equal opportunities in education, fair employment, dismantled glass ceilings in the professions, and a host of other vital values of our society express our faith in justice as an evenhanded guarantor of a playing field on which contestants may compete unencumbered by extraneous disabilities.

The other conception is more positive: fairness is the conscientious judgment of immersed and thoughtful people as to how the interests of both parties are best served. In this view of it, some inequalities are tolerated in the interest of other values. In the larger world it may be seen in various manifestations, from the graduated income tax to fire trucks and ambulances speeding through red lights. In our sphere of interest, we might conclude that because the hazard of convicting an innocent person is so repugnant, the prosecutor should bear the burden of proof. It's not an even distribution of risks, but, most of us would probably agree, it is fair.

The two ideas are nicely presented in the doctrine of *waivability*.

At least once during a course I teach on the law of evidence, I ask my class just what is the Law of Evidence? They get two choices. Is it, I ask, a set of rules that the parties can assert anytime they wish, but inactive until asserted? Or are the rules "law" that governs the conduct of a trial regardless of the wishes of the parties? Can the parties rewrite the rule against hearsay, for example, simply by declining to object to a piece of excludable hearsay offered by adverse counsel? Are the rules of evidence waivable at will or are they enforceable as our considered, collective effort at fairness?

Until recently, my best resolution of this conundrum was to report that trial judges differ. Some will rarely, if ever, exclude proffered evidence in the absence of objection; others will regularly say "objection sustained" though no objection was heard from counsel. Still others follow an erratic course, leaving it to counsel until the offense to the rules of evidence gets intolerable.

Then, in 1995, to my surprise, the Supreme Court took a swipe at the question. At issue in *United States v. Mezzanatto* was Rule 410 in the Federal Rules of Evidence, which provides that statements made by a defendant to a prosecutor on the way to a guilty plea are not admissible against him if the plea bargaining should come to naught. The obvious purpose of the rule is to encourage plea bargaining by assuring the criminal defendant that he need have no fears of prejudicing his case if the negotiation falls through. Unless you are a dedicated opponent of plea bargaining—the prevailing system of disposing of criminal cases in our great nation—it's a sensible rule.

In the Supreme Court's customary brisk, dispassionate tone, Justice Clarence Thomas told the story of the *Mezzanatto* case:

> On August 1, 1991, San Diego Narcotics Task Force agents arrested Gordon Shuster after discovering a methamphetamine laboratory at his residence in Rainbow, California. Shuster agreed to cooperate with the agents, and a few hours after his arrest he placed a call to respondent's [Gary Mezzanatto's] pager. When respondent returned the call, Shuster told him that a friend wanted to purchase a pound of methamphetamine for $13,000. Shuster arranged to meet respondent later that day.
>
> At their meeting, Shuster introduced an undercover officer as his "friend." The officer asked respondent if he had "brought the stuff with him," and respondent told the officer it was in his car. The two proceeded to the car, where respon-

dent produced a brown paper package containing approximately one pound of methamphetamine. Respondent then presented a glass pipe (later found to contain methamphetamine residue) and asked the officer if he wanted to take a "hit." The officer indicated that he would first get Mezzanatto the money; as the officer left the car, he gave a prearranged arrest signal. Mezzanatto was arrested and charged with possession of methamphetamine with intent to distribute. . . .

On October 17, 1991, respondent and his attorney asked to meet with the prosecutor to discuss the possibility of cooperating with the Government. The prosecutor agreed to meet later that day. At the beginning of the meeting, the prosecutor informed respondent that he had no obligation to talk, but that if he wanted to cooperate he would have to be completely truthful. As a condition to proceeding with the discussion, the prosecutor indicated that respondent would have to agree that any statements he made during the meeting could be used to impeach any contradictory testimony he might give at trial if the case proceeded that far. Respondent conferred with his counsel and agreed to proceed under the prosecutor's terms.

Respondent then admitted knowing that the package he had attempted to sell to the undercover police officer contained methamphetamine, but insisted that he had dealt only in "ounce" quantities of methamphetamine prior to his arrest. Initially, respondent also claimed that he was acting merely as a broker for Shuster and did not know that Shuster was manufacturing methamphetamine at his residence, but he later conceded that he knew about Shuster's laboratory. Respondent attempted to minimize his role in Shuster's operation by claiming that he had not visited Shuster's residence for at least a week before his arrest. At this point, the Government confronted respondent with surveillance evidence showing that his car was on Shuster's property the day before the arrest, and terminated the meeting on the basis of respondent's failure to provide completely truthful information.

Respondent eventually was tried on the methamphetamine charge and took the stand in his own defense. He maintained that he was not involved in methamphetamine trafficking and that he had thought Shuster used his home laboratory to manufacture plastic explosives for the CIA. He also denied knowing that the package he delivered to the undercover officer contained methamphetamine. Over defense counsel's objection, the prosecutor cross-examined respondent about the inconsistent statements he had made during the October 17 meeting. Respondent denied having made certain statements, and the prosecutor called one of the agents who had attended the meeting to recount the prior statements. The jury found respondent guilty, and the District Court sentenced him to 170 months in prison.

The problem in *Mezzanatto* arose because federal prosecutors routinely insist on "terms" whenever a defendant offers to furnish information against others in exchange for leniency. Rule 410 is not really addressed to ordinary plea bargaining. In the usual case, defendants don't talk to prosecutors; that's what they have lawyers for. But in the occasional case, where a defendant wants to cut a deal for himself by spilling the beans on a buddy, he may find himself sweating on a worn leather chair in the prosecutor's office, his lawyer sitting silently by, as the prosecutor invites him to tell the whole story, from the beginning. The whole story may put our hero's neck in the noose. Can't I just leave out the part that would really cook my goose if this thing should ever go to trial? What if my deal falls apart, I'm sunk. (There's no shortage of tropes to describe the plight.) Rule 410 replies, not to worry. This conversation you are about to have is so important to the system that we will encourage full disclosure by promising that whatever you say will not be used against you in any way if you should ever come to trial on the matter. A special little privilege specially crafted for a very special situation.

Of course, the prosecutor does not have to enter into such a negotiation merely because a desperate defendant offers his assistance. Before the office will consider such cooperation, the Assistant United States Attorney usually gets a hint from defense counsel of what help can be expected. The prosecutor may reject the overture, deciding that the offer comes from a bigger fish than the criminal who might be inculpated by his assistance. He might decide that the highly biased testimony of the wannabe stool trying to buy his way out of heavy time will be hard for the jury to believe, and corroborative evidence is nowhere in sight. For any number of reasons, the prosecutor has unilateral authority to accept or reject the offer. Just why the prosecutors in *Mezzanatto* decided to deal with Gary Mezzanatto in the first place when they already had Shuster, the lab man, who had given them Gary, the salesman, does not appear from the Court's decision and is left to our imagination. Perhaps prosecutors are, by nature, optimists, and they figured Gary just might give them a great case against an even bigger fish.

If the prosecutor thinks the offer is worth exploring, she spells out the deal (usually in writing): no promises, no bargained-for reduction in sentence, just a report of the extent and value of the cooperation to the court for such consideration as the judge deems appropriate. It's not much, but it's all an ill-positioned defendant can hope for. From the defendant, the prosecutors demand candor above all. They will not believe—and they certainly will not ask a jury to believe—their defendant-cum-witness's accusations against others if the accuser is not truthful about his own criminal trespasses. (This was the standard stipulation that Gary Mezzanatto flunked.)

In addition, the prosecutors will typically require their snitch to waive a portion of his right under Rule 410 of the Rules of Evidence to exclude the self-inculpatory evidence given during these face-to-face, exploratory interviews if, for some reason, the plea arrangement fizzles and the defendant/witness goes to trial. These "queen for a day" agreements stipulate that whatever the would-be witness, the queen, says of her own criminal complicity will not be used directly against her at trial (thus recapitulating the promise of Rule 410). But they also provide that the day of grace does not prevent prosecutors from using the statements as leads to other incriminating evidence or using them at trial to impeach the queen—now the defendant—should she be so improvident as to testify to a version of the facts different from that tendered to the prosecutors. To this extent, the contract requires the queen to waive protections to which she is entitled under the law of evidence: the option to testify free of impeachment by statements given during a failed plea negotiation. Whether she is entitled by law to freedom from the fruits of her statements to the prosecutor (other evidence learned of or found by virtue of the queen's disclosures) is still somewhat unclear. Few courts have addressed the question, but the indications are that fruits are not excluded by Rule 410.

There's nothing sinister or oppressive about the agreement. The feds see it as a device to help keep their informant—whose reliability is not generally of the highest grade—diligently cooperative. Once the criminal has fully and candidly described her crimes, the thought is, cold feet will be warmed by the knowledge that, facing trial, she cannot diverge from the inculpatory account she furnished to the prosecutor. I can't really blame prosecutors for setting these conditions for those who want to play the game; anyone who doesn't like it can dive back into the tank and get the trial she or he deserves, no hard feelings. I do not even pause to dispose of any lame contention that this contract offers an undeserved "advantage" to the prosecution.

The issue in the *Mezzanatto* case was simple: could Gary Mezzanatto waive the "privilege" that Rule 410 had constructed for his benefit, or was the rule an expression of policy for the general good of the system and beyond the control of any particular defendant? While it might be argued that all privileges can be relinquished by the party benefited (or else they are not *privileges* but *obligations*), it might also be claimed that Rule 410 omits mention of waiver for a good reason: if allowed, prosecutors would, as a term of any cooperation contract, routinely exact a waiver—extending, ultimately, to the direct use as well as the impeachment use of statements to the prosecutors. The government could thereby effectively nullify the congressional policy expressed by the law. (In fact, it is my impression this has already happened in many places [though it has not been loudly proclaimed].) It's a classic case of the broader question: does litigation law exist wholly for the benefit of the parties, to be remade at will, or is it expressive of a more immutable policy enforceable by the court despite the will of the parties?

The Ninth Circuit Court of Appeal had taken the latter view in Mezzanatto's case. Law is law. Seven of the nine justices of the Supreme Court disagreed. Justice Thomas, in the opinion signed by most of his colleagues, quotes a decision 125 years old and repeats: "A party may waive any provision, either of a contract or of a statute, intended for his benefit." Thus, provisions like Rule 410 are not immutable, the Court holds. And they recite a host of diverse provisions that have been held likewise waivable. At least in this context, then, there is no substantive fairness; what's fair is what works for the parties in the particular circumstances. A negotiated rule, fairly arrived at, is as fair as a legislated rule.

Nonetheless, the Court agreed that not everything may be waived. "There may be some evidentiary provisions," Justice Thomas wrote, "that are so fundamental to the reliability of the fact-finding process that they may never be waived without irreparably discredit[ing] the federal courts." In searching for examples, Thomas resorted to one cited earlier by a lower court: "No doubt there are limits to waiver," the Court of Appeal for the Seventh Circuit had conceded; "if the parties stipulated to trial by 12 orangutans the defendant's conviction would be invalid notwithstanding his consent, because some minimum of civilized procedure is required by community feeling regardless of what the defendant wants or is willing to accept." Justice Thomas's resort to the ludicrous only illustrates how difficult it is to come up with some sensible baseline standards of unwaivable fairness.

In its broader scope, the Court's resolution of the *Mezzanatto* dilemma appears to reject the concept of litigation law as legislated fairness. The overtones of the decision suggest that, within generous bounds, fairness is in the hands of the participants. All the law has done is provide the playing field on which they exercise their choices. Ordinarily, benefits they willingly relinquish are, for that reason, not essential to a fair trial. Obviously, this is a Type A conception of fairness: if the parties are free and comparably empowered, their elections—the *processes* of the encounter—dictate the contours of fairness. Therefore, to ensure justice, all we need do is put the parties in equally endowed opposition and let them hammer it out. The contours of fairness are whatever emerges from that forge.

In part because of forgivable reluctance to enter the murky realms of positive fairness, one is drawn gratefully to this pure process approach, the Type A fairness. No hard questions about irreducible core values. Just the purportedly neutral faith in the fair, free market of process. Agonistic parity. Maintain that, and the product will be greeted as fair.

Of course, no one who thinks about it for more than a moment would argue that agonistic parity means complete, perfect, literal equality of resources or prerogatives. Surely, in the criminal context, we do not believe that whatever one party may do, the other must be allowed to do the same. That way lies absurdity. What we must mean is balanced empowerment, the allocation of respective prerogatives appropriate to the different roles of prosecution and defense in criminal litigation. Each is entitled to what best serves the peculiar functions of each in the business of bringing a criminal case to a just conclusion. Not "equal," perhaps, but "appropriate."

If we thought that by electing Type A fairness we could leave all the hard choices to the free "market," pounding out perfect fairness in the competition of litigation, we are quickly brought to our senses. There is no free market, only a market structured by our choices regarding the appropriate distribution of prerogatives. Loping off down the path of procedural balance, we soon stumble over the insight that the job of maintaining appropriate parity is fraught with value judgment. Should the prosecutor have the burden of proof on all issues? Should the prosecutor have exclusive powers of court-sanctioned, intrusive investigation? Should the defendant have the right to decline to testify without adverse inference? Should defense counsel be free of any obligation to promote an accurate verdict? Such questions bring us unwillingly back to the sticky examination of just what the respective roles of the contending parties are, and what prerogatives are appropriate to them.

In addition, what you consider the appropriate balance of forces may depend, in large measure, on whether you view the question from the perspective of the innocent accused, the guilty accused, the persuaded prosecutor, or whether you (like me) still insist that the primary function of a criminal trial is to separate the guilty from the innocent with the highest degree of accuracy consistent with some few overarching public values. I grant you—as all my tribe must—we are still confronted with the task of identifying those "overarching public values." And pursuing that inquiry, we will quickly find ourselves down on our knees, prospecting for transcendental nuggets. But I fear there's no escape. Even those of us who reject the criminal process as a vehicle for righting social wrongs, even those of us who believe that the Constitution is not offended by the conviction of a guilty person though he is poor, talkative, and not too shrewd concerning his own best interests, we find we must explore the purposes of the functions that we would like to consider essentially neutral.

To our dismay, we discover that pure process is not the whole story. We seek escape by insisting that the constraints on the truth-seeking function of a trial must be few, clear, and essential to the basic tenets of our liberal democracy. But you don't have to be a dedicated Realist to spot the weakness in that protestation. Somebody's preferences are going to have a big part in drawing up that list of the essential basics.

In the chapters ahead, I shall describe what I consider the principal areas in which it might be argued that one side or the other is unfairly disadvantaged. In each, it might be said that the law has failed to maintain agonistic parity between the parties to assure that the contest will be fair (and the verity of the result suffers accordingly). In most cases, I will respond by insisting (temperately) that inequality is not necessarily a mark of unfairness. I will attempt to lead the discussion away from that friendly, familiar, facile metaphor, the sporting event, and into the darker realms of Type B fairness: role-determined, purpose-enhancing entitlements. In that murky mode, I shall attempt to assess claims of unfairness.

For, though I am a devoted process person, I can't allow the fairness of the criminal justice system to be appraised in terms of a clash of well-matched forces on a level playing field. For one thing, we can't ignore the indisputable fact that there are one-sided advantages—perhaps many and substantial—that are not only tolerable but valued components of a fair system of adjudication. The presumption of innocence and the burden of proof are prominent examples. I much prefer the more drab version of the fairness principle: neither side should have an advantage that is not rationally based on the sound principles of the enterprise. I admit that, to be put to use, my good gray precept—Type B fairness—requires a bit of assembly. First, you must identify (and class as sound) the governing principles of criminal adjudication. Then, you must assess the rationality of the connection between the supposed advantage and the principle it serves. This is a project made to order for any field-hand academic type. It may not be the exercise of choice for everyone, but it's exactly the sort of thing we do (with relish!) every day. Even Justice Thomas, though hard-pressed to articulate the principle or come up with a real example, conceded that the free market of justice is constrained by some positive elements. Whether we can recognize baseline precepts of justice more useful than the jury of apes to guide the allocation of prerogatives remains to be seen.

For the moment, let me simply argue that, much as we might like to avoid the arduous—and perhaps somewhat arbitrary—business of relating fairness to function, it is inescapable. At the top, let's acknowledge substantial differences in function. For our basic premise is that the two sides in a criminal case are not like parties to a civil litigation: two similarly situated contenders in a freely interactive world, who have come up against each other with some adverse claims and defenses.

In court, during a criminal trial, the casual observer of the customary routine might mistakenly believe that she is seeing two sides of a symmetrical form—just like the civil trial. Dressed alike, each lawyer examines witnesses, introduces exhibits, cross-examines, and argues to the court and jury. But looks are deceiving. Prosecutor and defender have virtually nothing in common with civil litigators beyond certain linguistic and sartorial conventions.

The prosecutor is a government official, an agent of the executive branch. This gives him public responsibilities while freeing him from the constraints of loyalty to any private individual. Large among those responsibilities is the sworn duty to react to evidence or suspicion of criminal conduct by investigation and, where appropriate, prosecution. The job calls for *initiation,* a careful, considered, leading move in the contest. Defense counsel is private. Even where appointed by the court, paid from the public treasury, or a servant of a public defender office, each lawyer is the private advocate of the individual client's interest. Her job is *responsive:* what is the charge? What is the supporting proof? What is our best answer?

The public prosecutor's job is essentially constructive. Constructive in the literal sense of building a structure, fitting pieces together into a coherent, plausible whole. Having brought the accusation, the prosecutor is obliged to prove it. While a good defense often involves the construction of an alternative scenario, this is not the essence of the job. Mainly, and in most cases, the defense will be bent on destruction; it will lean on weak joists of the prosecutor's structure, poke holes, rain through the roof.

Moreover, unlike the public prosecutor, the private defense bar has only occasional interest in the accuracy of the verdict. Usually, representing guilty clients, their object is quite the contrary. And normally, defense counsel has neither reason for nor interest in discovering for himself whether the client who professes innocence is actually innocent. The prosecution can be counterattacked quite as effectively by a lawyer laboring under the delusion that his client is actually innocent. And, in light of counsel's function, the true facts *should be* of little concern to the defense in most cases. They are of overriding importance to the prosecutor, in every case.

In those relatively rare instances in which the client is truly innocent, of course, defense counsel has an acute interest in an accurate verdict. And, as with the fire extinguisher, rare use does not diminish the importance of availability. We must be sure that the means are at hand for the defendant caught in the toils of a false accusation to advance the evidence of his innocence, or to demonstrate the falsity of the evidence against him. So fairness requires that all defendants have the ordnance by which some few—the innocent—can most effectively fight back. Many of these are provided by the Sixth Amendment of the Constitution: the rights to receive full notice of the charge, to confront and challenge adverse evidence, to call favorable witnesses, and to have the assistance of counsel, naming but a few. Statutes and cases grant others: the right to learn helpful evidence from the prosecutor's files, for example, or the right to consult with a psychiatrist where mental condition may become an issue. Some critics assert that the abuses of these entitlements have given unfair advantages to the guilty defendant bent only on delay and befuddlement. Others claim with matching vehemence that the defense is still overwhelmed by prosecution advantages.

I'm surveying only the surface to name a few of the most prominent differences in the topography of the territory occupied by the opposed sides in a criminal case. But it should be obvious that to talk about a "balance of advantage" as though it were a simple comparison of armament, without taking account of the differing functions of the parties, is foolish. The best way to assess fairness in these circumstances is to explore the peculiarities of the multiple roles of prosecution and defense and to consider the implements accorded by law for the accomplishment of these differing objectives. An unfair disadvantage in this scheme is a disabling impediment inappropriate to the task of the party suffering it. It is in search of these unnecessary and unwise handicaps that I pursue this project. In thus setting my course, I confess that the pitch of the playing field is important only insofar as it sets off an inquiry into the purposes served—or disserved—by the inequality.

My endeavor, I expect, will make some controversial calls. I will not be able to escape the necessity of setting markers of tolerable and intolerable exercises of authority, of virtuous and pernicious defenses. And I am sensitive to the criticism that I have dropped my buoys by my own reckoning, that channel norms that seem just and proper to me may be abhorrent to others. Sensitive, but undeterred. I have no choice. I am ill-equipped to propose any set of incontrovertible first principles and then to develop a just criminal system from them. Some intrepid jurisprudents have made attempts at such grand schemes. Bless them, the postmodern utilitarians, the secular theists, post-Marxist republicans, the gender-role feminists, the neorealist critical theorists, and the rest. I am not optimistic that a unified, value-free field theory will emerge. So to talk about the subject of fairness at all, I must risk the distortion of personal perspective.

With this acknowledgment firmly inscribed, I will, of course, make every effort to describe the struggles of prosecution and defense truly and fairly, and to judge their purposes according to fundamental tenets of criminal law enforcement, the liberal democratic ethic, the cultural norms (as I read them), and perhaps even some precepts of fairness perceived as "universal." In this challenging project, we will want to know whether the devices of investigation, publicity, argument, and the law itself enhance or diminish the likelihood that a criminal trial will "come out right" without endangering any "precious rights" of the parties concerned. Fairness, we might say, is the justice-enhancing aspect of the implement itself, modified by the way it is used. It's like getting from here to there: we find justice in having the right vehicle—a vehicle capable of traversing the distance, fueled, responsive, and sturdy enough to overcome impediments to the journey—and driving it well, conscientiously, and with educated determination.

The difficulties with this approach are obvious. By what sixth sense can we perceive the dictates of the liberal democratic ethic? What are the cultural or universal precepts of fairness? Do children everywhere protest, "But that's not fair!" when someone else gets a treat they are denied? Has everyone everywhere in all ages at some time thought it was unfair that accidents of birth should dictate their fate? And even if we could respectably hypothesize a few basic tenets, such as "likes should be treated alike" and "punishment only for behavior previously defined as wrong" and "judgment without fear or favor," could we derive an entire, complex mechanism for the delivery of criminal judgments from a few such stripped down premises?

Perhaps this is the place where I should insert an apologetic disclaimer. There are surely many people who detect a pervasive toxin that subverts fairness at every stage of the criminal justice system, and that factor is racism. To these observers, it is virtually impossible to discuss criminal justice in America without talking about race. They see the taint in the cop's decision to stop a car and question the driver (are young black men more frequently stopped, and routinely asked to get out while the trooper peers into the interior of the car?). The critics perceive differential zeal of investigation (is the black-on-white rape more vigorously pursued than black-on-black?) and read racism in the legislative allocation of punishments (why is possession of crack cocaine—used mostly by African Americans—so much more heavily punished by federal law than powder cocaine—used by whites too?). Race, they say, accounts for disparities in the punishment of violent and economic crimes, and especially the selection of cases for imposition of the death penalty. The claim is made that the minority races and ethnic subgroups are routinely, systemically, unfairly oppressed by the system. To these commentators, courtroom fairness is an arid abstraction in a profoundly unfair society. Even such a thoughtful and moderate commentator as Professor Randall Kennedy has concluded, "Racial bigotry has been and remains a significant pollutant within the administration of criminal justice."

Actually, the claim that racial considerations unduly influenced death sentences was pressed in the United States Supreme Court where, in 1987, it almost carried the day. Warren McCleskey, a black man, was convicted in 1978 in Georgia of murder for killing a white police officer during a store robbery. The jury, considering mitigating and aggravating factors in the penalty phase, as required by law, recommended death, the judge followed their recommendation, and the state courts affirmed. Seeking review in federal court, McCleskey argued that capital sentencing was racially discriminatory in Georgia. The argument relied upon a famous statistical report, called the Baldus Study, that examined more than two thousand murder cases in Georgia during the 1970s and concluded that black defendants who had killed white victims were far more likely to get the death penalty than any other racial combination.

Justice Powell, writing for a bare majority of five, held that neither the Baldus Study nor any other evidence indicated that the purpose of the system of capital sentencing in Georgia was discriminatory. Merely by showing that others similarly situated did not suffer a death sentence does not prove McCleskey's sentence was "wanton or freakish," "arbitrary or capricious," or imposed on the basis of unlawful racial prejudice. Each jury decision, concerning a unique individual, predicated on desirably flexible discretion, must be taken on its own merits. Thus the appropriateness of any given death sentence cannot be judged by comparison with others which may have been influenced by various, unknown, and particular factors. Collective judgments, moreover, colored by individual experience, are often difficult to explain.

Perhaps most interesting—and provocative—in the majority opinion in *McCleskey v. Kemp* is the Court's recognition that sentencing disparities that correlate with race "are an inevitable part of our criminal justice system." The Court cites several ways they have attempted to minimize the pernicious race factor in the system. But realistically, such discrepancies must be tolerated because no system can be entirely free of "imperfection." "Where the discretion that is fundamental to our criminal process is involved," Justice Powell wrote, "we decline to assume that what is unexplained is invidious. In light of the safeguards designed to minimize racial bias in the process, the fundamental value of the jury trial in our criminal justice system, and the benefits that discretion provides to criminal defendants, we hold that the Baldus study does not demonstrate a constitutionally significant risk of racial bias affecting the Georgia capital sentencing process."

Notwithstanding such good authority that—at least in the many discretionary aspects of the criminal justice system—race counts, I do not, in these pages, examine the impact of race on fairness. Race is an enormous and enormously complex, invisible, and largely ineradicable parameter of the process. And I know little about it. I cannot answer the most troublesome questions with any confidence. Apart from the capital punishment question, I cannot account for the indisputable fact that blacks and Hispanics are grossly overrepresented in our prison population. I have little to offer on the deeply disturbing association of certain elements of our society with violent crime, or the response of prosecution agencies and courts to their prominence. To the extent that criminal law enforcement is in fact disproportionately directed at members of minority races, beyond what is demanded by their disproportionate involvement in particularly pernicious crime, it goes without saying that the system suffers from inexcusable and intolerable unfairness. If I had set out to learn the answer to this important question, or to describe the ways in which it is and is not true, or to account for my discoveries in terms of social pathologies, I would be writing a different book. I am thankful that others who have wrestled long and hard with this intractable subject have published their thoughts, notably Professor Randall Kennedy in *Race, Crime, and the Law* (Pantheon, 1997).

As for my own project, I can only leave this possibly distorting element in a shadowy configuration. If racial bias permeates the system and the way we think about it, I have necessarily put it on hold as I discuss other sources of unfairness. Perhaps, even if I tried, there is little I could say to the reader who finds the race factor overwhelming. For me, racism is like luck, aura, and mendacity—a grievously deforming factor, the distribution and prevalence of which is largely random and unknowable. Failure to purge these wild cards of unfairness, however, does not detract from the effort to identify and analyze other endemic, systemic features that some might characterize as unfair.

In law, as already noted, fairness in the process of criminal justice is found in the concept of due process. The Constitution, in two places, expresses the stern injunction that there will be no adjudication of guilt except by due process of law: once in the Fifth Amendment, directed to the federal government, and again in the Fourteenth, directed to state trials. As one might imagine, considerable discussion of the origin of the term and its core meaning has enlivened the pages of scholarly journals. Although there is some uncertainty, it appears to derive from Magna Carta in the early thirteenth century and the precept there written that criminal judgments must be according to "the law of the land."

In current jurisprudence, the term *due process of law* is read as "basic fairness." The Supreme Court opinion spelling out the content of the concept most candidly and fully is probably that great old classic from the pen of Justice Felix Frankfurter called *Rochin v. United States*. Reciting from the trial record, here's how Frankfurter told the story:

> Having some information that [Rochin] was selling narcotics, three deputy sheriffs of the County of Los Angeles, on the morning of July 1, 1949, made for the two-story dwelling house in which Rochin lived with his mother, common-law wife, brothers and sisters. Finding the outside door open, they entered and then forced open the door to Rochin's room on the second floor. Inside they found petitioner sitting partly dressed on the side of the bed, upon which his wife was lying. On a night stand beside the bed the deputies spied two cap-

sules. When asked "Whose stuff is this?" Rochin seized the capsules and put them in his mouth. A struggle ensued, in the course of which the three officers jumped upon him and attempted to extract the capsules. The force they applied proved unavailing against Rochin's resistance. He was handcuffed and taken to a hospital. At the direction of one of the officers a doctor forced an emetic solution through a tube into Rochin's stomach against his will. This "stomach pumping" produced vomiting. In the vomited matter were found two capsules which proved to contain morphine.

Although Justice Frankfurter would have dearly loved to exclude the evidence as the product of an unlawful search and seizure, in 1952 the Fourth Amendment exclusionary rule was not yet applicable to the states. His only way of condemning the crude tactics of the LAPD was to find that they violated due process. He had to find a denial of fundamental fairness. Still, he was sensitive to the charge that the Constitution must be more than a reflection of the sensibilities of a particularly squeamish Court. Here's how he went about it.

First, citing prior authority and disclaiming any disrespect for state proceedings, he explains the objective basis for the concept of due process:

> Regard for the requirements of the Due Process Clause inescapably imposes upon this Court an exercise of judgment upon the whole course of the proceedings (resulting in a conviction) in order to ascertain whether they offend those canons of decency and fairness which express the notions of justice of English-speaking peoples even toward those charged with the most heinous offenses. These standards of justice are not authoritatively formulated anywhere as though they were specifics. Due process of law is a summarized constitutional guarantee of respect for those personal immunities which, as Mr.

Justice Cardozo twice wrote for the Court, are "so rooted in the traditions and conscience of our people as to be ranked as fundamental," or are "implicit in the concept of ordered liberty."

How generations of law students have chortled over those eloquent phrases! Only the canons of decency of English-speakers count? And how do Frankfurter & Company presume to recognize the dictates of conscience of an entire people? The particulars of the concept of ordered liberty? Are the justices of the Supreme Court in some special correspondence with the divine lawgiver? Are the first ten amendments to the U.S. Constitution some form of the holy decalogue, returning our nation from enlightened rationalism to Natural Law? Frankfurter anticipated the retort:

> The Court's function in the observance of this settled conception of the Due Process Clause does not leave us without adequate guides in subjecting State criminal procedures to constitutional judgment. In dealing not with the machinery of government but with human rights, the absence of formal exactitude, or want of fixity of meaning, is not an unusual or even regrettable attribute of constitutional provisions. . . .
>
> The vague contours of the Due Process Clause do not leave judges at large. We may not draw on our merely personal and private notions and disregard the limits that bind judges in their judicial function. Even though the concept of due process of law is not final and fixed, these limits are derived from considerations that are fused in the whole nature of our judicial process. These are considerations deeply rooted in reason and in the compelling traditions of the legal profession. The Due Process Clause places upon this Court the duty of exercising a judgment, within the narrow confines of judicial power in reviewing State convictions, upon interests of society pushing in opposite directions.

Due process of law thus conceived is not to be derided as resort to a revival of "natural law." . . . To practice the requisite detachment and to achieve sufficient objectivity no doubt demands of judges the habit of self-discipline and self-criticism, incertitude that one's own views are incontestable and alert tolerance toward views not shared. But these are precisely the presuppositions of our judicial process. They are precisely the qualities society has a right to expect from those entrusted with ultimate judicial power. . . .

Applying these general considerations to the circumstances of the present case, we are compelled to conclude that the proceedings by which this conviction was obtained do more than offend some fastidious squeamishness or private sentimentalism about combating crime too energetically. This is conduct that shocks the conscience.

So there it is, spelled out with disarming candor. We have not returned to natural law. But our judges, to discern the dictates of fundamental fairness, must be an ascetic, priestly class with a mystical connection to contemporary currents of social imperative. Vintage Frankfurter. And who is to say he was wrong? How else can we make a legal principle of the inchoate reaction of people sharing the same ethical heritage? We do need a special group, schooled in tradition and forswearing purely personal preference, to inform us when we have—perhaps with the best of intentions—transgressed the bounds of cultural tolerance.

For those who thought they could discover the configurations of fundamental fairness by watching the cases as they came down from this specially endowed tribunal, the pickings were lean. We did learn a few years after *Rochin* that, while the stomach pump shocked the conscience of English-speaking people, forcible extraction of blood to learn whether an automobile driver was inebriated was, at worst, an offense to fastidious squeamishness. Between that case and Justice Thomas's twelve good orangutans and true there was precious little instruction from the Court on the mapping of the canons of decency and fairness.

The most we should expect from the Supreme Court, of course, is an occasional tip that some specific event in a prosecution went beyond the pale of tolerance. It happens rarely. Now that we have nearly the full array of specific injunctions of the Bill of Rights applicable to states as well as the feds, there is little work left for the due process clause. Thus, when some states used juries of fewer than twelve or accepted verdicts of conviction from a jury that was less than unanimous, the Court did not need to consult the vague contours of due process but could assess tolerance under the more specific guarantee of trial by "jury" in the Sixth Amendment. When police tricked a murder suspect into leading them to the victim's body in a snowy field in Iowa, the Court could condemn the ploy as a violation of the right to counsel. When southern white sheriffs without a warrant ransacked the rural farmhouse of a elderly black woman looking for the murder weapon used by her nephew, the Court called it "unlawful search and seizure in violation of the Fourth Amendment."

Due process under the Fifth and Fourteenth became a fail-safe provision reserved largely for the truly outrageous cases. As such, it is not our best guide to the dictates of fairness; various procedures may be unfair in the sense of unwise or unduly restrictive without amounting to an offense to due process, without denying *fundamental fairness* to a defendant. It might be unfair, for example, to try a defendant without affording him and his lawyer an opportunity to review the statement he gave to the police at the time of his arrest. But denying him access to that evidence in advance would probably not shock Frankfurter's English-speaking conscience.

We are, then, returned to our own instincts. Fashioning principle from inclination is a daunting—to say nothing of risky—undertaking. But there is no escape, we cannot flee to the illusory safety of a simple process-enhancing alternative.

I would much rather be the groundskeeper, responsible only for maintaining a smooth and level playing field with no concern for the outcome of the games played upon it. But we all know there is more to it than that. The hard question of substantive fairness cannot be avoided. So we may as well plunge right in.

$$\left(\begin{array}{c}2\end{array}\right)$$

DISCRETION AND THE ADVANTAGE OF INITIATION

Choosing a Target, Bringing a Charge

THERE IS VERY LIKELY some real advantage to being cast in the responsive role. It is often easier to parry than to thrust. Once the decision is made to do legal battle on a particular field over a chosen set of issues, the defender may find himself in a good position to deflect the charge. A variety of tactics offer defensive zing, including self-righteous scorn ("This whole trumped up charge is nothing but a cheap political shot"), the security of a presumption-fortified position ("You *say* I did it, but you'll never be able to *prove* it"), counter-attack by accusation of ill-motive or human frailty ("She never got a good look at the perp, and I have been identified only because of racial stereotyping"), or (most effective) the accumulated errors and omissions of the attacking forces ("How can you believe police officers who were so careless in gathering and preserving evidence?" "The official version has changed twice since this cop made out his first report at the scene." "Sure, he says I was involved; that testimony was bought and paid for by the deal he made with the government in his own case." "Would any cautious person ever rely on a forensic result from a lab as sloppy as this one?").

But there is undoubtedly a substantial advantage in being the one to decide—and to decide without interference from anyone else—which case should be developed and pursued to trial. Particularly where the prosecutor can select a target from a variety of lawbreakers, focus investigatory energy on it, name the most vulnerable or notorious actor as principal defendant, perhaps induce cooperation from lesser but also vulnerable players, frame charges that are most readily proved, and then hold off filing until the investigation has sewed up all the loose strands; in cases like that the advantage is with the party who calls the shots. And in most American jurisdictions this advantage is compounded by broad license to try several defendants together—or several different charges against a single defendant. Talk about synergy! And in our system, this choice—the power to bring, compose, and consolidate criminal charges—is traditionally an executive prerogative. Subject to minimal check by a judge or a group of citizens sitting as a grand jury, the prosecutor decides what to investigate, whom to charge, with what crime, and often when and where to bring the case.

The question that engages us here is whether this one-sided power of initiation amounts to unfairness in the system. To Professor Bennett Gershman, writing in 1992, the answer is clear:

> Commentators have described the prosecutor's discretion as potentially "lawless," "tyrannical," and "most dangerous." The prosecutor carries out his charging function independent from the judiciary. A prosecutor cannot be compelled to bring charges, or to terminate them. A private citizen has no standing to bring a criminal complaint if the prosecutor decides not to prosecute. And the judiciary has shown a remarkable passivity when asked to review the prosecutor's charging decisions.

Indeed, some courts have deferred absolutely to the prosecutor's discretion, even though that decision has been shown to be demonstrably unfair. Thus, overcharging crimes, discriminating against defendants for prosecution, improper joinder of charges or parties, vindictiveness, coercive dismissals, plea bargaining abuses, and immunity violations, continue to occur regularly, without meaningful judicial review or correction.

It's certainly true that charging decisions are, in the main, discretionary (which is just another way of saying there is no "meaningful judicial review" if Gershman meant by that close and regular supervision by a court). But I am dubious about the claim that vindictiveness, coercion, abuses, violations, and other improprieties in the charging process are not subject to concerned review by a judge. Also, whether abuses occur regularly (by which I assume Gershman means frequently) is another matter, difficult to prove or disprove, depending largely on whose courtroom stories you listen to—and how much credit you accord the storyteller. But apart from these problems with the assertion, the question it raises should be addressed: does the exclusive, unreviewable, executive power to initiate charges betoken some inherent and unfair imbalance in the American system? To approach an answer, we should look more closely at the process of accusation, the prosecutor's role, and possible challenges that might be made to keep the exercise of the prosecutorial prerogative within the bounds of fairness.

To begin, we must recognize that many—most—crimes come into the local prosecutor's ken by an arrest. The choice, if any, to prosecute was made initially by a line officer. In some few cases, police discretion in this decision is openly acknowledged, though even in the most notorious of these situations—domestic disputes—police are increasingly under orders to make the arrest automatically. That's the official line anyway.

In fact, if pressed, cops will tell you that in many cases of various grades the arrest is far from automatic. Of course, arrests for serious crime at the scene, by chase-and-capture, or following an incriminating statement rarely invite discretionary forbearance. But I have had detectives tell me that they would not make an arrest on a face-to-face robbery if the victim told them she was "75 percent sure" that the suspect she saw in a lineup was the robber. Their "90 percent or better" rule can be found nowhere in the law. And for minor crimes and offenses, street discretion is a central feature of policing. Losers in barroom brawls can be encouraged to "press charges" or—if it's late in the tour, you don't need the overtime, or the case is equivocal—discouraged. A person who waves a beer bottle and shouts insults on a street corner might be arrested for "attempted assault" or "disorderly conduct," or simply told to cool it and sober up. A man who stuck his hand in a woman's handbag might be arrested for grand larceny "from the person" (a felony) or "jostling" (a minor offense). Angry words in a dispute over a parking place can be sorted out by tin-badge diplomacy or can result in a motorist in handcuffs charged with "resisting arrest," "menacing," or "obstructing" an officer. For the innumerable petty offenses that are increasingly drawing the attention of urban police policymakers—noise, public drinking, graffiti defacement, urinating or sleeping in public places, hanging out, soliciting, panhandling—for all those neighborhood-destructive activities, discretion is the buzzword.

Zero tolerance is a term one hears today to announce a policy now gaining prominence: police will treat many minor, "quality-of-life" offenses seriously. Zero tolerance implies no option to overlook. But a police force of letter-of-the-law automatons is hardly the desirable troop to enhance community well-being. We need thoughtful, human, compassionate peacekeepers—wise discretion behind the badge. Long and learned articles are being written on the troublesome question of how to encourage situational responses without inviting arbitrary enforcement. Underlying the issue is the evident fact that, in those many cases in which the executive prerogative of initiating a criminal prosecution resides with line officers—and, for many good crime-deterrent and community-enhancement reasons, we wish it to be thus—discretion should be guided by some sort of "rule of law" to keep police decisionmaking fair.

Even with the cases, serious and trivial, frequently thrust upon local prosecutors by police response to the street commerce of crime and disorder, the decision of whether to take the case forward and, if so, in what configuration, resides with the prosecutor in the exercise of second-level discretion. Should the case be prosecuted as a felony or a misdemeanor? Perhaps it should be tossed outright as an improvident collar. Or maybe a more serious crime lurks beneath the surface of a routine arrest. Are there accomplices who might be discovered by further investigation? Should several participants be joined as codefendants? Is there another side to this story that should be checked out? Maybe the first defendant can become a useful witness in a case against others? Where the prosecutor decides to go with the case is his call.

That's most cases. When the case is one of those numerically few but substantively important prosecutions, state or federal, that are begun from scratch by the prosecutor, the elements of choice multiply and the prosecutor's authority to initiate prosecution becomes a major factor in shaping the case to come. These are the prosecutions for complex conspiracies, major frauds and other financial crimes, political corruption, drug smuggling, or racketeering. Often invisible, frequently without an individual victim to complain, these major cases would go unnoticed by the criminal justice system without the interest, energy, and perseverance of the prosecutorial agencies. Protracted investigation, multiple choice points, and options of all sorts are the hallmarks of these prosecutions. The special prerogatives of the public prosecutor are most vivid in the development of these special cases.

Almost anything can spark the interest of an alert prosecutor: an item in the news about the mysterious collapse of a recently constructed concrete overpass; a bit in testimony at a legislative hearing about kickbacks to unions in the food trades; a merchant's comment about gang intimidation; a locker-room gripe about prevalent payoffs to inspectors in the building industry; the report of a prison snitch concerning smuggling of contraband with the connivance of the guards. Virtually anything. All the prosecutor has to do is call in an assistant and a couple of agents and say, "Have a look." As soon as a witness is located or a couple of documents are turned up—something to confirm mere hunch—the assistant will probably decide to put the case into a grand jury. It costs nothing, it may pay off big. Enlisting the grand jury in the case is easy. Bring a witness in, swear him, and have him say hello—the case is "before" the grand jury.

Instantly, the investigation is jacked up a wide notch. The prosecutor now has subpoena power. The subpoena comes in two shapes. The *subpoena duces tecum* calls for the production of documents. Secret books and records are opened to the unfriendly inspection of the prosecutor and staff on little more than a direction to produce them. The *subpoena ad testificandum* calls a witness before the grand jury. And with subpoena power comes not only the authority to compel attendance and testimony from reluctant witnesses but (in the name of the grand jury) the power to confer immunity.

Along with espionage, immunity is the prosecutor's most important investigative tool. The grant of immunity overrides the assertion of the Fifth Amendment privilege of silence. It is the only legal device by which the reluctant witness can be forced to answer questions—and on penalty of perjury. In exchange, the immunized witnesses receive a binding promise that neither what they say nor things learned from their testimony will be used against them in any criminal prosecution. "Use immunity," it's called. There aren't many places today where witnesses get true immunity ("transactional immunity") in the sense that they are immune from future prosecution for the crime they divulge.

So now the prosecutor's assistants can call for testimony, under oath, and for the production of virtually any private documents on no more than the proverbial stroke of the pen. Unlike a search warrant, the grand jury subpoena needs no supporting affidavit of probable cause, no judicial imprimatur. Just, "We'd like to hear it or see it; so come in and tell and show—or else." Or else off to jail for contempt until you decide to comply.

As counsel to the citizens' primary investigatory panel—the ancient grand jury—the prosecutor acts without adversary and with precious little court oversight. Courts have extolled the right of the grand jury, guided by the prosecutor, to explore whatever channels look remotely promising. True, the proceedings are secret (and this secrecy shrouding the grand jury proceedings, reinforced by law, seems to be one of the few that really holds against the omnivorous press—though there always seem to be anonymous "sources close to the investigation" who leak tidbits about the underlying case). And true, too, at this stage, it's only an investigation. Still there is no denying that the authority to lead the probe is a powerful prosecutorial endowment.

At some point down the road, maybe many months down the road, the prosecutor and his staff must make a decision: do we have enough evidence of a crime here to go with? Not just sufficient to support an indictment, but enough to take the indictment to court with substantial assurance that we can prove the case beyond a reasonable doubt to a petit jury? Of the many and diverse odors to this mess we have uncovered, what crimes should we charge and against whom? This may seem a simple matter, but when the players fade in and out of the criminal scenario, when the activities are sketchy and records are scarce and equivocal, questions of blame are not always easy to answer. Late hours are spent figuring out who did what, on whose orders, with whose help, for what purpose, and just how much can be pinned on the shadowy figure who might have been at the head of the whole operation.

So choices are made. Strength of evidence, moral judgments, and (no doubt) some thought of how it will play on the evening news enter the decision. The indictment is drawn. Usually long and multi-count, the document is meticulously crafted. The conduct alleged to constitute each of the crimes charged is described in detail. And since many of the crimes recited by name and statutory definition sound a bit vague (for example, "racketeering activity," "criminal conspiracy," or "wire fraud"), the factual part of the count is important to inform the defendant just what he is accused of doing.

But there is another reason for the exacting specificity of the indictment in these cases as contrasted with the usual three-line counts in an indictment for common street crimes. The language of the filed accusation (language, nominally, originating in the grand jury's findings) will probably be the only message to the press and public of what the prosecution believes to be the case against the defendant—at least until the evidence is adduced at trial. The prosecutor and the grand jurors are bound by law not to reveal anything that happened in the grand jury. The prosecutor, moreover, is ethically commanded to keep to himself his opinions on the merits of the case. The conscientious prosecutor reads the Canons as forbidding virtually any out-of-court, pretrial, public statement on the evidence he expects to produce, the character of the accused, or the likely outcome. So the scrupulous prosecutor can have his press conference only by reading aloud the language of the filed indictment, a public document.

This press conference is, incidentally, the advantage the prosecution gets in the public forum from the specified allegations of the indictment—in effect, displaying its strongest case in the form of allegations—that gives attorneys of the defense their best excuse for standing up before the microphones to declare their clients' innocence, their outrage, and their complete confidence in ultimate vindication. It's their answer, they will say. Criminal cases, unlike civil, do not allow defendants formally to answer allegations. They can only enter a plea: guilty or not guilty. So the obligatory defense press conference serves as the elaborated reply to the charges in the indictment. If defense counsel wants immediate access to public prejudice, this is the only way he can get his detailed denial out there while the magma is hot. Ethical constraints (such as they are) are often ignored, and the only inhibition may be a tactical reluctance to tell the prosecution too much too soon.

The main difference between the assertions of the accusation and the curbside defense is that the prosecutor must stick to the factual allegations of the indictment. However detailed the story told by the counts of the indictment may be, it is more than a story. These are the allegations of accusation. They are the specific acts and intentions that the grand jury asserts make out the offense charged by the count. They are designed to notify the defense just what he is accused of, filling out the bare bones of the statutory language. The statutory definition of murder, for example, might be (as it is in New York): causing the death of another person with intent to cause the death of such person or another person. The indictment will customarily, at a minimum, inform the defendant of the county in which the crime was committed, the date, the means by which death was caused, and, probably, the name of the victim.

Not every detail must be specified in the indictment, but enough should be spelled out so a defendant charged, for example, with breaking and entering who might have committed several burglaries knows just which one he is called upon to contest. To convict, moreover, the government must prove the facts alleged in every material particular. Deviations between allegation and proof are tolerable only where the court finds them trivial to the preparation of a defense.

By contrast, the defense story, delivered before a bank of microphones on the courthouse steps, is not a binding undertaking. Counsel, if given to such oratory, can say anything. Outright (and outraged) denials, coupled perhaps with counterallegations, are de rigueur. Promises of proof, assertions of malicious prosecution, they are all just words cast, cost-free, onto the evening news screen. If any claim stands the test of trial, so much the better; if it is abandoned in favor of some more promising line of defense, no one even remembers what was said, much less calls the defense to task for shifting ground.

In addition to inviting the defense to put its counterallegations in a binding "answer," there is a simple fix for the routine cries of wounded innocence. It wouldn't take much—the canons of professional responsibility are part way there already—and it would do great service to the beleaguered guild. We might simply adjust the ethical constraints of the bar to prohibit all lawyers, acting in a professional capacity, from making any false statement to anyone about anything. Enforcement would surely be a problem, as it is with virtually all violations of the canons of ethics, but it would stand as a clear and unequivocal announcement to lawyers of collegial expectations. And who knows, in time it might come to mean as much to the practicing bar as other commonly observed tenets defining their professional stature. I know if I were in the trenches, I would welcome an excuse to tell my client, "Sorry, but I can't plead your case to the media. No fee can purchase my word—that's the law."

So the case comes to court. Many motions will be made and determined, perhaps seeds of disposition will be sown and the case may end quickly and neatly in a guilty plea (the earnest defense professions of wounded innocence forgotten). Perhaps a jury will be selected and that great glory of the American adversary system, the trial, will begin. In any case, it will be a game played on the prosecutor's chosen field, by defendants selected by the prosecution, and often at a time and place of the prosecutor's designation.

Does this one-sided advantage signal some unfairness in the process? I can read unfairness only if both of two conditions can be established. First, we would need evidence to confirm Ben Gershman's supposition of actual, frequent, and irremediable abuse of the prosecutorial prerogative. Potential for abuse will not do. Is there the opportunity for oppressive exercise of the charging decision? Sure, wherever any agency of the government has discretionary authority to take action that may destroy the lives and fortunes of selected targets, that hazard lurks. And libertarians are not the only ones who go on alert whenever they think of it. But at the same time, we know that not every allocation of power—even in a liberal democracy such as ours—can be (or should be) checked and balanced. Excessive checking yields isometric freeze. It's hard enough for the U.S. government to get anything done with its three branches busy trying to undo or supersede each other's decisions. Where action is important, we must judge responsibility by its actual exercise, not by the hypothetical tyrant in control.

In addition to evidence of abuse, I would need some convincing demonstration that sharing the charging power was both feasible and promising. The promise I would look for would be either a meaningful check on the actual abuses or some useful supplement to the exclusive authority that would pick up cases otherwise ignored.

It would be extremely difficult to establish either of these predicate conditions—and hence to demonstrate that the power of initiation as presently lodged is unfair. As to the first, there is little to add to what I have already noted. While there are surely examples of bad judgment in the decisions of whom to charge with what, which crimes to overlook, whether guilty participants should be turned into all-but-forgiven friendly witnesses, and so on, it is almost impossible to make a quantitative or systematic analysis of the errors, much less reach a conclusion on the motivation for such calls.

When it comes to redistribution of the power of commencement, we need first to consider adversary sharing, and then we will look at collegial sharing. Is it conceivable that the defense could initiate, or cause to be initiated, a criminal charge that the prosecutor has declined to bring? Imagine, for example, a case in which the defense contends that a named person other than the defendant committed the crime with which the defendant is charged. Even if some mechanism could be devised to bring the competing case before another grand jury, or a special prosecutor be inducted to bring it to trial, could we countenance the state in a position of simultaneous inconsistency, charging by two agents in adjacent courtrooms two different people with the commission of the same solo crime? A hundred other anomalies crowd the mind. The very notion of defense-initiated prosecution induces instant vertigo.

But the idea of privately instituted prosecution is not quite so weird when the victim rather than the defendant is the instigator. In the ancestral form of our criminal process, charges were brought by individuals, generally victims of the crime or others injured indirectly by it. This system of private prosecution is virtually obsolete, however, in most countries belonging to the Anglo-Norman heritage, and certainly in the United States. In constituting the modern state, we have all yielded our ancient role of vindicator to the public prosecutors, who now bring criminal accusations not in the name of the victim but in the name of us all. Calling a crime a public wrong, an injury to community rather than individual security, we have designated public officers to take full authority over criminal prosecution.

Of course, that leaves the wronged victim full recourse to the civil side of the law to win compensation for the injury done by the criminal to the victim's private interests. And—at least in those rare cases involving a wealthy defendant—the civil suit for damages is becoming a more common sequel to the criminal prosecution. In one notable example, victims' families were awarded substantial recoveries for two deaths wrongfully caused by O. J. Simpson, notwithstanding the defendant's acquittal of the same two murders.

We have become increasingly sensitive to the victim's aggrieved feelings of exclusion from the criminal process. And today the victim is regarded as more than the mere witness he was when I was prosecuting criminal cases. Thanks to a number of "victim's rights" laws enacted over the past decade, the victim is accorded a somewhat greater role in the prosecution of cases against her assailant. But it doesn't come down to much. The right to be informed, to be consulted, to make a statement in open court—far from any meaningful control. Despite the deference we now accord the wounded, we have no intention of sharing with them any of the responsibility allocated to the prosecutor. This may seem unfair to some victims who feel that the case is theirs and resent the unaccountability of the prosecutor's choices. But from a broader perspective, I think we can agree that the victim's private feelings of forgiveness or vindictiveness, while pertinent, should not control the disposition of the case. So we leave it to the tact and goodwill of the prosecutor to afford the victim the satisfaction of believing that he or she is a critical part of the prosecution "team." And in fairness, we should be content with that.

Though not much is left of the atavistic idea of private prosecution, we do have a substantial overlap between peer public prosecutors within a state, often covering the same criminal incident. Many states have local as well as state police forces, and some have more than one public agency with some prosecutorial authority. The county-bound district attorney, for example, may be displaced—at least in some cases—by the state attorney general. But as far as I can see, this dispersion of authority does little to inhibit the discretion of the primary prosecutor.

There is also the recent—and growing—overlap between state and federal prosecutors. It used to be that these two bears lived in different dens, rarely competing for the same forage. Today things are different. More and more crimes fall within the jurisdiction of both offices. Various informal accommodations are reached. Some cases are purposely assigned to the jurisdiction with the heaviest sanctions or the most accommodating rules of evidence. But often it's a simple competition, a race for the case, where the first agency on the scene takes the full responsibility for prosecution. We need not examine the competition here except to note that from it we are unlikely to derive a serious and workable inhibition of the discretion of either office. Only the other day, I read in the papers that a state prosecutor had appeared in federal court to object to the entry of a guilty plea to a federal charge on the grounds that it would interfere with a long-standing and ongoing local investigation into the same corrupt scheme.

There are, of course, some structural controls on abuses of the charging prerogative. Again, not much, perhaps, but frequently cited by the formalists. To begin with, executive officers—including, in most states, local prosecutors—are periodically up for election. If the public dislikes the way their servant has been exercising discretion, if the people think targets for prosecution have been unfairly chosen or wrongly charged, the remedy is at hand. True, abuse of authority by the regional United States Attorney may have a marginal effect, at best, in the election of the President of the United States—the appointing authority. But perhaps it is not so far-fetched to think that the President's political party will suffer to some degree for the visible excesses of the prosecutor. After all, other executive officers wield considerable discretionary authority with considerably less visibility and no accountability other than the party's periodic review by voters.

If the ballot, even in the best of democracies, is too remote to be an effective constraint on prosecutorial discretion, administrative remedies are still available. Every self-respecting government office—and prosecutors are nothing if not self-respecting—has some mechanism for integrity review. Admittedly, reliance on such internal controls is a little like relying on the bar to "police itself"; it risks the designation "naive." But for one skeptical observer, at least, this is the place to put some attention and energy to work. Let's make administrative control a serious undertaking.

Like the accreditation committees that visit law schools from time to time, ad hoc groups of senior assistants from U.S. Attorneys offices are sent on periodic inspection tours of peer offices in other parts of the country. I assume exercise of discretion is one of the items on their agenda. A great idea. In a somewhat less successful effort, some local prosecutors' offices have tried to articulate the considerations that should enter various discretionary choices: target selections, plea bargains, bestowals of immunity, and the like. Some offices also try to obtain collective judgment from within the office on some of the more difficult calls—seeking the death penalty, for example. None of these devices diminishes the discretionary authority of the office, but they do damp some of the swings in its exercise.

It's difficult to conceive of a working system of external peer or public review of the discretionary decisions of a prosecutor's office. Who would be qualified to do the reviewing? And by what standards would it be done? The only system that occurs to me is already in place: judicial oversight of prosecutorial discretion. As we have noted, discretion implies a large dose of deference in the judicial review of the executive choices. And that makes the bulk of prosecutorial charging decisions virtually unreviewable. But, significantly, it leaves the atrociously bad calls vulnerable. For asserted abuses of discretion, prosecutors remain answerable to courts. Neither peer nor public, courts are nevertheless external to the prosecutors' preserve. Most of the prosecutors' decisions surface in one way or another in court, and most prosecutors feel that they must be prepared to answer for them should a hostile adversary challenge them as abuses before a suspicious judge. Though rarely invoked, this oversight is a powerful constraint, particularly insofar as it carries the potential for public disgrace.

There's really no satisfactory answer to those who reply: we are not concerned with the offices that run on justifiable professional pride; we worry about the meanest of them, the vindictive, mendacious, corrupt, or politically ambitious. And such there surely are. About all I can say is, we are—and should be—concerned with such offices, and we should fortify such controls as we have to deter official arrogance. That may mean heightened supervisory scrutiny in the administrative mode, more generous access to judicial review of alleged abuses, and (as I shall argue) perhaps articulated standards for the discretionary decision of initiation.

Some may reply to this rather dull prescription that the construction of a trial defense appealing to the jury's sense of fair play is the best way to keep a sharp eye on executive prerogatives. Maybe there is no better forum than a courtroom to expose abuses in the charging choice. If so, then it is perfectly appropriate to allow an African-American defendant, defending against a charge of slaughtering his white former wife and a chance companion, to bring up an alleged history of racial bigotry on the part of a white officer who testified that he recovered damning evidence against the defendant. It may have little direct bearing on the issues of the case, but it does suggest that the case was brought at its inception for improper purposes. If the jury agrees, it might acquit the defendant just to teach the prosecuting authorities that the power of initiation must be dispassionately exercised. Too, a young, female bomber pilot in the air force might defend before a martial court on the ground that, although she had committed adultery and lied about it, other officers, male, had done the same thing without facing a prosecution. Again, without relieving herself of guilt, the defendant might use the forum to challenge the fairness of the decision to prosecute.

Strictly speaking, these assertions (and a host of others that might be imagined) are not defenses to the criminal charges brought. They don't really go to the issue of culpability. Rather, they are little votes of no confidence in the professional judgment of the prosecutor. Regardless of guilt, the jury in effect declares, by our verdict of not guilty we reject prosecution as an improper exercise of the discretion with which we entrusted our servant.

In this sense, I suppose, it might be said that affording the defense an attenuated basis for attacking improper prosecutorial choice balances the advantage enjoyed by the state in the initiation of criminal charges by enhancing the inducement to make these decisions fairly. It won't exactly level the field, but it might inhibit an oppressive slant. And, in fact, vehicles are waiting at the curb to carry claims of unfairness in initiation into the trials themselves.

Let's look next at a couple of real defenses. Sometimes, when a prosecutor chooses to initiate a criminal prosecution by the selection of a target—individual (his political rival's financial adviser) or generic (corruption in a poverty program administered by blacks)—the very choice may give rise to a defense of selective prosecution. We are thinking now of cases in which the interest of the prosecutor was aroused by general suspicion rather than the report of a specific crime, where no victim has come forward to raise the hue and cry. In sniffing around for traces of these all but invisible crimes, the prosecutor may employ undercover espionage agents who, in their zeal, may stimulate (rather than merely observe) the conduct later charged as the crime. Such tactics may support the defense of entrapment. The defensive responses to prosecutorial initiatives—the defenses of selective prosecution and entrapment—might be thought, then, to enhance fairness in the initiation of charges, to counteract the hazard of wanton, vindictive, or creative initiation. Do these devices offer any assurance of responsible exercise of discretion?

The defense of selective prosecution (such as it is) is predicated on a rather odd notion. Since all prosecution—and especially prosecutor-initiated prosecution—is by nature selective, how can selectivity be a defense? The idea is that where the prosecutor's reason for choosing a particular target is somehow beyond the scope of professional discretion, the resulting prosecution—regardless of the defendant's guilt—should not be allowed. A personal vendetta, racial antagonism, inappropriate political objectives, things like that might be said to transform a prosecution into an act of official oppression antithetical to the ideals of a liberal society.

You will note that I say nothing about the abuse of charging discretion from the standpoint of the likely guilt or innocence of the soon-to-be accused. That is because, at this point in the process, guilt is a marginal issue. The law says that a person should not be accused unless there is some reason to think he might be guilty. It would have to be an egregious abuse indeed for a prosecutor to charge someone without some evidence of his guilt. But we are not yet engaged in the full-scale inquiry of who actually did what to whom. That's for the trial, where the forum is equipped for intense, adversary examination of that issue. So the defense of selective prosecution cannot be asserted on the grounds that the prosecutor wrongly chose to accuse a person who was probably innocent (or not as guilty as someone else who was not charged). Rather, the defense claims that in initiating the case, the prosecutor was driven by inappropriate considerations—which, of course, might be the explanation if the prosecution was supported by only flimsy proof, but might also explain a well-founded charge.

But the law is extremely reluctant to examine the motivation behind any move that is itself perfectly legal. As a result, and despite frequent challenge, prosecutors in fact enjoy broad license. Repeated prosecutions, for example, for no better reason than the prosecutor's firm belief that the defendant is a really bad guy are usually not deemed oppressive. Jimmy Hoffa and John Gotti were both prosecuted over and over until the government finally put them away. So, too, in those rare instances where the federal Department of Justice decides to go after a person who was acquitted in a highly publicized local trial, the charge that the case was selected from all the many dubious local acquittals only because of its publicity value will probably fail.

In 1985 the Supreme Court considered a claim of selective prosecution. On July 2, 1980, the President of the United States issued a lawful proclamation directing all men born during the year 1960 to register with the Selective Service System. A number of them, including young David Alan Wayte, refused to do so. Wayte, opposed to the draft, chose to write several letters to the President and other government people identifying himself as a nonregistrant, announcing his opposition to the draft, and challenging the government to do something about it. The Selective Service, meanwhile, had adopted a policy of "passive enforcement," by which it would move only against those who flouted their noncompliance or were brought to the government's attention by others. These people Selective Service would then "beg" to register. Only if that failed would the government initiate criminal prosecution. Wayte, when the government got around to him, challenged this policy as selective prosecution that discriminated against those who exercised their constitutional right of protest. It was an ingenious argument, and he won at the trial level, where the judge dismissed the government's case against him.

Justice Powell, however, writing for the Supreme Court in *Wayte v. United States,* thought otherwise. Noting first that the decision to initiate a prosecution is generally left to the wisdom of the prosecutor, Justice Powell allowed that discretion in the matter is not "unfettered." The decision, the Court said, could not be based upon an impermissible standard, such as race, religion, or the exercise of rights. Powell went on to say that under the Constitution, a claim of selective prosecution should be treated as a claim of denial of "equal protection of the laws." Meaning, the Court explained, that Wayte had to show "both that the passive enforcement system had a discriminatory effect, and that it was motivated by a discriminatory purpose." Reviewing the operation of the passive enforcement policy, the Court concluded that there had been no discriminatory selection by the government. The Court also found no undue interference with Wayte's freedom of expression by reason of the selective enforcement policy. "Passive enforcement," they concluded, "was the only effective interim solution available to carry out the Government's compelling interest."

Obviously, the Court's reasoning does not have the reassuring rumble of inevitability. Actually, it looks downright conclusory. But it is indicative of the customary welcome accorded to claims of selective prosecution. And the Supreme Court reaffirmed *Wayte* as recently as May 1996. In a case called *United States v. Armstrong*, the Court quoted itself with approval: "In the ordinary case, 'so long as the prosecutor has probable cause to believe that the accused committed an offense defined by statute, the decision whether or not to prosecute, and what charge to file or bring before a grand jury, generally rest entirely in his discretion.'" Such discretion, the Court went on, is subject to constraints, of course. One such would be a decision to prosecute based on "an unjustifiable standard such as race, religion, or other arbitrary classification."

Actually, Armstrong was claiming just that sort of unjustifiable discrimination. Citing figures to show that, in the local district, virtually all federal prosecutions for crack cocaine were brought against African Americans, he argued impermissible selectivity. The Court, refusing to indulge the presumption that all crimes are committed by a representative distribution of all races, rejected Armstrong's contention. To sustain such a claim, they wrote, the defendant must show that "similarly situated individuals of a different race were not prosecuted." That means that for the young air force lieutenant to prevail on a selective prosecution claim, she would have to show not only that female officers were court-martialed more frequently for adultery than males but that males who had lied under oath about the nature of the relationship and disobeyed direct orders to discontinue it were not brought up on charges.

Everybody knows: selective prosecution is a long-shot defense, a very long shot. Hardly a counterweight to the power of initiation, it is simply a faint reminder that the prosecutor's choice may be challenged in court for gross and demonstrable bad faith. At the same time, it must be said that courtroom clout is not the only measure of the efficacy of a claim. The charge itself so deeply impugns prosecutorial integrity that any self-esteemed agency will exert itself to be above suspicion. The highest levels of the United States military felt called upon to deny even the hint of discriminatory prosecution of female officers. And just try even the mildest hint that a prosecutor might have considered the factor of race in indicting some poverty pimp and you'll smell the dander smoking.

Maybe we have located the defense of selective prosecution in exactly the right place. Acknowledgment that such a defense exists affirms our commitment to standards, feeble enforcement confirms that executive discretion is not easily supervised by courts. The self-protective instincts of the public agency do the rest. We want the government to know that it would be unacceptable to focus an investigation of corruption on Asian lobbyists on the basis of racial stereotyping, even if no one is prosecuted without good evidence, and particularly if a corrupt Euro agent caught in the sting would not be prosecuted as well.

At the same time, we know that we cannot have courts distracted from the business of adjudicating criminal cases to review the internal motivations and external impact of every government decision to bring a problematic case. I, for one, do not want my courtrooms tied up with the contentious pursuit of imponderable questions. Was this, the third consecutive prosecution of a Sicilian for mob-related racketeering, the manifestation of an impermissible ethnic bias on the part of some federal prosecutor? Does some government drug buster harbor a private conviction that Latinos of Central America are the major exporters of cocaine to the United States? And does that belief result in excessive concentration of prosecution energy on Spanish-speaking people? Did a Los Angeles detective express hostility to African Americans in unrelated circumstances? Insofar as abuse of fiduciary authority actually drives some maverick agent of the government to unfair selection of targets, it is best left to political and administrative remedies.

Entrapment is only slightly more effective than the defense of selective prosecution as a courtroom tool for the assurance of fairness in the charging choice. It is—as the pros say—a claim frequently made but rarely proved. In essence (in the construction persistently adhered to by the U.S. Supreme Court and most other courts and legislatures), the defense of entrapment should succeed, and conduct otherwise criminal be excused, when a jury believes that the conduct in question was performed at the inducement of a law enforcement officer by a person not otherwise disposed to such criminal behavior.

In this reading of it, the defense of entrapment is a genuine anomaly; it is the only instance in the criminal law in which the defendant's propensity to criminal conduct is a legitimate issue. Elsewhere, the law steadfastly insists that—despite all common sense and ordinary experience to the contrary—conduct may not be proved by proving that the actor had a predisposition to such conduct. Jurors may not reason (as we all do all the time): he must have done it because it's just the sort of thing a person like him would do, or she's just the sort of person who would do a thing like that. But by the prevailing notions of entrapment, only those who are not otherwise disposed to commit such a crime are entitled to the defense of excessive government stimulation. Here, propensity counts.

What this means is that when investigating police go undercover and engage with their suspect in the activities being investigated, they must take care not to persuade the target to make a criminal move that he or she would not otherwise make. In all those cases where agents pose as buyers for drugs or the armaments of war, as fences for stolen property or crooked inspectors soliciting the fix, as coconspirators in underworld commerce or clandestine terror gangs, in all those many cases, the prosecution may be lost if the agent steps over a blurry line and *creates* the crime with which the defendant is later charged, a crime the defendant himself would not have committed but for the agent's inducements.

Partly because of its queer focus on whether the particular defendant was pure at heart, the theory of the defense of entrapment is in some dispute. The prevailing judicial view of it is challenged by a chorus of academics. We see the issue not as one of the inclination of the particular target (the subjective theory) but of the acceptability of the police tactics. Excessive stimulation should be measured, we say, by its likely effect on a hypothetical person: the ordinary, moderately stubborn, average citizen not otherwise inclined to criminal behavior (an objective standard). If the agent's encouragement was so persuasive that it would have made a criminal out of virtually anyone, suckered any but the most supremely virtuous, then the police have gone too far; the government has truly created a crime in order to prosecute it.

In this view, moreover, entrapment probably should not be a "defense," an issue for the jury that, if resolved against the government, operates to cancel culpability altogether. To many academics, establishment of entrapment calls instead for exclusion of the evidence thus acquired. It would be like any other exclusionary rule by which evidence acquired by excessive zeal is kept out of the case. The sound and sensible suggestion, as I have said, has had remarkably few takers among our many American jurisdictions, each of which may have its own rule since freedom from entrapment is not a constitutional right.

It is highly frustrating. Even the members of the Supreme Court, our most impervious (to say nothing of influential) adversaries on the subject, seem to flirt with the objective idea, only to reject it. On one occasion, when they were considering the claim that government agents had supplied an ingredient without which the manufacture of a controlled drug would have been impossible, the Court hinted that someday such a case might succeed. Nothing said about subjective disposition, just too much government participation. Sounded for a moment as though they'd seen the light. But it was left at that: perhaps, maybe, someday, but not in this case.

Their most recent venture into the land of inducement and over-reaching was little more than a cry of judicial outrage at the years of persistent, deceptive, wheedling efforts by government agents to trap a fifty-six-year-old Nebraska farmer into an expression of interest in juvenile pornography. The fairest reading of the Court's reaction is a finding that the government had gone too far, exceeding tolerable limits of restraint in the investigation. Again, we wanted to shout, Bravo! At last you've got it. Actually, it sounded almost as though the Court was ready to pronounce such government tactics a violation of the constitutional right to due process as that idea was expounded by Justice Frankfurter in *Rochin*—official behavior that "shocks the conscience." In other words, the tenor of this decision is just what we academics have been clamoring for: no evidence obtained by police overreaching to the unconscionable extent that any law-abiding person would be induced to criminal conduct. But to the screech of tires rounding a sharp logical curve, the Court managed to adhere to the subjective test, holding that the farmer's inclination to commit the crime (in this case, order the photos) was itself induced by the government's encouragement. Thus he should be treated as a person, subjectively disinclined to accept the government's mail-order solicitation. So what seems neat to us academics has, as yet, eluded the good justices of the highest court who continue to insist on the doctrinally dubious maxim focused on the mind of the defendant rather than the propriety of the government's pursuit of him: no individual culpability for artificially implanted disposition to criminal behavior.

Forgive the digression. For present purposes, the gauge of entrapment matters not. By whatever measurement, on whatever theory, the defense of entrapment does not provide a meaningful check on the prosecutorial charging authority. For one thing, the power to initiate a criminal prosecution is not inhibited by the defense of entrapment simply because 99 percent of the prosecutor's initiatives are not susceptible to challenge on those grounds. And the minute fraction remaining are thrown out because of peculiar circumstances— such as the criminal inclination of the target—that have little deterrent effect on the temptation to overreach the power of initiation.

Still, the defense of entrapment serves as a valuable boundary on the authority of the state to "develop" a case against the quiet suspect. Every now and then, it is good to remind the law enforcement people that there are limits in common decency (to say nothing of the theory of culpability) on official prerogative. And the defense of entrapment, rarely successful though it be, nonetheless exerts some moderating influence on the enthusiasm of undercover agents to get the goods on their assigned quarry.

So let's face facts. The criminal justice system works best when the prosecution is energetic and resourceful in discovering subcutaneous crime and bringing powerful and evasive criminals to book. Whatever sense of security we enjoy in the protection of the law is sustained by the initiative of law enforcement agents at all levels to nudge the punitive process into action and, undeterred by all its cumbersome obstacles and frustrating defeats, to do it over and over again.

The problem is how to maintain the energy of initiation while discouraging improper motivation, how to inspire aggressive prosecution while detecting and short-circuiting abuse of authority. It's the oldest riddle in the management book, writ large here because of the importance of the enterprise and the enormity of the failures.

If curbing abuse were the only objective, it could be easily accomplished. Tie up the law enforcement agents in sufficient paperwork and administrative hassle, visit them with an occasional arbitrary, personal forfeiture (such as loss of vacation days), and you will soon have a perfectly tame—and wholly inert—band of civil servants wearing useless badges. Taxes will decline as vacant prisons are shut down and judges take early retirement. On the other hand, if aggressive prosecution is the only goal, it is almost as easy to convert the forces of law enforcement into an irresponsible gang of thugs. The neat trick is to achieve the goals of both zeal and restraint without diminishing either.

Like most people, I am worried about unbridled discretion in the hands of the prosecutor. I am suspicious of the neutrality of many of these offices; they are, after all, political, usually headed by ambitious or beholden people, and frequently staffed by the young and the inexperienced. No telling what sorts of bees are in those bonnets. But I don't see any way a court—or a competing agency—can exert any real control on the executive choice. A court can't dismiss a charge for which there is supporting evidence because the judge believes the prosecutor should have investigated or charged someone else.

But there is one notable—nay, agonizing—example of how the charging authority evolved from broad license to tight control and back to a sort of directed discretion. I mean the death penalty. Before I write the first sentence on this subject, I'm sorry I brought it up. It is extremely difficult for most people to talk or think dispassionately on this, the most troublesome of all subjects in the field of criminal law enforcement. Almost no one says a word about it who does not have a deep and conscientious commitment in favor of, or (more likely) against the extreme penalty. I think I understand the fervor, though I should probably admit that I don't share it. I find, after many years of thought, even participation in the death penalty process, that I have no strong views one way or the other on the moral issue. And just as I find my gorge rising at the mindless call for death whenever a good guy (a hero cop, a child, a beloved schoolteacher) is killed, I find myself content with a judgment of death against a man who chose to express his political anger by the deliberate slaughter of 168 innocents. Not that my strange detachment—or vacillation—on the issue gives me any advantage in writing about it; it remains just as difficult for me as for anyone else to come to grips with the core issues.

A brief report on the constitutional status of the death penalty: In the seventies, the Supreme Court handed down some very important opinions. The first, *Furman v. Georgia* (1972), held murder statutes unconstitutional where the imposition of the death penalty was either automatic or purely discretionary. Many state laws were thereby invalidated, many sentences pronounced under them were commuted. For a few years, people thought that the Court had effectively abolished the death penalty. But in 1976, in a case called *Gregg v. Georgia,* the Court corrected that impression. Where the law provides for a second proceeding for the determination of punishment (after the defendant has been found guilty), and sets forth the aggravating and mitigating factors that should guide discretion in deciding whether to impose the penalty of death, the law is constitutional. Some forty American jurisdictions currently allow for capital punishment under some variant of the permissible procedure.

In my state, New York, the newly minted capital punishment law also addresses the charging decision. Other than federal capital punishment laws, few jurisdictions have comparable provisions. In New York, the law is that no sentence of death may be imposed upon a first-degree murder conviction unless, within 120 days of indictment, the prosecutor files with the court a notice of intention to seek the death penalty. No standards or procedures have been laid down, and prosecutors' practices vary greatly from county to county. Some can hardly wait for the corpse to cool before firing off a news bulletin that they will seek the death penalty; other offices agonize while internal advisers weigh moral, political, and circumstantial considerations, and the prosecutor wrestles with his conscience.

It's an odd device (with which we have no experience since New York hasn't had a capital case yet in the post-*Furman* era). It puts exclusively into the prosecutors' hands, and within their unguided discretion, a choice normally made by the citizens assembled as a grand jury. New York, being one of the slowly dwindling number of grand jury states, still entrusts to the people the ultimate power to charge a fellow citizen with a felony—and back when I was in the prosecutor's office, that included the decision whether to charge a homicide as a capital crime. The extent to which the grand jury exercises independent judgment is open to some question. But it did seem fitting that the decision to press for death should be made by fellows. The grand jury still has the responsibility to decide whether to charge murder in its highest degree, but defers to the discretion of the prosecutor whether to pursue capital punishment.

The grand jury, by its indictment, gives notice of the facts constituting the crime, but neither it nor the prosecutor gives notice of the factors deemed aggravating enough to warrant the penalty of death. Presumably, the prosecutor takes into consideration the aggravating, along with the mitigating, factors spelled out in the statute for the guidance of the petit jury that will ultimately decide the issue. But the law is silent on whether the prosecutor's charging decision should anticipate the jury's sentencing decision. As written, the law of New York would allow the prosecutor to assign weight to the competing factors—or to deviate from them—according to some personal chart of moral navigation.

"Seeking the death penalty" in a first-degree murder case in New York is part of the charging decision, and as a wholly unstructured, unilateral, virtually unreviewable exercise of discretion, it is worrisome. Far more consonant with the customary powers of initiation would be a decision by the prosecutor in the first instance to charge the case as a capital crime, followed by a submission of that choice to the judgment of the citizens sitting as a grand jury. Virtually all the other American jurisdictions with capital punishment laws lodge the final charging authority with a neutral body, judge or grand jury. Too, the absence of standards and procedures is troublesome. Even to someone like me who has no enduring objection to the death penalty as such, the open-ended statute appears to be an invitation to arbitrary (or politically expeditious) choice. At a minimum, the law should require that to seek the death penalty, the prosecutor must be convinced that there is a substantial likelihood that a jury, weighing the factors enumerated by statute, would conclude that capital punishment was merited. And procedurally, New York (or any jurisdiction that places discretion in initiation of a capital case in the prosecutor's office) should—like the federals—make formal provision for the defendant to submit to the prosecutor, or to some special committee established by her for the purpose, evidence of factors in mitigation and to reply to alleged factors of aggravation.

I have alluded to the grand jury. Once upon a time, it was regarded as a vital check on the potentially abusive powers of initiation, a citizens' oversight commission reviewing every royal charging initiative. This Anglo-American paradigm of initiation might be contrasted with the European model. In most European systems, to this day, the method allows broad investigative powers to the initiating authorities, but puts the investigation under the supervision of a judicial figure—a magistrate of sorts. It is that supervising judge—the *juge d'instruction* as he is generally called—who has the responsibility to manage the investigation and to frame the accusation with full supporting data in a dossier prepared by him for the purpose. The trial that follows is little more than a verification before another judge of the facts set forth in the dossier. The emphasis is on thorough, unfettered, and dispassionate investigation at the outset rather than on postaccusation contention.

This inquisitorial alternative to the Anglo-American adversary system has from time to time attracted envious interest among domestic scholars. I am among them. But at the same time, I know in my bones that we are too deeply enmeshed in our own history and tradition to abandon any essential component of our own method. Not only must we live with the heritage of our own cultural development, but I think the hope of borrowing some feature of a foreign plant and grafting it onto the local variety is doomed. When the basic structure is antithetical to the engrafted feature, it will not thrive in the new host.

Those who love parallels might point out that the American plant is not as inhospitable as it might superficially appear. While to some, the inquisitorial design is of a different genus, others might say that in the adversary system, the public prosecutor performs a role not so different from the juge d'instruction. At least at the initial stage, the prosecutor often directs the investigation and should be neutral regarding the outcome, as energetic in exploring exculpatory as inculpatory data. The indictment, then, is the domestic version of the dossier, the document reflecting the findings of a thorough and dispassionate inquiry, to be tested at trial (or, more often, conceded by guilty plea).

But this nicely drawn parallel has more formal than actual verisimilitude. Prosecutors on the scent are rarely the neutral and detached counterpart of even the quasi-judicial figure who presides at the European investigation. Role counts. And prosecutors generally see themselves primarily as partisans, a mantle that is not easily shed when they are in the guise of investigator. As they see it, the job of investigation is mainly to choose an adversary wisely and, having chosen, to build strength for the government's case.

Moreover, we really do not want to give up our own free-ranging conception of the grand jury—a panel of regular inhabitants, advised by a public prosecutor—digging wherever curiosity leads, directing the prosecutorial focus of the government, and ultimately responsible for the accusatory decision. So important did the Founders deem this prerogative of citizens—and protection for the target—that they wrote it into the Fifth Amendment as obligatory upon the federal government. The provision did not, however, make it into the Fourteenth as a command directed to the states—one of the few that twentieth-century courts thought inessential to "ordered liberty," and hence not implicit in the "due process" called for by the nineteenth-century amendment. Today, only nineteen states continue to accord their defendants the right to indictment by grand jury for the ordinary felony.

It's a little hard to know why so many jurisdictions have decided to live without the grand old lady of our criminal tradition. There were, of course, many jokes in disparagement of the grand jury. The sobriquet "rubber stamp" seemed inseparably associated with its name, embellished by a former Chief Judge of the Court of Appeals of the State of New York, who once said that a grand jury would indict a ham sandwich if the prosecutor asked for it. There's a lot of truth to the homily. Certainly most cases go in and out of the closed grand jury room in a matter of minutes with a predictable result. The prosecutor, as the official guide of the grand jury, is the grand jurors' only source of evidence and their primary source of law. As such, she enjoys considerable influence in their deliberations. Still, a friend of mine—a thoughtful, intelligent, and free-minded soul—who recently completed service as a grand juror declared the work engaging, independent, and important.

In those states that have decided to live without it, the device substituted for the abolished grand jury (in the ordinary case) is an abbreviated adversarial hearing before a magistrate. Here the judge listens to a short version of the state's evidence, allows brief challenge by the defense, and decides whether the evidence provides a strong enough likelihood of guilt that the entire case should be presented to a petit jury at trial. The function of the magistrate here is analogous to the role of the European juge d'instruction only by the crudest measurement. The American charging judge has no part in the development of the case, has no responsibility for preparing the details of the charge, and has only the most cursory acquaintance with the underlying facts. But I've never heard it said that a magistrate would hold a sandwich for trial after a preliminary hearing, so one can assume that some greater independent judgment is being exercised in the charging decision by this post–grand jury system.

But the system is surely less efficient than the expeditious, *ex parte* grand jury hearing. In some jurisdictions (notably California), the preliminary hearing can take as long, or longer, than a long trial. And the preliminary hearing is still far from the judicially directed investigation of the European model. Thus despite the rising popularity of this alternative to the grand jury, I find it hard to cheer the emergence of the American magistrate as an intake screen.

Apart from the many citizens relieved of duty they (unlike my friend) regard as dull and useless, the only participant to applaud the demise of the grand jury must be defense counsel who hope to obtain some early bootleg discovery of the prosecution's case from the magistrate's hearing. Discovery, as we shall see, is thought by many practitioners to be the Essential Equalizer, the defendant's best chance to put himself in a tactical position as close as possible to the prosecutor's vantage. Any opportunity to hear, to pin down under oath, and perhaps to challenge by cross-examination an early (and only lightly coached) version of a critical adverse witness's story is golden.

But whether it be by grand jury or committing magistrate, some preliminary check on the prosecutor's charging authority is probably a good thing. We should have—as we do have—some baseline principle that people should not be required to defend themselves against a criminal charge unless there is some good reason to believe they are guilty. Not the converse, of course: the prosecutor is not required to prosecute everyone who may be guilty.

Within the baseline, however, and reserving judicial prerogatives to guard against the rare, conjectural instance of gross abuse, external oversight of the prosecutor's license is not really a necessary component of a fair system. Indeed, the Supreme Court said as much in 1975, and reiterated it in 1994 in *Albright v. Oliver,* where they wrote: "We have said that the accused is not entitled to judicial oversight or review of the decision to prosecute."

The best protection against facile or biased accusation is the prospect of trial, and the embarrassment potential of the unwinnable case. The cautious prosecutor tailors the charge to the rigors of courtroom proof. If witnesses are uncertain about critical events, if the inferential linkages are weak, if the credibility of the prime witness will crumble under challenge, don't indict. Try to look at your case through the eyes of the jurors.

The irony, of course, is that in the American system, few cases will ever be unrolled before the eyes of any jury. Nevertheless, it might be said that one reason the guilty pleaders plead guilty is that the cases against them would withstand jury scrutiny if submitted to them. So the prospect of trial, as much as the trial itself, probably operates as some deterrent to the reckless exercise of the charging prerogative.

Where the grand jury really comes into its own is in the few hard cases—the complex, protracted investigations and the tough calls. Even the states that have converted to magistrates retain the reserve option of summoning twenty-three ordinary folk into a grand jury for these extraordinary cases. It must be so. It's hard to imagine how, in a really serious pretrial investigation, the prosecution could use the subpoena power—much less the power to confer immunity—without the backing of this secret, ex parte assembly of empowered citizens.

Does the American grand jury—in its lively or dormant form—provide any protection against prosecutorial overreaching? Some may claim that, true to its early design, the grand jury still provides a citizen check on government zeal. There are famous cases where a grand jury refused to do what the prosecutor wanted. There are even cases in which the grand jury "ran away": took the bit in its teeth and—disappointed in or suspicious of the prosecutor's agenda—expelled the prosecutor and proceeded with specially appointed independent counsel. There are close and sensitive cases where a prosecutor, grateful to have a wide receiver to whom he could pass the buck, sincerely appealed to the grand jury after the evidence was in, "Tell us, what should we do in this case? Is it go or no go?" And I am certain there are many undocumented cases in which the grand jury asked the prosecutor some hard and embarrassing questions in the privacy of the grand jury room, questions about the investigation, about methods, about policy priorities that probably stimulated some urgent self-examination in the prosecutor's office. But serious challenges to prosecutorial priorities are few and decades between. Does the prosecutor's nominal position as servant of the grand jury actually inhibit the initiative of the office to make cases as they choose?

To most observers, I think, the answer is no. The grand jury, for all its earnest and upstanding members, is still perceived as essentially passive, sturdily bound to the office that serves as its guide. And, it should be added, the examining magistrate—for all her judicial independence—probably has even less impact on the prosecutor's exercise of his executive authority to initiate prosecution. The magistrate may reject a few cases, here and there, on insufficient evidence to hold for trial. But the effect is simply to force the police to go back and look further; it does not call for them to modify in any way their own prerogatives. The grand jurors, in some small way, participate in the investigation as it unfolds, asking questions, making suggestions from time to time.

Before wrapping up the subject of control, we must add one more ingredient. The press, the news media generally, like to think that they are the true guardians of public values. Consistent with that lofty mission, they are ready to take credit for keeping prosecutors honest and diligent. Even the self-important prosecutors, they like to imagine, cringe before the power of print and pixel. When these organs of public outrage get wind of prosecutorial oppression, when it becomes apparent to reporters that the government has abused its powers of accusation, they can exercise the lethal power of exposure. It works as deterrence, the theory goes, for most of this media-sensitive tribe, and for the undeterred, disgrace is a great corrective.

Undeniably, there's truth in the claim. While not exactly—or universally—craven, prosecutors' offices do take their rectitude seriously. They do not like bad press and, particularly, they don't like to see themselves portrayed as abusive, insensitive, vindictive, or politically motivated. Even if they do not face or fear electoral contests, the image of professional virtue is precious.

Unfortunately, the news media do not everywhere or always live up to the high ideals they claim. Their reporters are not always tuned to the right event, their perception of abuse may be flawed, and—most important—the editorial policy of the news outlet may itself be disinclined—or overinclined—to criticism of law enforcement agencies. After all, the media also have constituencies. So their reactions may be shrill, passive, or simply mistaken, and many veteran prosecutors shrug and say: "I'll march to my own drummer. Let the media get in step with me." It often works.

When it comes right down to it, of course, there is no institutional substitute for personal integrity. The devices we have—the possible defenses of selective prosecution and entrapment, the shadow of a critical grand jury panel, the specter of public humiliation—all working in various and subtle ways on professional pride and the gratification of success, do a pretty good job of keeping the temptations of excess under control. Few critics of the system today would claim that the government regularly abuses its authority to initiate criminal prosecution. Some may quarrel with the prevailing emphasis on violence, street crime, quality-of-life offenses, or drug dealing; others may think too much time and energy is wasted on racketeering, official corruption, or white-collar crime. But, with pockets of dissent here and there, I think most people approve of the prosecutorial choices being made—as do I.

Perhaps injustice hides unseen in the interstices of law enforcement—racism, for example, might be an uglier factor than is generally recognized. Perhaps greater resources might be successfully deployed against some underprosecuted crime—burglary comes to mind, or family abuse. Maybe whole categories of invisible crime await discovery: bank fraud, misuse of poverty funds, corruption of regulatory inspectors, consumer scams, adoption rackets, cybertheft, who knows what else. Perhaps better-trained, more conscientious young prosecutors would make better decisions when a raw case slides across the desk for processing.

There are surely ways to improve the government's justly touted authority to choose the crime, choose the defendant, and choose the time and place of trial. Many of these improvements require investment of greater resources here at the front end of the process. Perhaps, for starters, we should insist on the articulation of standards for the exercise of discretion in initiating not only capital prosecutions but all. The very process of formulating such criteria might induce an insightful focus by the prosecutors on the importance of these decisions, and the casual customs involved.

When, as a young prosecutor, I was deeply involved in the plea-bargaining process, I would have loved to have had a set of office guidelines to help me learn the subtleties of a just settlement. But helpful as it would have been to me, I was convinced that such a document would have to be top secret. While published standards for the exercise of discretion open the process to public debate (presumably healthy), they may develop a secondary purpose: to make the office look good, which soon obliterates the original idea. Inevitably, the cosmetically correct guidelines would be ignored, and we would have to revert to the true, hardscrabble, subtextual discretion. But more pernicious, articulated standards tend to convert discretion into obligation. It presents the disappointed adversary with a point of contention: "You didn't even heed your own standards!" And in our overheated adversary mode, the public officer is soon defending herself against a charge that she deviated from her own, internal, gratuitously formulated policies. All in all, I came to appreciate the wilderness of unguided discretion, where each case was a new challenge, and the grunts and smiles of older colleagues were the only means for the transmission of the discretionary ethic.

Today my neat garden of prerogative has become somewhat overgrown and tangled in uncertainty and complexity. So much for the vantage of detachment. I continue to believe in the virtue of discretion and vice of superfluous contention. And insofar as articulated standards for the exercise of prosecutorial choice inhibit the former and encourage the latter, I'm against them. But I also believe that the articulation of guidelines and considerations in the exercise of discretion can be a healthy exercise for all parties—including us, the public.

To avoid their deleterious emanations, we must be sure that standards do not become (as some commentators have advocated) regulations, promulgated by the Department of Justice as a regulatory agency might in the effectuation of congressional purpose. I, at least, do not want to turn the administration of the criminal law into an echo of the awkward and protracted process characteristic of agency regulation. In my opinion, there are already too many ill-considered intrusions by legislatures—state and congressional—aiming to control prosecutorial and judicial discretion in plea negotiation and sentencing. Rigidity and predictability are not values esteemed as highly in law enforcement as in administrative law. Rather, I imagine articulated standards to be skillfully drawn somewhere between the ignored bromide and the binding effectuation of bureaucratic policy.

Think this is impossible? The Department of Justice has published a twelve-volume, loose-leaf "manual" for the guidance of U.S. Attorneys' offices around the country, four and a half volumes of which relate to criminal prosecutions. There may well be more modest counterparts in some few state offices as well. Chapter 27 of the *DOJ Manual* sets out the "Principles of Federal Prosecution." After setting forth its purpose as the promotion of "reasoned exercise of prosecutorial discretion" and stipulating that its provisions should not be relied upon "to create a right or benefit," the manual takes prosecutors gently through the delicate discretionary decisions of their office.

Starting out the section on "Initiating and Declining Prosecution," for example, the manual advises that if the government has probable cause to believe that a person has committed a federal offense, it should (not indict, but) consider whether to investigate further, commence, or decline prosecution with or without reference to other jurisdictions. Grounds for this consideration of options are then set forth, but always with operative terms that preserve the discretionary nature of the choice. The government should prosecute if the attorney believes that the conduct amounts to a federal offense and the admissible evidence will suffice to obtain and sustain a conviction, unless prosecution should be declined because:

(1) No substantial federal interest would be served by the prosecution;

(2) The person is subject to effective prosecution in another jurisdiction; or

(3) There exists an adequate noncriminal alternative to prosecution.

The words *substantial, effective,* and *adequate* leave much of the judgment to the wisdom of the prosecuting attorney, while the balance of the provision directs the inquiry to designated considerations.

The text goes on, in like vein, to spell out the several factors that should be considered in evaluating each of the designated grounds. Thus, for example, determining whether a "substantial federal interest" pertains requires weighing such elements as "law enforcement priorities," "seriousness of the offense," the "deterrent effect of prosecution," "culpability," "history," "willingness to cooperate." A collation for cogitation, not a formula for resolution. Admirable.

I see several benefits in the articulation of standards concerning the prosecution prerogative—the choice of case, the appropriate charge, the use of extraordinary devices of investigation, and a host of other components of the array of discretionary options. There is, for one, the benefit of articulation for its own sake. Just for the prosecutor to sit down and write out his multiple responsibilities, to try to formulate the appropriate considerations in the utilization of this awesome arsenal of power is worthwhile. It focuses the mind of the prosecutor, it tempers the temptations to arrogance, and it invites the examination of values implicit in the structure of public entitlement. Moreover, it provides the agenda for perpetual revision, as well as the heritage bequeathed by one office to its successor.

But apart from the utility of the process itself, published standards serve a votive function. They are an affirmation of obligation, a commitment to the public to discharge the prosecutorial commission responsibly. I know, people disparage the ceremonial gestures as meaningless P.R., or worse, self-congratulatory feel-good exercises. And there is surely some of that in all ceremony. But I must confess, I feel the emotional weight of occasion. I am moved by school commencements, weddings, inaugurations. I even like to hear a speaker get up at some renewal event and pledge adherence to the basic tenets of an endeavor. And I can't help but believe that, to some extent, public confidence in the prosecutorial enterprise is enhanced by the promulgation of sound and well-articulated precepts.

In addition, there is a double return from the bureaucratic process. Bureaucracy, I know, is synonymous with heedless, wasteful, and inept governance. And I know that excessive, meaningless paperwork can chill the ardor of the most devoted public servant. So I feel a bit strange putting in a good word for the bureaucracy. Much of the opening of the *DOJ Manual* speaks more of procedures than standards. When the local United States Attorney must consult with the attorney general in Washington, for example, who has to approve what sorts of decisions in what kinds of cases? Touching bases and signing off, that sort of thing. The lifeblood of the bureaucratic method. But there are benefits to be had from it.

First, the signature system brings information to the supervisory staff. Even if they rarely make any decisions, the top level should know what the troops are up to. And applications submitted by the line attorneys for this and requests for approval for that are excellent means to keep the brass in touch. The second benefit is to the applicants. Multiple, complex obligations—even among the conscientious—beget corner-cutting. And to the less than meticulous, the slide to slovenly is the easy way to go. Instructing the ground troops that for this or that necessary ingredient, they must pause, marshal their reasons, and write them out for submission to a superior is an effective way to keep them conscientious.

Finally, though it might be acknowledged that top drawer offices probably do not need written reminders of the elements of a sound decision on whether to go forward with a case, not every drawer is at the top. Newly appointed prosecutors, fledgling assistants might be helped by a recorded catechism. Knowing the expectations of the DOJ, reading the legacy of experience in the field, these things surely help to bring the performance of the weak prosecutor up to norm.

So, all in all, I find my emphasis on the cultivation of sound discretion consistent with the articulation of standards for the commencement of prosecution. Precepts can be—and should be—formulated, revised, and passed along. Inherited wisdom, along with perpetual rethinking, are helpful in discharging the awesome responsibility of choice.

3

ACCESS TO INFORMATION, FIRST- AND SECONDHAND

You Are What You Know

INFORMATION IS WHAT TRIALS are about. Trials are not about law. Disputes may arise on questions of law, trial judges may be called upon to make some dicey initial calls on legal issues, but the heart of the trial is the determination of who did what to whom and in what frame of mind. Appeals are about law; trials deal with facts.

So, understandably, at the trial stage, the parties are vitally interested in the raw factual data that can be produced in court. Of course, skill counts. The lawyers are not cold, dispassionate fact packers. They are in the business of persuasion—modern rhetoricians—and presentation is an important part of the job. But as any experienced trial lawyer will tell you, technique gets you only so far; to win, you must produce evidence.

Evidence, good and bad, sometimes falls from the sky. And important cases are occasionally won or lost by the unexpected fact that suddenly materializes in the courtroom. But for the most part, facts are dug out of the hard-crusted world. And when it comes to the tools for excavation, we hear most of the talk about the prosecutors' advantage and the unfair tilt it gives to the playing field.

In this chapter, I will be paying more attention to the tools—the legal empowerment to dig facts out of places and people (including the files of your adversary)—than to the skill and dedication of the people wielding the spades. This is not for a moment to be taken as disparagement of the human factor, the lawyering factor, in this business. There is a world of difference in the production of evidence between the indolent, inept, or overextended lawyers and those who are gifted strategists, devoted to the case, and imaginative in assembling the elements of a persuasive story—or puncturing a phony one. The point I shall attempt to make, a bit further along, is that superior lawyering skills cannot be conjured by the glint of gold. In the teeth of powerful mythology, I shall argue that excellent and desultory counsel seem to appear for the rich and the poor defendants or for the prosecution more or less at random.

But the lawyers' endowments are not the only human elements in the effective pursuit and accumulation of evidence. Lawyers work with investigators, accountants, model makers, chemists, psychologists, pathologists—forensic experts of all sorts. Surely, weak financial resources must be felt acutely in seeking information and advice from such indispensable accessories. Here is the pressure point where it is most vehemently protested that the defendant suffers an unfair deprivation in comparison with the broad resources available to the prosecution. And who can deny that experienced and trained investigators and experts stand by, only a telephone call away from the prosecutor's cluttered desk? Access to information is, in large measure, access to those who can scare it up or distill it down.

Not every defendant is indigent, of course. And many local prosecutors' offices hardly boast the opulent array of talent the glossy image accords them. But by and large, it is probably fair to say that the prosecutor—whose job it is to make the case, after all—has resources vastly superior to those available to the ordinary defendant.

The disparity of trial resources has long been a concern of the Supreme Court. They are not concerned primarily with the disparity between the defendant and the government, oddly enough. What they worry about is the disparity between the sort of justice the rich and poor defendants can hope for (an interesting question outside the scope of our present undertaking). Ever since Justice Hugo Black wrote, in 1956, "There can be no equal justice where the kind of trial a man gets depends on the amount of money he has," his legatees have been on a quest for the elusive ideal of perfect equality of resources before the law.

Justice Black's words were in his opinion for the Court in *Griffin v. Illinois,* a decision in which every indigent defendant was promised a free transcript of the record of the trial for use on appeal. The basis for the Court's decision was the clause in the Fourteenth Amendment that forbids the states to deny any person "equal protection of the laws." Although this and other equal protection decisions of the courts focus on the comparison between defendants, the notion of equality of access to information sometimes modulates into a comparison between the defense and the prosecution. It is no part of the egalitarian ideal that inspires the Reconstruction Amendments, but somewhere, deeply engraved in our Shadow Constitution, is the liberal precept that no individual should stand disfavored and disempowered before the forces of government. And the principle of equal justice under law is often read to mean that, as between adversaries, the playing field should be level. And that notion can be as readily applied to access to information for use at trial as to transcripts for appeal.

Take the leading case in the Supreme Court, *Ake v. Oklahoma,* decided in 1985. *Ake* involved the question of whether, in a capital case, the state must provide a psychiatric expert to examine the defendant, advise his lawyer, and testify on his behalf. For the overwhelming majority of the Court, Justice Marshall wrote that wherever the issue of sanity is likely to arise in a case, the defendant must have the means to hire his own psychiatric expert. This right to expert assistance arises, the Court held, not as a matter of equal protection vis-à-vis other defendants capable of paying the fees but as a matter of due process. The comparison—if any was needed—was to the position of the prosecution which, one way or another, has access to psychiatric experts. The importance of having a psychiatrist at your elbow, Marshall wrote, can be read in the widespread reliance on them by prosecutors (along with those defendants who can pay the fees).

Talk about facts! What are "the facts" of a case? Once a case has gone all the way through appellate review, the facts (for all practical purposes) are the summary of the trial evidence provided by the last appellate court. Scholars all know that this version may have a dubious correlation with the record itself and is likely to be a quite different story from the actual occurrences of the criminal event as it happened. There is hardly a more vivid demonstration than the opinions in *Ake* of the way in which an appellate judge can recite facts to set us up for the legal conclusion he wishes to reach.

As Justice Marshall tells the facts, the emphasis is entirely on the defendant and his mental instability; the victims and the crime itself are all but forgotten. Glen Burton Ake, Marshall tells us, was arrested and charged with murdering a couple and wounding their children. He behaved in a bizarre manner from the start; was committed by the judge for observation; was found by the psychiatrist to be "frankly delusional"; and was diagnosed as a paranoid schizophrenic. After a few months of psychiatric treatment he was found competent—with the help of hefty doses of Thorazine—to stand trial. Since the defendant was without funds, his counsel requested the trial court to have him examined, or to provide funds for the defendant to have himself examined, for the purpose of mounting a defense of insanity. During his pretrial psychiatric evaluation, apparently, no one had asked him a question relating to his mental condition at the time of the crime. The trial judge refused on the theory that he was not obliged by law or the Constitution to make this expenditure on behalf of the defendant. Marshall and the majority of the Supreme Court set him right.

Justice Rehnquist was the only dissenter and he told the same facts to lead us to his conclusion that the defendant in this case neither required nor deserved an expert-assisted psychiatric defense. Notice, for example, how instead of the dry recital that the defendant was "arrested and charged" with some anonymous murder, Rehnquist personalizes the crime in all its horror. There is no better way to capture the flavor of Rehnquist's rendition than to quote it. Besides, it is only fair to evaluate the majority position in the light of the facts taken at their worst:

> Petitioner Ake and his codefendant Hatch quit their jobs on an oil field rig in October 1979, borrowed a car, and went looking for a location to burglarize. They drove to the rural home of Reverend and Mrs. Richard Douglass, and gained entrance to the home by a ruse. Holding Reverend and Mrs. Douglass and their children, Brooks and Leslie, at gunpoint, they ransacked the home; they then bound and gagged the mother, father, and son, and forced them to lie on the living room floor. Ake and Hatch then took turns attempting to rape 12-year-old Leslie Douglass in a nearby bedroom. Having failed in these efforts, they forced her to lie on the living room floor with the other members of her family.
>
> Ake then shot Reverend Douglass and Leslie each twice, and Mrs. Douglass and Brooks once, with a .357 magnum pistol, and fled. Mrs. Douglass died almost immediately as a result of the gunshot wound; Reverend Douglass' death was

caused by a combination of the gunshots he received, and strangulation from the manner in which he was bound. Leslie and Brooks managed to untie themselves and to drive to the home of a nearby doctor. Ake and his accomplice were apprehended in Colorado following a month-long crime spree that took them through Arkansas, Louisiana, Texas, and other States in the western half of the United States.

Ake was extradited from Colorado to Oklahoma on November 20, 1979, and placed in the city jail in El Reno, Oklahoma. Three days after his arrest, he asked to speak to the Sheriff. Ake gave the Sheriff a detailed statement concerning the above crimes, which was first taped, then reduced to 44 written pages, corrected, and signed by Ake.

Ake was arraigned on November 23, 1979, and again appeared in court with his codefendant Hatch on December 11th. Hatch's attorney requested and obtained an order transferring Hatch to the state mental hospital for a 60-day observation period to determine his competency to stand trial; although Ake was present in court with his attorney during this proceeding, no such request was made on behalf of Ake.

On January 21, 1980, both Ake and Hatch were bound over for trial at the conclusion of a preliminary hearing. No suggestion of insanity at the time of the commission of the offense was made at this time. On February 14, 1980, Ake appeared for formal arraignment, and at this time became disruptive. The court ordered that Ake be examined by Dr. William Allen, a psychiatrist in private practice, in order to determine his competency to stand trial. On April 10, 1980, a competency hearing was held at the conclusion of which the trial court found that Ake was a mentally ill person in need of care and treatment, and he was transferred to a state institution. Six weeks later, the chief psychiatrist for the institution advised the court that Ake was now competent to stand trial, and the murder trial began on June 23, 1980. At this time Ake's attorney withdrew a pending motion for jury trial on present sanity. Outside the presence of the jury the State produced testimony of a cellmate of Ake, who testified that Ake had told him that he was going to try to "play crazy."

The State at trial produced evidence as to guilt, and the only evidence offered by Ake was the testimony of the doctors who had observed and treated him during his confinement pursuant to the previous order of the court. Each of these doctors testified as to Ake's mental condition at the time of his confinement in the institution, but none could express a view as to his mental condition at the time of the offense. Significantly, although all three testified that Ake suffered from some form of mental illness six months after he committed the murders, on cross-examination two of the psychiatrists specifically stated that they had "no opinion" concerning Ake's capacity to tell right from wrong at the time of the offense, and the third would only speculate that a psychosis might have been "apparent" at that time. . . . In addition, Ake called no lay witnesses, although some apparently existed who could have testified concerning Ake's actions that might have had a bearing on his sanity at the time of the offense; and although two "friends" of Ake's who had been with him at times proximate to the murders testified at trial at the behest of the prosecution, defense counsel did not question them concerning any of Ake's actions that might have a bearing on his sanity.

However they may be recited, the facts require the Court to apply constitutional principles to resolve the issue they raise—or, at least, to appear to do so. Thus, citing *Griffin* and a series of later cases along the same lines, Marshall finds that due process assures that a charged defendant will have "meaningful access" to "the raw materials integral to the building of an effective defense." Not that the state need purchase for the indigent "all the assistance that his wealthier counterpart might buy." But he must have the "basic tools," and in a case like Ake's, one of those tools is a psychiatrist.

At Ake's second trial in Oklahoma, a psychiatrist was appointed for him and testified that the defendant was insane. The jury convicted him again and recommended an endless prison term. That conviction was affirmed. Thus the crime was punished, the killer's life saved, and the important principle of equal assistance established. Neat trick.

Now if *Ake* means anything outside the narrow ambit of its facts, it means that any defendant is entitled to expert assistance in developing the defensive case. Not just experts like psychologists, but forensic examiners, clue-hounds, and experienced witness interrogators. In short, the decision can be read as the Magna Carta of defense investigation. To date, however, courts have been extremely reluctant to construe *Ake*'s import broadly enough to entitle the defendant, at state expense, to mount a thorough pretrial investigation of the case. Indeed, Marshall himself—no shrinking violet when it comes to criminal defendants' entitlements—was careful to say nothing about what those basic tools might be (beyond the head doctor in Ake's case).

A few years later, however, in 1987, Marshall, dissenting from the Court's refusal to hear an appeal from a capital conviction, lamented the lost opportunity to develop *Ake*'s command that the state provide for the indigent defendant the basic tools of a sophisticated defense. In *Johnson v. Oklahoma,* he wrote:

> This Court long has acknowledged that when a State brings criminal proceedings against an indigent defendant, it must take steps to ensure that the accused has a meaningful opportunity to present a defense. Although the State need not pur-

chase for an indigent defendant all of the services that the
wealthy may buy, the State must provide the defendant with
the "basic tools of an adequate defense." We recently have begun to confront the questions whether and when expert assistance is such a basic tool. . . . This case demonstrates the
pressing need to consider and resolve those questions.

The denial of petitioner's request for the appointment of an
expert chemist resulted in a fundamentally unfair trial in two
respects. First, the denial prevented petitioner from raising
doubts about the strength of the State's evidence against him.
The prosecution's case against petitioner rested largely on the
testimony of the police chemist that petitioner's bodily fluids,
hair, and clothing comported with samples found at the scene
of the crime. . . . Without expert assistance, a defendant will
usually be powerless to create doubts in the jury's mind about
such testimony's strength or correctness. As Justice (then Chief
Judge) Cardozo once stated, a defendant is "at an unfair disadvantage if he is unable because of poverty to parry by his own
[expert] witnesses the thrusts of those against him." Reilly v.
Berry, 250 N.Y. 456 (1929). Petitioner here was at such a disadvantage with respect to testimony that the prosecutor termed
the "real crux" of the State's case. Second and equally important, the denial of the request for expert assistance prevented
petitioner from gaining potentially conclusive exculpatory evidence in support of his affirmative alibi defense. As petitioner's
counsel explained to the trial court, petitioner desired expert
assistance partly because he wanted to undergo a test that could
have conclusively disproved his commission of the crime.

It's a vision of fairness still in the bud. How far will the state go to
assure that no defendant, by reason of poverty, will lack the means for
presenting an effective defense? The principle has been proclaimed;

application is still uncertain. If we are serious about providing the accused with a fair opportunity to meet the accusation as effectively as possible, serious thought must be given to providing the means to do so.

Serious thought begins with an imponderable. It's easy enough to say resources count. Especially if you are an accused innocent, your freedom depends on having the means to get at the facts—not just the contents of the prosecutor's files (such as they may be), but the facts in the field. And it is even easier to see that most of those accused of crimes do not have the wealth to conduct a full investigation of the raw data. But it does not follow from there that justice demands free defense access to field facts. The imponderable is just how impaired is the defense by limitations of resources in the development of a persuasive defense for the wrongly accused?

We're on the dark side of the moon here. Most thinking about investigation has focused on two topics: control of the government's power of intrusion and sharing the product of it. Little thought has been given to sponsoring independent defense fact gathering. But we can start somewhere. Every Moll, Nell, and Sue knows that a well-heeled criminal—a major drug smuggler, racketeer, corrupt pol, or financial crook, for example, to say nothing of a celebrity former footballer—brings to his defense assets that the vaunted power of the state is ill-funded to match. Investigators of various sorts, experts, and other consultants help prepare the case for trial, and thereafter hired jury pickers, spin doctors, drama coaches, and others assist a team of veteran lawyers in the trial of the case. Meanwhile, in many of these cases, the threadbare prosecutor has the help of the pair of agents or cops who made the case, an overworked lab technician (who doesn't really remember this case), the occasional advice of a supervisor or legal researcher, and, if she's lucky, the assistance of a novice sitting next to her in the courtroom to run errands and sort documents while learning the ropes. We needn't worry about the war chests of these and defendants similarly situated.

We also know that a substantial portion of the criminal docket is represented by institutional defenders of one sort or another—public defenders, legal aid, capital defense projects, various privately funded rights offices, and so forth. It's fair to assume that such outfits have investigators on staff. Perhaps not the best or the most numerous, but for the necessitous case, there is probably some ex-cop on payroll who can go out and hunt up witnesses with the best of them. For those indigents represented by individual assigned counsel, applications to the court for reimbursement of the expenses of investigation by specially retained sleuths are generally granted. And to a considerable extent—heeding the words of Marshall and others—the state will pay for independent defense experts to reexamine prosecution evidence, as well as evidence acquired by the defense investigators. So even the indigent defendant is not utterly helpless when it comes to investigation.

Parenthetically, we must note that here, as with provision of counsel, the really deprived, the truly disadvantaged defendant is not the legally indigent but the thinly funded working person who must reach into his own meager bank account for the cash to defend himself or his child. If you can scrape up the thousands for legal fees, and maybe a few hundreds left over for an investigator, you may be substituting debt for money painfully saved over many years for the kids' college education or your own retirement. It's the old story; those with modest assets are in the greatest peril. Close parenthesis with words of neither hope nor solace.

The hard question, then, comes down to this: how often are deserving cases lost for lack of an independent investigator or expert who might have turned the tables had funds been available to retain him? I suppose we could go out and ask a hundred randomly selected defense counsel around the country, "Have you ever had a case where an innocent client was convicted because you lacked resources to conduct a thorough investigation of the facts? How often has it happened?" We might get some answers, but would we think them trustworthy? How does the lawyer know that her client is innocent? What did the lawyer know that led her to that belief, and why could she not demonstrate it even to the extent of instilling a reasonable doubt among the jurors? How does she know that the investigator would have discovered better means to prove it? How can we be sure that the lawyer is not just hoping for a miracle strike to confirm a generous hunch? Or looking for an assistant who can turn up a false alibi or phony character witness for a guilty client?

I can't begin to answer the imponderable, but I suspect that if truth were told, most conscientious defense lawyers today go to trial with about all they can hope for: some basis for attacking the prosecution case, an exculpatory version or alibi from the defendant or a friend/relative, and maybe an expert witness. Even the innocent defendant—even the well-funded innocent defendant—usually cannot hope for much more than that.

The real disparity in resources does not stem from the defendant's relative financial disability, I would guess, but from his legal inability to force stories from the disinclined and documents from the reluctant. The defendant has power to subpoena witnesses and documents to court, of course. That's constitutionally guaranteed. But no authority to call for evidence for investigative purposes, and no power to conduct searches and seizures or electronic surveillance, or to compel evidence by grant of immunity. These are serious disabilities.

But are they unfairly imposed? In part, I guess the answer depends on how seriously you take the oft-heard claim of defense counsel that they bear the de facto burden of proof, a contention I shall explore. The burdened party is generally accorded the means to discharge that obligation. Allowing that the defense shoulders a shadow-burden, I suppose it is conceivable that they should have access to the privacy-penetrating, reluctance-defeating devices at the command of the prosecution. We might, with some interpretive strain, expand the reading of "compulsory process" in the Constitution's Sixth Amendment beyond its present limitation to the subpoena and allow the defense to petition directly to a judge for orders allowing searches and seizures, physical or electronic. Private defense investigators could conceivably be authorized to carry them out as private process servers today serve defense subpoenas.

It's a stretch. Even if there were compelling reasons (which I'm not sure there are), the entitlement would incur some severe anomalies. Prime among them is the basic design of the Fourth and Fifth Amendments as constraints upon the investigating powers of the government. Defendants would operate in the privacy-piercing business free of constitutional restraint. Whether a statutory substitute, implemented by judicial supervision, would do the trick is open to question.

But in any case, such entitlement to pursue the raw facts would accrue only after the state had filed its formal accusation. It's a bit late in the game for searches and seizures, wiretaps, and such. And it would be difficult at this point for defense counsel to specify just what evidence he was seeking to exonerate the defendant—an important constitutional safeguard. Defense-led, law-bound evidence hunts are not utterly inconceivable, but it's not going to happen soon.

Earlier, before accusation, it is difficult to see how, as a practical matter, defense counsel could even participate in the prosecution's investigative decisions. In most cases, there is no defendant as yet and hence no defense counsel. And insofar as some possible target feels himself in the cross-hairs of suspicion, the prosecutor can hardly be expected to consult his counsel before seeking a covert surveillance order from the court or immunizing a witness before the grand jury. So, for both structural and practical reasons, it seems inescapable that the prosecution, in service of the charging authority, should have unilateral access to the compulsory forms of investigation. And the comparative disability that the defense surely suffers in some cases cannot be called unfair.

Coming around to a more conventional way of thinking of the fair balance of access to pretrial information, we approach with trepidation the subject known in every courtroom by the made-for-television appellation *Discovery!* Despite its relatively limited scope in criminal cases (compared with the civil variety, where discovery litigation virtually consumes all other issues), we find plenty to argue about. The allocation of obligations, the matters to be disclosed and when, and the consequences of breach have bedeviled advocates and demanded grudging judicial attention down through recent years. And the discovery issue can be a buried time bomb. I read recently about a former Black Panther, imprisoned for twenty-seven years on a murder conviction, whose conviction was just set aside for failure of the prosecution to disclose a material fact about its principal witness.

The discovery issue, as I see it, has two aspects. The first is simply a matter of the respective entitlements of each side to know what the other knows. Or to put it another way, the extent to which the unearthed facts are secrets to be held by the party who dug them up until the most effective moment for divulgence. Contrary to principles of neutral resolution (facts are facts, they don't belong to anyone), this view of partisan preemption is consistent with our adversary system of litigation, which puts a premium on party control of evidence. Plus, some would surely argue that evidence is fragile. Put it out there where the adverse party can have a crack at it, and its integrity is at risk. Shielding your delicate shards and susceptible messengers from the harsh effects of premature exposure is not, some would insist, a matter of maximizing explosive effect. It is rather the best way to assure a clean wash of evidence at the trial.

The second aspect of the discovery issue is the reciprocal or conditional right to discover something comparable to what you have been forced to divulge. This odd notion, with roots in the level playing field ideal, supposes that to keep the contest even, each party should be required to purchase facts from his adversary only at the price of revealing something he could otherwise keep hidden.

The issue of reciprocity has been squarely addressed by the Supreme Court in a case called *Wardius v. Oregon* decided in 1973, some twelve years before *Ake.* Oregon had a law (as many other states do) that required a criminal defendant to notify the prosecution before trial if he intended to put on an alibi defense (that is, present evidence that he could not have committed the crime charged because he was elsewhere at the time). This gave the prosecutor an opportunity to prepare in advance to disprove it, disproof of the defense being part of their burden to prove guilt. Because Wardius failed to give notice, his evidence of alibi was excluded (as the law required).

Unlike *Ake,* the facts in *Wardius* were a picture of simplicity. Wardius, charged with a sale of narcotics, proposed to call Colleen McFadden to testify that at the time the sale went down, she was at a drive-in movie with Wardius. He was not allowed to call her, and Wardius himself, on the witness stand, was precluded from saying he was with McFadden.

That is heavy medicine. Perhaps a defendant's most important trial right is to give and to adduce evidence of his own innocence. Think due process. How would our collective, English-speaking conscience tolerate a rule that excluded defense evidence of innocence? Failure to give notice seems a pretty technical omission to override such a fundamental, substantive entitlement. But that was not what the Court found defective about Oregon's law.

Noting that it fully approved of pretrial discovery laws—and, indeed, had recently upheld such a statute in the state of Florida—the Court in *Wardius* went on to note that "although the Due Process Clause has little to say regarding the amount of discovery which the parties must be afforded, it does speak to the balance of forces between the accused and his accuser." In contrast to Oregon's, the Florida notice-of-alibi law, the Court reminded us, "is itself carefully hedged with reciprocal duties requiring state disclosure to the defendant." The Florida statute provided that five days after getting the defendant's list of alibi witnesses, the prosecutor must serve the defendant with a list of witnesses it intends to call to rebut or discredit the evidence of alibi. Oregon had neglected to burden the prosecution with such reciprocal disclosure. For that reason, the law was struck down. Fair is fair.

"Discovery must be a two-way street," Justice Marshall put it with disarming simplicity. But what he really meant was that, to balance the state's advantage in acquiring damning evidence, the defense must be given broad rights of discovery. The point is buried in a footnote and further concealed in a student note quoted, with evident approval, by Marshall. Footnote 9 reads as follows:

> Indeed, the State's inherent information-gathering advantages suggest that if there is to be any imbalance in discovery rights, it should work in the defendant's favor. As one commentator has noted: "Besides greater financial and staff resources with which to investigate and scientifically analyze evidence, the prosecutor has a number of tactical advantages. First, he begins his investigation shortly after the crime has been committed when physical evidence is more likely to be found and when witnesses are more apt to remember events. Only after the prosecutor has gathered sufficient evidence is the defendant informed of the charges against him; by the time the defendant or his attorney begins any investigation into the facts of the case, the trail is not only cold, but a diligent prosecutor will have removed much of the evidence from the field. In addition to the advantage of timing, the prosecutor may compel people, including the defendant, to cooperate.

The defendant may be questioned within limits, and if arrested his person may be searched. He may also be compelled to participate in various nontestimonial identification procedures. The prosecutor may force third persons to cooperate through the use of grand juries and may issue subpoenas requiring appearance before prosecutorial investigatory boards. With probable cause the police may search private areas and seize evidence and may tap telephone conversations. They may use undercover agents and have access to vast amounts of information in government files. Finally, respect for government authority will cause many people to cooperate with the police or prosecutor voluntarily when they might not cooperate with the defendant." Note, Prosecutorial Discovery under Proposed Rule 16, 85 Harv. L. Rev. 994, 1018–1019 (1972) (footnotes omitted).

There it is. Justice Marshall has tipped his hand. Taking his point far beyond the rather nice—but narrow—celebration of symmetry, he summons up the general arguments of the balance of advantage contenders. Because the prosecutor has first dibs on a scene search, the power of subpoena and immunity, and the rest, the defendant deserves a compensatory break—like full discovery, presumably. Let's try to level this playing field, they say; we can't have a fair adversary confrontation when all the evidence-gathering advantages lie with the government. The anonymous student author of the Harvard Note (ecstatic, one can imagine, to find himself or herself elevated to the status of a quoted authority) is hardly the first nor yet the last to make this argument. But it seems to me seriously flawed.

Pretrial discovery wasn't always the norm it is today. Until the latter half of the twentieth century, a defendant was expected to "discover" the prosecutor's case against him as he heard the witnesses' tales unfold at the trial. That's what the trial was, in essence: a parade of evidence openly displayed for the first time. Given the high interest of the defendant in destroying, hiding, or altering that evidence (to say nothing of his presumably low scruple to employ criminal means to that end), it was generally thought that the wise prosecutor should keep the case under close wraps until unveiled before the jury for whose eyes and ears it had been assembled.

The first small crack in this heat shield appeared in 1957, when the Supreme Court decided a case involving a labor union leader named Jencks who had been convicted of lying in an affidavit in which he swore he was not a member of the Communist Party. Two FBI informers, Matusow and Ford (both Party members), gave evidence against Jencks. Jencks was denied access to their written reports, filed with the FBI, that might have contained statements that could have been used on cross-examination to impeach these witnesses. The Supreme Court found that to be error. The rule was later codified in federal law and, although not expressly founded on due process, the *Jencks* rule became standard practice everywhere. At the least (the rule provides), after direct examination is concluded, the defense in a criminal case is entitled to have all prior recorded statements of government witnesses that have some bearing on the witnesses' testimony.

The next, more substantial crack in the government's protective shield came a few years later, when the Supreme Court decided the case that, to this day, keeps a murderer's name securely attached to a doctrine cited in almost every criminal case, state and federal. "Brady material" is lawyers' code for any information known to the government that might tend to exculpate an accused and which the government (for obvious reasons) does not intend to adduce fully at trial. The case in which the doctrine was born, *Brady v. Maryland* (1963), involved a robbery during which the victim was killed. In separate trials, Brady and his partner, one Boblit, were convicted and sentenced to death. Oddly, Brady—who was tried first—took the stand

and admitted his guilt, asserting that Boblit, not he, had strangled the victim and asking only that the jury, on that account, spare his life. Before trial, Brady's lawyer had requested a copy of a statement made by Boblit to police in which he admitted being the one who strangled the victim. There was at the time some question whether that statement, even if counsel had it in hand, would have been admissible at Brady's trial, and defense access to one of Boblit's several statements was denied.

On the third appellate round, the Maryland Court of Appeal finally held that withholding the document amounted to a violation of due process of law. At the same time, they made it clear that such evidence would have been admissible to assist the jury in deciding the capital punishment issue, if not on the question of guilt (where the identity of the actual killer did not affect the culpability of the defendant).

The United States Supreme Court approved. In its memorable conclusion, Justice William O. Douglas wrote for the Court: "We now hold that the suppression by the prosecution of evidence favorable to an accused upon request violates due process where the evidence is material either to guilt or to punishment, irrespective of the good faith or bad faith of the prosecution." It has been expanded, contracted, and suffered all variety of exegesis in state and federal courts since, but the original doctrine remains the nub of the constitutional discovery rule in every jurisdiction in the United States. As evolved, the Brady Rule today goes something like this: if the prosecution knows (or should know) of any data that might be used by the defense to develop a helpful response to the accusation—a response that has a significant chance of affecting the outcome—and if the prosecution does not intend to adduce that evidence as part of its own case, the information must be turned over to the defense, even without specific request, in sufficient time to allow for its most effective use. With the help of a case known as *Giglio,* the *Brady* doctrine was expanded to include material tending to exculpate by impeaching the credibility of a prosecution witness.

These cornerstones of discovery in criminal cases, *Jencks* and *Brady,* hardly support the sort of discovery that defendants claim is necessary fully to compensate for prosecutorial advantages. It's all very well to have material useful for impeaching a prosecution witness, and thank you very much for the possibly exculpatory material, but really to prepare this defense we need a preview of the prosecution case. Which prosecution witness will say what, just how good is the witness, just how bad is the evidence—that's what we want to know.

Many believe—as Thurgood Marshall did—that in a trial the element of surprise, of unexpected probative superiority issuing from an unsuspected source, is a perversion of the adversary system (especially, Marshall might add, when it is the government that has the aces up its sleeve). "Trial by ambush" is the conventional trope. Prosecution force that is overwhelming may be commendable, but not force that overwhelms because surprise precludes effective probative challenge. The idea that seems to have gained fairly universal acceptance is that prior notification—indeed, open prosecutorial files—affords the defense the opportunity to strike the prosecution proof with the sort of challenge or contradiction that will best assist the fact finder in determining the ring of truth.

There's a lot to be said for this idea, at least for those who maintain faith in the jury's ear for truth—faith born either of true belief or the imperative of necessity. The full opportunity to meet adverse evidence with questions concerning its authenticity or probity, to assemble evidence that directly contradicts expected adverse proof, these are the only ways to assure ourselves that the trial is not just a ritual validation of an accusation. Preparation is everything, the experienced trial lawyer will tell you. So it is not enough to inform the defendant, "You are accused of using the mails to defraud; patience, you'll hear the details in court." Our accusatory system demands that the state notify him in advance of just what particular deception, when, and of whom, he is charged with promoting by post so that he can muster his defensive forces for a focused courtroom confrontation.

Why then do we still not have mandatory "open files discovery"? In the European model, the inquisitorial system, the defense gets pretrial access to the whole dossier on which he will be tried. Some few local prosecutors in the United States, as a matter of state law or office policy or individual choice, also make fairly broad disclosure to defendants. In addition to a highly particular description of the crime, the prosecutor will tender copies of documents, reports by experts, lab reports, all prior statements of the defendant himself, together with a list of property seized from the defendant or by search warrant, and any identification of the defendant by an eyewitness at a lineup. It's not everything, but it's quite a package; not only are the disclosures useful in preparing for trial, but they probably stimulate more than a few guilty pleas. Still, most prosecutors will hold out what the defendant wants most: the names and statements of the prosecution witnesses.

From the prosecution standpoint, they are withholding only unusually sensitive evidence—witnesses who might be subject to harassment or corruption. In addition, there is the matter of simple decency. Why should the victim of a savage rape have to meet with her rapist's champions? Or fear visits from his friends? Why should any witness have to face hostile examination by those who would break the story if they could and, at the very least, confuse and embarrass the teller? Let the defense do their cross-examining in court, where the witness is protected to some extent by the judge and the rules of evidence.

From the defendant's perspective—especially the perspective of the innocent defendant, learning the details of the accuser's story or the supporting evidence well before the trial begins is probably the only opportunity to check them out. Does the witness harbor a grudge? Does anything in his background caution against credence? Is the story inconsistent with, or contradicted by the accounts of others? Did the witness have the vantage claimed? Does the paper trail support the live recitals? These are some of the vital clues to testimonial error—and the guideposts for the construction of a persuasive alternative scenario—that can make the difference when the case plays out before the jury. If not afforded pretrial, the information can rarely be drawn from the witness when he gets up to render his smooth, coached, and well-defended account from the stand.

The principle of notification is important enough to be included in the Sixth Amendment to our precious Constitution among the basic elements of a fair criminal trial. Right up there with the rights to a speedy and public trial by an impartial local jury, the assistance of counsel, confrontation of adverse witnesses (including the right to cross-examine them), and compulsory process to produce supportive evidence, the Sixth Amendment promises defendants the right "to be informed of the nature and cause of the accusation." I have not seen any authoritative construction of the words *nature and cause.* I believe they are universally taken to mean that the defendant must receive clear and explicit notification of the specific allegations of the accusatory instrument, the indictment upon which he will be tried—that the language in the indictment describing the crime must "descend to particulars," as the Supreme Court once put it. No more.

Perhaps one day an imaginative lawyer will stand up and argue that the detailed specifications of the formal indictment might satisfy the requirement for information on the *nature* of the accusation, but that information on the *cause* of the accusation goes beyond the four corners of the pleading to the statements of named witnesses upon which the charge was founded. The two words are not, after all, synonymous. If *cause* is to have any meaning apart from *nature,* it must be in the precipitating basis for the accusation, rather than its particulars. A short step in logic but a great leap in doctrinal reform. To discern in the landscape of the Sixth Amendment a defense entitlement to know, in advance of trial, the statements of witnesses that caused his accusation is a radical challenge to conventional construction. But as I say, as a matter of linguistic interpretation, I think it has considerable force.

I fervently hope it does not succeed. Yes, I can see merit in the argument that free defense access to prosecution data enhances the adversary process. Up to a point. But I would hate to see the judicial powers that be persuaded that the Constitution commands advance disclosure of the various inculpatory stories of witnesses. Any such blanket rule would soon accumulate a number of exceptions—the bit in question is immaterial or cumulative, or disclosure would expose a frightened or vulnerable witness to intimidation or misgiving (to name just a few). Yet another pretrial courtroom wrangle would be invited to sort it all out, with ultimate review in the Supreme Court itself. Just the reform we need! Even if reciprocity were possible (which it is not because of the peculiar privileges of the defense), I would be wary of bringing to the criminal arena the protracted, contentious power game that full discovery has become on the civil side.

Curiosity does not control the law of discovery. And due process has never meant—cannot mean—that the defendant is entitled to whatever material might enhance his defense at trial. History has read due process with an eye toward the fairness of the trial itself, and although deep discovery might improve the defense position at trial, it does not necessarily enhance fairness.

For my money, *Jencks* and *Brady* had it just about right. Exculpatory and impeachment material must be disclosed. But the bulk of the prosecution's case—the evidence that the prosecutor thinks will convict the defendant—generally need not be disclosed until adduced in court. The defendant, courts and lawmakers still believe, may construct his defense on what he knows of his own behavior at the critical time without regard for what the prosecution has learned by its investigation. A defense should be founded on independent truth, not on contrived hole punching. It's not an outrageous position.

One of the prime arguments in opposition to full discovery is the adaptive perjury claim. I suppose cynics are not altogether off the mark when they note that broad defense discovery is often nothing more than a navigational chart for plotting a perjurious defense. Pretrial discovery of the details and particulars of the inculpatory evidence affords the lively imagination of the defense a leisurely opportunity to set a course to sail through the weak features of the prosecution position while tacking around the irrefutable components. With a lift from a fabricated breeze, the defense should be able to emerge, unscathed, in open waters.

For those who worry greatly about the hazards of an effective perjurious defense, no argument reciting the virtues of defense preparation to "meet" the anticipated adverse evidence will be persuasive. Better (they will reply) to go back to trial-as-slow-discovery and rely on honest but ignorant efforts by the defendant to reconstruct his own actions in a way that will contradict any inculpatory evidence only as convincingly as his independent story warrants.

Futile to remind them that the contrived defense is not necessarily the product of perverted pretrial discovery. Still, it is true that a defense may be fabricated almost as easily the old-fashioned way: by listening to the prosecution case as it comes out at trial. A criminal defendant is not required to commit himself to a theory of exoneration by an opening statement to the jury before hearing from the prosecution witnesses. Hence, even if he received no advance inkling of the shape of the prosecution case against him until the trial began, agile counsel would still enjoy the opportunity to tailor his defense. And the adversary design of allegation-followed-by-defense contemplates this reserve option of untruth.

Our adversary model, of course, does not condone perjury by the defendant or her witnesses, or the subornation of it by defense counsel. Destruction of evidence or interference with adverse witnesses is still a crime. But short of these transgressions, as I shall attempt to demonstrate farther along, the lawyer for the defendant is largely unconstrained by any ethical imperative to respect the truth as he believes it to be. And the defendant herself is not likely to be deterred from offering what she thinks is an effective story by the remote possibility that a prosecution for perjury will be her next hazard. Thus, some space has been built into our conception of a trial for the defendant to pursue persuasion with scant regard for probity. It is one of the largest advantages enjoyed by the defense. Exploration of the question whether it is unfair will have to await a later chapter.

Neither I nor anyone else can venture even a wild guess about the dimension of the problem of perverted pretrial discovery. Are these contrivances commonplace (as some believe)? And do they fool juries? Or are the occasional attempts artfully to build a false defense around the discovered evidence far outnumbered by instances of truth enhancement by virtue of informed preparation? Does discovery encourage perjury? Or does it—even where generous and unilateral—serve to focus attention on disputed issues, improving trial efficiency and encouraging guilty pleas from the guilty? Is there any control possible on the perjurious defense without sacrifice of the benefits (whatever they may be) of open prosecution?

It is difficult to devise a way to pin the defendant down to a story before he learns of the evidence against him. My old friend the late Judge Harold Rothwax, in his otherwise polemical book, *Guilty: The Collapse of Criminal Justice* (Random House, 1996), has playfully proposed that we require the defendant seeking discovery to record his version of events before learning the contours of the prosecution's case, his account to be sealed and used against him only if he shifts his ground after discovery. It's a cute idea.

A closer look discloses some troublesome problems. How, when, and by whom is this naive statement of guilt or innocence to be obtained? And how does this obligation square with our fabled Right of Silence—the constitutional privilege not to be compelled to serve as a witness against oneself? It is true that the Supreme Court has held (in *New York v. Viven Harris*) that a self-inculpatory statement unadorned with *Miranda* warnings and waivers—and on that account inadmissible as part of the prosecution's proof—may nonetheless be admitted to impeach a contrary version delivered by the defendant from the stand. But that doctrine affords scant support for Rothwax's idea since the inadmissibility of the defendant's sealed pretrial statement is not due to any mere Miranda flaw but to the simple fact that it was required—hence compelled—from the defendant. Compelled statements—even those compelled only by a grant of immunity—may not be used to impeach a contrary version told by the defendant from the stand.

Rothwax would probably reply that the sealed statements of his proposal were not compelled from the defendant but freely tendered as the price for the discovery he seeks. But if discovery is itself a right (and at least *Brady* and *Jencks* discovery is), requiring the surrender of the right to silence as the price of enlightenment is unconstitutional. So whatever its merits, the idea confronts some serious obstacles of established law.

In addition, the Rothwax solution allows only the impeachment of the testimony of the defendant himself. The scripted defense that worries Rothwax can be played by actors other than the defendant. To contradict a contrived story told by others, Judge Rothwax would have to admit the defendant's pretrial declaration even if the defendant himself were not on the stand to be impeached. The solution is, after all, designed to keep the defense honest, not just the defendant. So here the proposal ventures beyond the scant security of the *Harris* precedent, skating off on very thin ice.

In fairness, it should be noted that while the idea of requiring a rendition from the suspect is bizarre to a common-law lawyer imbued with the ideology of the adversary dialectic, the idea of soliciting a fresh and truthful account from the person who should know most about his own whereabouts and conduct at the time in issue is not inherently weird. As already noted, the traditional European model allows the investigating *juge d'instruction* to call and examine the suspect as part of the preliminary inquiry. Thus if his proposal is poked a bit, it sounds as though Judge Rothwax (like many of us) is expressing some attraction for the inquisitorial alternative to the American adversary system. In this, I would like to share his optimism. Is there any hope that we can import the inquisition feature of the European model to engraft on our own mechanism of controlled contention? Alas, as I have said, I don't have much confidence in these cross-cultural grafts. Ironically, as many of us peer enviously at their model, several European systems are being refitted to look more like the Anglo-American adversary system. If jurisprudence survives the cross-Atlantic voyage in one direction, the old warrior's ghost might say, perhaps it can travel the other way too. Perhaps.

There are other, more traditional ways to keep the defendant honest as he spins his defense in court. The most obvious implement is rarely employed. Lying under oath is a crime. But prosecutors are reluctant to charge defendants with perjury. Part of the reason is surely the Next Case Syndrome: when you have put your all into a case and the verdict comes down, you want to leave it behind and get on to something else.

In addition, if the verdict is *guilty,* the prosecutor may figure that the punishment for the perjury that failed can be picked up by the court in deciding the sentence for the underlying crime. It's one of the clearly legitimate bases for the exercise of judicial discretion or the application of standardized guidelines. If the jury bought the perjury and acquitted, the prosecutor might figure that retrying the case on the falsity of the defense would likely reproduce the same outcome. Hardly worth the effort.

Of course these rationalizations do not apply to prosecution of a mendacious defense witness, and such perjury cases are not unknown to the courts. But if the reasons of fear, loyalty, or love are strong enough to induce the false exculpation in the first place, the remote possibility of prosecution for perjury probably will not inhibit the gesture of support. For I am convinced that, as defendant or witness for a cherished other, even the most honest—and innocent—among us will lie under oath to the extent that we believe the lie will divert a guilty verdict. And the possibility of enhanced punishment if the lie fails, or the remote chance that we might be prosecuted as a perjurious witness, exerts only slight inhibition.

I have strayed from the point. I was discussing discovery and the means of preventing this fair play procedure from fueling a deceptive gambit. It occurs to me that there is one way to control defense license to some extent—not in order to make the playing field level but because perjury is a foul corruption of the process. I have not seen this idea proposed or discussed anywhere. Perhaps that is because, although I don't think it does serious violence to the basic constraints of fairness in our adversary system, it does require adjustment of one critical component. I'll try it out here.

We could simply require that the defendant formally commit himself earlier in the process to a particular line of exculpation. Not by a sealed account of himself, but by pleadings. Today, a criminal defendant does not answer a charge, he enters a plea. Some defendants plead guilty right at the outset. And for the rest, with only one rare exception, the plea is just two words long: not guilty. We could require the accused to meet the formal accusation with an answer (as it's called in civil pleadings), a formal contention that declared just why he denied the charge. Today's unelaborated plea is no more than a formality. It is not taken as a statement of the defense position but merely as a device for "joining issue," for bringing the allegations of the accusation into contention. We could, I suppose, insist that this answer be meaningful, at least to the extent of electing a defense from among several rather broad categories. We could receive a plea of "not guilty by reason of nonparticipation," "not guilty by reason of lack of criminal intent," or "not guilty by reason of provocation, justification, or excuse." In most places, we already require a special plea of "not guilty by reason of insanity." (This is the rare exception to the general rule allowing undifferentiated denial.)

And this formal plea might be augmented with a brief, sworn, exculpatory allegation: "It wasn't me, I was in Cincinnati at the time"; "I may have ended up with the property in my basement, but it was pledged to me by the owner as security for a loan"; "Sure we had sex together, but she wanted it as much as I did"; "I did hit him with my knife but only to save my own life when he put a lamp cord around my neck and pulled." Such responsive allegations of innocence could be used to keep the eventual trial theory of the defense in line with the defendant's initial, prediscovery position.

The major problem with my cool idea is this: Our system lays on the prosecution the burden of proof to match the authority of accusation. And that means that no obligation may be placed on the defendant to demonstrate his innocence. A criminally accused person is "not guilty" when the prosecution has failed to sustain its burden of proof to the high level of "beyond a reasonable doubt." He may also be factually innocent, but that is by no means an essential element of being "not guilty." This feature of the system, the Supreme Court has held, is sufficiently fundamental that it is implied by the concept of due process of law. So the defendant enjoys a constitutionally derived right simply to plead, "Prove it." If, to accommodate this right, I included a plea category of "not guilty by reason of the presumption of innocence," I think I would scuttle the whole idea. Everyone would elect that plea and we'd be back where we started.

And if some foolhardy defendant, eager to state his case, elected a more specific plea of denial, coupled perhaps with a defensive scenario, we would still require the prosecutor to prove all the material allegations of the charge. Thus if a defendant initially pleaded consent to a rape charge, and at trial the prosecutor failed to prove penetration, the burdened prosecution must fail regardless of the defensive shift required. Under current standards, at least, the defense cannot relieve the prosecutor of the burden of proving all material elements by the implicit concession of a selected defense. So my proposal has problems.

Still, I think we might expand somewhat on the special plea of insanity and require defendants to plead certain affirmative defenses like entrapment or self-defense at the outset. Before they learn the prosecution case by discovery. This suggestion is not so radical; many jurisdictions already require the defendant to file early notice of an alibi defense (remember *Wardius*). Within these special pleas, of course, there is lots of room for maneuver in the details of the defense story, details that may be constructed to take account of the state's evidence that was learned by discovery. But I see no legal impediment to a requirement that, where such a special plea is entered, the defense make an opening statement to the jury, outlining the specifics of his affirmative defense as the prosecutor must detail her affirmative case. This at least would inhibit maneuver to adjust to postdiscovery discoveries. While I am dubious about devices to inhibit defense perjury—which we will have as long as we have guilty defendants and a virtually risk-free opportunity to lie under oath—I am sympathetic to any scheme that might improve chances to discredit these ploys.

Finally, to return to the idea of reciprocity, is there some virtue in a plan that would require the defense to share with the prosecution the product of its own investigation? Especially where the defense is gold-plated, should discovery run the other way with the lean prosecutor living off the fat of the defense budget? Let's think seriously for a moment about this idea. Is there any support in concepts of fairness or in the peculiar doctrine of level fields of combat for the idea of mutual or reciprocal discovery? To the extent that a defendant, by luck or labor, turns up information—inculpatory information, let us say—missed by the vaunted (but often clumsy) forces of the state, should the defense be forced to disclose it? A reverse *Brady* doctrine? The same considerations of fairness and service of the interests of truth-in-verdicts should greatly enlarge the discovery owed the prosecution in all jurisdictions.

Or reverse *Jencks* for that matter. If a defense witness has given counsel a statement that might be used to impeach her credibility, why not require the defense to turn it over to the prosecutor for use in cross-examination? Actually, there is some solid law supporting the idea of reverse *Jencks*. When Robert Lee Nobles was tried for robbing a bank with three others, the main evidence against Nobles (who had allegedly stood under the surveillance camera during the robbery and thereby missed the photo-op) was the testimony of two men, a teller named Peter Van Gemesen and a person described as a "visiting salesman," Gary Hoffman. Both, as we may imagine, were vigorously cross-examined concerning their asserted recognition of Nobles. Going after Van Gemesen, defense counsel asked him about an interview with John Bond, an investigator for the Federal Public Defenders' office. Van Gemesen said he did not remember telling Bond that he had seen only the fourth robber's back and, after refreshing his recollection by consulting Bond's report, continued to insist that regardless of what the report said, he had seen enough of the man to identify him as Nobles. Hoffman, under cross, denied that he had told Bond that "all blacks looked alike" to him.

These were obviously central matters in discrediting the identification testimony of the two witnesses who were, in essence, the whole of the prosecution's case against Nobles. The defense proposed to put Bond on the witness stand, but the trial judge ruled that if Bond were called, the defense must turn over to the government Bond's report for possible use in discrediting Bond's testimony. The defense refused and the judge precluded Bond's testimony. Nobles was convicted.

When the case reached the United States Supreme Court in 1975, Justice Powell, speaking for the Court, upheld the trial judge's ruling. Justice Powell described just how the prosecutor's access to Bond's report might enhance the jury's search for truth (his example: if Bond had testified that Hoffman had said all blacks look alike, but the report contained no such statement). Powell then went on to reject the several protests of the defense—along with the opinion of the Court of Appeals for the Ninth Circuit, which had reversed the trial court.

No, the Supreme Court explained patiently, Nobles's Fifth Amendment privilege was not violated by compelling him to turn over the statement of his agent, Bond, reporting what the witnesses had told him. The privilege protects Nobles only against the forcible extraction of his own statements. Rejected too was the defendant's argument that the law that excuses him from pretrial disclosure of his investigator's memos should carry over to exempt him from post-testimonial tender as well. And, no, turning over Bond's report would not compromise the defendant's Sixth Amendment right to counsel's effective assistance by sapping the professional relationship of trust and confidence, nor would it impair the ability of the lawyer to investigate thoroughly (this argument received summary disposition in a footnote).

The Court had considerably more trouble with the claim that surrender of the investigator's report would violate the so-called work-product doctrine. This doctrine, well known and much beloved by the bar, exempts from discovery an attorney's notes reflecting the lawyer's impressions, judgments, and other reactions jotted down in anticipation of litigation. And as a practical matter, the salutary purposes of the exemption require that the doctrine shield material prepared by agents of the lawyer too. Recognizing all this (whether or not it be underscored—as I would have thought—by the special Sixth Amendment importance of legal assistance for a criminal defendant), Powell held that the work-product privilege, like others, may be waived and, by offering the testimony of the agent, Bond, the defense relinquished any protection otherwise due Bond's confidential report on the same subject.

The Supreme Court emphasized that its holding in *United States v. Nobles* was limited: defense disclosure need be made only of that portion of the report "related to the testimony the investigator would offer to discredit the witnesses' identification testimony," and only in the special circumstances of waiver by "testimonial use." The Court made no attempt to peg its conclusion on some notion of reciprocity, to match the defense obligation with the government's duty under the so-called Jencks Act to turn over any statement by the witness that "relates to the subject matter as to which the witness has testified." The governing federal rule of criminal procedure—Rule 26.2, to be exact—burdens both the government and the defense, simultaneously but not reciprocally, when it directs that upon request following the testimony of a witness, the party shall produce for examination and use on cross-examination any statement of the witness that relates what the witness has testified.

But even if the assistance to cross-examination is roughly comparable, the Court in *Nobles* made it clear that we are not talking discovery here. Rule 16 of the Federal Rules of Criminal Procedure is explicit. The defendant shall not be called upon to produce for pretrial inspection by the prosecution either his lawyer's-work-product or any prior statements the defendant or witnesses might have made to the defendant, his attorneys, or agents.

To any lawyer schooled in the traditional ways of the adversary machine, the idea of reciprocal or mutual discovery is anathema. The prosecutor, sure. He is a public official with an obligation to fairness and no client to serve except the community as a whole—which includes the defendant. But defense counsel? Commanded to aid his adversary even to the extent of turning over notes that fit *Nobles'* narrow criteria, defense counsel would instinctively respond by taking a page from the prosecutors' book and simply declining to keep a written record of discoverable material. What it comes down to is that, with all respect to the ghost of Justice Thurgood Marshall, discovery is not a two-way street. Sorry, Thurgood, it just does not run in this direction. It may be that where the defense must disclose, the prosecution must do likewise; but it is not the case that where the prosecution must disclose, the defense must reciprocate.

The simple and plain reason for this is that symmetry is only the dullest form of balance and inappropriate when roles differ sharply. One would not insist, in the name of a just balance, that where the violins have the tune, the horns must be given the same tune. And there are good reasons—in tradition if nowhere else—why the defense in a criminal case should not be inhibited in its independent investigation by the possibility of shooting itself in the foot.

Maybe it does come, in some indirect way, from the idea that the defendant should not be made to cooperate in bringing about his own downfall—even where that outcome is richly deserved—and should not have his champion pressed into the service of his accusers. So whatever discovery of the prosecution case the defense deserves in the interests of fairness need not be purchased by reciprocal disclosures. And once again, it is the notion of fairness (keyed to the different roles and duties of the parties in a criminal case) rather than the notion of reciprocity inherent in the image of the level playing field that dictates different access to information.

Having said all that, I must note (with some surprise) that the law does, in some places and to differing degrees, impose upon the defense some obligation to make advance disclosure of its case. Not as a matter of reciprocal obligation, either, but in the interests of fairness. As I noted above, in most places, defendants must tell whether they intend to raise a defense of insanity and in many they must disclose an alibi. In many jurisdictions, the defense must also deliver to the prosecutor a list of expert witnesses they intend to call, together with their expected testimony. In California, discovery is open and mutual.

California, California, what would we do without you? The cradle of Participatory Democracy, the home of Alternative Arrangements. In June of 1990, the State of California had one of its voter initiatives, a referendum, that included Proposition 115. And the people of California, at the ballot box, "adopted" a new law that was then passed by the legislature as Section 1054 of the Penal Law. The first subdivision of Section 1054 sets forth the obligations of the state as follows:

> The prosecuting attorney shall disclose to the defendant or his or her attorney all of the following materials and information, if it is in the possession of the prosecuting attorney or if the prosecuting attorney knows it to be in the possession of the investigating agencies:
>
> (a) The names and addresses of persons the prosecutor intends to call as witnesses at trial.
>
> (b) Statements of all defendants.
>
> (c) All relevant real evidence seized or obtained as a part of the investigation of the offenses charged.
>
> (d) The existence of a felony conviction of any material witness whose credibility is likely to be critical to the outcome of the trial.
>
> (e) Any exculpatory evidence.
>
> (f) Relevant written or recorded statements of witnesses or reports of the statements of witnesses whom the prosecutor intends to call at the trial, including any reports or statements of experts made in conjunction with the case, including the

results of physical or mental examinations, scientific tests, experiments, or comparisons which the prosecutor intends to offer in evidence at the trial.

Aside from the expected *Brady* and *Jencks* provisions [(e) and (f)], the law directs disclosure of names and addresses of prosecution witnesses—though not their expected testimony—and physical evidence and prior statements of the defendants that the prosecutor intends to introduce at trial. Pretty good, not perfect but more generous than most.

The third subdivision of Section 1054, containing the defendant's reciprocal obligation, really stakes out new ground. It reads like this:

> The defendant and his or her attorney shall disclose to the prosecuting attorney:
>
> (a) The names and addresses of persons, other than the defendant, he or she intends to call as witnesses at trial, together with any relevant written or recorded statements of those persons, or reports of the statements of those persons, including any reports or statements of experts made in connection with the case, and including the results of physical or mental examinations, scientific tests, experiments, or comparisons which the defendant intends to offer in evidence at the trial.
>
> (b) Any real evidence which the defendant intends to offer in evidence at the trial.

The first time a prosecutor requested disclosure from the defendant—a man accused of rape—he declined and protested all the way up through the California courts that the obligation imposed upon him was unconstitutional. The California Supreme Court was unimpressed. In *People v. Izazaga* (1991), the court answered each of the defendant's constitutional claims. On the assertion that the reciprocal discovery law violated his right against self-incrimination, the

California high court recalled that the United States Supreme Court had approved of a notice-of-alibi discovery law in *Williams v. Florida* and went on to say: "Discovery of the names and addresses of the witnesses that the defense intends to call at trial, whether or not in support of an alibi defense, merely forces the defendant to divulge at an earlier date information that the [defendant] from the beginning planned to divulge at trial. Under the rationale of *Williams*, such discovery does not constitute compelled self-incrimination, and therefore does not implicate the privilege." The court opined that, even apart from the *Williams* theory, those incriminating statements of witnesses, pried from the defendant by the law of discovery, were not obtained in violation of the Fifth Amendment because they are not the statements of the defendant himself. And the Fifth prohibits only forced *self*-incrimination.

On the argument that the disclosure was a violation of due process of law insofar as it unfairly tilted the playing field against the defendant, the court recalled that *Wardius* read due process to require a "balance of forces between the accused and his accuser." "That is," the California court explained, "when the prosecution is allowed discovery of the defense, that discovery must be reciprocal." Examining the statute in detail, the court concluded, "the new discovery chapter enacted by Proposition 115 creates a nearly symmetrical scheme of discovery in criminal cases, with any imbalance favoring the defendant as required by reciprocity under the due process clause."

Though the provisions may not look identical at first glance, they are very close. Each side must disclose to the other the names, addresses, and statements of witnesses, including experts, whom it intends to call at trial; and both sides must turn over "real evidence" (by which is meant physical, as contrasted with testimonial, evidence). These are the principal elements of proof. The provisions diverge in that the prosecutor must turn over the defendant's statements, if any, and the prior criminal records of critical witnesses, information the state alone would have. The more critical difference is that, while the state's *Brady* obligation is spelled out [in paragraph (e)], no comparable duty is placed upon the defense. So even in California, if the defense's investigation turns up a witness it would never call—because he supports the prosecution's theory—it can sit on the unfortunate find and hope the prosecutor doesn't bump into him.

Back to Mr. Izazaga, protesting the uncomfortable and unfamiliar obligations imposed on him by California's new law. He also argued that his constitutional right under the Sixth Amendment to the effective assistance of counsel was violated by the reciprocal feature of the discovery law. Counsel's diligent investigation might be chilled by the obligation to disclose the results, he asserted. In response, the court noted that the law required only disclosure of witnesses that the defense intended to call to the stand at trial—presumably only the helpful witnesses. So exhaustive investigation is not "penalized" or "chilled." In line with other cases on the point, the court rejected the Sixth Amendment argument.

So the State of California, at least, has responded to the call for matched sharing—first sounded back in 1963 by Justice William Brennan. Almost open-files discovery of the prosecution case is paired with an almost commensurate reciprocal disclosure by the defense. And on a careful review of what it had done, the state concluded that the structure of justice still stood. The new law—radical though it might be—had not trammeled any vital right of the parties under the Constitution. Yes, but even Justice Brennan abandoned his call for a level playing field as the principle upon which free discovery should be based and, reviewing that speech twenty-seven years later, said: "The essential purpose of permitting a criminal defendant to engage in pretrial discovery of the prosecution's case is to enhance the truth-finding process so as to minimize the danger that an innocent defendant will be convicted."

The idea that full mutual discovery, or even augmented defense discovery, offers a significant shield for the innocent is not readily apparent. The truly guiltless defendant probably has least need to know the prosecutor's case in advance. Unlike his culpable counterpart, who has little hope beyond discrediting prosecution evidence, the innocent defendant is probably busy assembling an independent scenario proving his innocence. And revealing his case in advance to the prosecutor is just asking for trouble. So if I were one of those rare souls about whom Justice Brennan is concerned, I'm not at all sure that I would choose to be tried under California's liberal laws.

The curious thing is why, given the obvious benefits to both sides (in the ordinary case) from the California scheme, other jurisdictions are so hesitant to follow. While the federal and state jurisdictions are all experimenting with their fundamental notions of discovery, no clones of Proposition 115 have yet surfaced elsewhere. Indeed, state courts around the nation are strangely silent on the California initiative: Section 1054 of the Penal Law is not discussed outside the borders of California.

The reluctance of the defense bar and their sympathizers in the academy may be understandable: defendants would probably give up more than they would gain by the reciprocal discovery feature. But where are the forces of law and order, those who share the sentiments of Judge Learned Hand expressed in 1923:

> Under our criminal procedure the accused has every advantage. While the prosecution is held rigidly to the charge, he need not disclose the barest outline of his defense. He is immune from question or comment on his silence; he cannot be convicted when there is the least fair doubt in the minds of any one of the twelve. Why in addition he should in advance have the whole evidence against him to pick over at his leisure, and to make his defense fairly or foully, I have never been able to see. . . . Our dangers do not lie in too little tenderness to the

accused. . . . What we need to fear is the archaic formalism and the watery sentiment that obstructs, delays, and defeats the prosecution of crime.

Would they not like to follow California and require the defendant to disclose at least the barest outline of his case in advance?

4

VOUCHER AND THE VIRTUE OF OFFICE

The White-Hat Factor

AN AXIOM OF DEEP GRAVITY in the trial of criminal cases is that the prosecutors, and the victims they speak for, are the good guys; the defendant and his lawyers are the bad. Among the jurors, exerting a pull you can almost feel, is a disposition brought into the jury box from real life, a disposition to identify with the victim, to regard law enforcement forces as the vindicators, and to suspect that all defendants are probably guilty (or else they wouldn't be there, would they?). And their lawyers are not to be trusted when they try to persuade you otherwise (since everyone knows they are only doing their job, and sincerity is not in the job description). To the defense bar, this hostile predisposition is the root of the actual, covert presumption of guilt that all but eclipses the overt, legal presumption of innocence in every criminal trial.

I know that when I was trying cases for the prosecutor, I relied heavily on the white hat to which I thought myself entitled. Clean shaven, conservatively dressed, I cultivated a courtroom demeanor of respectful rectitude. I spoke for the People of the State. "Your honor," I would say solemnly, "The People respectfully move for an adjournment of this matter until next Tuesday." I would swell with indignation at the slightest hint of dereliction. "Your honor, the People resent counsel's innuendo. We have been ready to proceed with this trial all along, and suffered the dilatory tactics of the defense only under protest." Before the jury, I would contrive in a dozen small gestures and inflections to reinforce what I assumed to be the inclination of my twelve stalwarts to favor truth and decency over brutality, deceit, and self-interest. I cannot imagine any prosecutor worthy of carrying the public pennant who would do otherwise.

In the past several years, a variety of surprising acquittals in highly publicized cases has fueled a growing apprehension that jurors are becoming harder to convince. Trial lawyers on both sides, along with the general public, have begun to sense that skepticism toward the prosecution is replacing long-standing confidence. We have all seen several items—no more than grains of sand blowing in the wind, perhaps—that must contribute to jurors' disillusionment with the diligence and the dedication to truth of the prosecution team.

It's hard to tell whether it's anything really new, or only the product of more intense scrutiny and heightened sensitivity. But who today can ignore, for example, signs of police bigotry? Whatever his private sentiments, Detective Fuhrman, late of the LAPD, certainly etched on the public consciousness the image of a racist cop. And how many instances have we seen in local and national news of shootings by white cops of unarmed black teenagers? Police have been accused, and once in a while convicted, of fabricating evidence, robbing drug dealers, and worse. Prosecutors, even a couple of judges, have been charged with corruption and bizarre personal crimes. The FBI lab, that bastion of unimpeachable integrity, has received official censure. We were mistaken, as it turns out, but all of us thought we could detect a disturbing, nationwide shift in juror skepticism; the white hat, we thought, was more frequently showing up on the wrong cranium.

For some time, of course, we have known that many residents of the inner city, people in minority communities, did not look on the local police as their friends. Especially where the defendants were African American or Hispanic, we knew that local lore or personal experience would incline jurors of a like background to suspicion or antagonism directed toward the police generally, and white officers in particular. Prosecutions in these neighborhoods were often uphill battles. We didn't like it, but we lived with it. For some few cases, in some few venues, sometimes, the prosecutor found she was not wearing the white headgear. Not the end of the world.

But who would have expected that in heartland America so many people would regard federal officers—the once-glorious FBI, along with ATF, DEA, INS, and the rest—as agents of a hostile power? Who would have guessed that in the communities where every family owns an American flag and patriotism is a religion so many good citizens would distrust law enforcement agents? Who would have expected that self-styled libertarians would be out there handing out leaflets calling law enforcement officers puppets of a foreign conspiracy?

What has come over America? we asked in our ignorant distress. It can't be the message of the fundamentalist "militia" people, of the murderous crazies like the Unabomber or Timothy McVeigh getting into the attitude of sober jurors across the land. Surely the ordinary folk considering the evidence in some common backyard burglary are not thinking of the shootout at Ruby Ridge or the attack on the Branch Davidians at Waco. Have the ever-popular police shows on TV subtly undermined the credibility of cops by making them all too human? I'm no expert on these shows, but I haven't noticed that the hero role has been transferred to the criminals. Has the remarkable statistical drop in crime rates changed attitudes so fundamentally and swiftly that the public generally now fears law enforcement officers more than predators? Hardly seems likely.

Scholars, laboring under the same delusion, have taken to the journals to explain the attitude shift. Dinner party experts have contributed their judgments. Journalists have had their say. Theories are not in short supply. We are witnessing the flowering of the liberal, permissive society in which nothing is blameworthy, everything is only an alternative lifestyle. Or, if you prefer, we are in the grip of a right-wing backlash against government in all its manifestations, including criminal prosecutions. Maybe it's the lawyers who are to blame. With their scientific jury stacking and high-priced consultants, they can put anything over on the twelve gulls whom they finally agree to allow to sit on the jury. Or else credit the imagination of the defense bar, which has come up with a blinding array of excuses, from premenstrual syndrome and the chemical effects on the brain of Prozac or junk food, to "black rage" and the abuse excuse as put to Officer Krupke in Leonard Bernstein's *West Side Story:* "Hey, I'm depraved on account of I'm deprived."

Lots of people had lots of ideas to explain what was, to many of us, a disturbing reallocation of the white-hat factor. But until 1997 we were all building on hunch, nourished by assumption, confirmed by general concordance. Then the rug was neatly pulled from under the confident pundits (including me) by some good and simple empirical data. Thank heaven for the occasional scholar who, leaving colleagues behind to speculate, goes out and has a look.

Two Duke Law School professors, Neil Vidmar and Sara Beale, with Mary Rose, a graduate student, and Laura F. Donnelly, a North Carolina court administrator, published their findings in *Judicature.* They surveyed the jury acquittal rates in five states (where good statistical records were kept) and the federal courts over ten to fifty years. Their conclusion: "The fact remains that the statistics from the federal courts and from the states of North Carolina, Florida, California, New York, and Texas show absolutely no support for critics' explicit or implicit assertions that juries are becoming too easily swayed by emotional appeals, soft hearts, or racial politics and consequently tend to acquit defendants at higher rates than in the past. If anything, the trend appears to be in the opposite direction." A welcome splash of cold water.

Specifically, Vidmar, Beale, and colleagues find that in the 2 to 3 percent of felony charges that are decided by jury trials, the conviction rate is remarkably steady: 68.3 percent in North Carolina in the past ten years; 58.9 percent during the same period in Florida; 82.1 percent in California over a fifteen-year period; 72.3 percent in New York over a ten-year period, with a slight upturn in the past five years; 84.0 percent in Texas over the past ten years. Various factors might account for the point spread among the states, but within each state, the graphs are astonishingly horizontal. The chart of federal dispositions is somewhat more jagged, but the trend, particularly in nondrug cases, is slightly upward, from an average of 63 percent between 1945 and 1960 to 82 percent in 1995.

Some diehards, reading these numbers, may say that, flat or not, dispositions other than guilty verdicts (mostly acquittals, presumably, with some disagreements and dismissals thrown in) at rates as high as one in three (North Carolina), to say nothing of better than two in five (Florida), demonstrate a high degree of jury skepticism. But let's remember that these rates occur in percentages of the criminal dockets in the low single digits. These are the rare cases that go to trial, a self-selected group composed of those with the weakest prosecution evidence, the strongest defenses, and (quite possibly) the highest proportion of the truly innocent. In that group, conviction rates of seven or eight in ten—while not the work of an utterly docile jury—

are surely nothing for the diligent prosecutor to worry about. And in any case, the important intelligence is that, whatever the level, prosecutors have suffered no recent loss in juror support.

Enlightened, then, and relieved by the Vidmar-Beale results, we can indulge the luxury of insight. The perception—misperception, as it turned out—of a growing predilection for disbelief was bracing. It forced us to look critically at the white-hat factor, to listen to the protests from the defense side. We had to confront the charge that the pervasive faith in government left a lot of injustice in its wake. Maybe the public knew best: maybe it was high time the false advantage of prosecutorial virtue was stripped from government. The criminal justice system is supposed to mirror a healthy public skepticism about the state. Oppression thrives where people trust the forces of law and order; freedom requires perpetual challenge to the rectitude of those who purport to act only in the public interest. Jefferson himself said as much.

Besides, the critics insisted, we're not just talking image here. This is no fickle shift in heroes from the accusers to the accused. We're talking truth here. The government has proved itself over and over to be a battalion of liars and incompetents. And not just in the gilt-edged prosecutions where the bungles are trumpeted from the ramparts by the gleeful news media. Have you watched the thousands of felonies tried to empty courtrooms all over the country? Cases in which police perjury, crude forensics, confused testimony, or inept presentation is apparent even to the casual observer? This is not the Lone Ranger, folks, this is a collection of bumbling civil servants on whose word you wouldn't open your umbrella.

There is surely some truth in all this. There's no documentation, of course, for the silent inclination of jurors to take the facts as the prosecutor serves them up. And judges and ex-jurors are understandably reluctant to say that a judgment of conviction was rendered on a prosecution case based mainly on faith. But listen to the chat of the prosecutors, the defense lawyers, or even the judges themselves and you have to believe that many guilty verdicts come down on sympathy for a likable victim—even as a vote of confidence in a personable prosecutor—and not much more. A terrible crime, these players will admit, demands a villain to condemn for it, and the accused at hand is often better than no one at all.

It sounds pretty scary. If the scales are really tipped by the inchoate advantage of a virtuous prosecutor, the gleam of a police officer's badge, or a general disinclination to credit anything an accused or his lawyer says, the government's advantage may be truly pernicious. Should we hope the next century will bring an era in which the legal presumption of innocence will be coupled with an actual predisposition to believe that the government has consciously fabricated evidence or carelessly brought the wrong person to trial? It's not a pretty prospect.

I heartily favor the presumption of innocence—but as an expression of the prosecution's burden of proof, not as a reflection of an actual distrust of all prosecution evidence. A juror attitude of skepticism toward all evidence—suspending credence until a close look is had—is a healthy way for a jury to approach its daunting task of distilling truth from the broth of half-lies, patched recollection, selective disclosure, and outright mendacity ladled out to them. But a healthy inquisitive skepticism is a different animal from a working belief that police distort facts, government experts are wrong, witnesses succumb to manipulation, and prosecutors hunt scalps—and any scalp at hand will do as nicely as any other.

Perversely, perhaps, it still seems right to me that the prosecution should receive the benefit of a favorable public disposition. A presumption of veracity does not seem misplaced to me—or inconsistent with the presumption of innocence. After all, the prosecutor has no client and no cause but the vigorous defense of the public tranquility; nearly all defendants are in fact guilty, nearly all defenses do aim to muddle truth. More important, by and large, people charged with crime are not a random assortment who look something like the real criminals, the reckless braggarts or terrified false-confessors, law-abiding citizens incriminated by forensic blunders and lab screwups, the innocent victims of police racism or perjury.

It's true, prosecutors depend a great deal on what others tell them, and those people could be careless, wrong, or vindictive. But the prosecutor knows his burden, is not eager to lose, and has the power of dismissal. So behind every case on trial, there has presumably been a conscientious effort by someone to assess the likelihood of true guilt, to appraise the tensile strength of the proof, and to consider alternative constructions.

I don't say every prosecutor's judgment in these matters deserves blind faith. But I do believe that, with rare exceptions, it warrants an inclination to credit prosecution proof. If we ever come to a time when the public can repose no confidence in the decisions of public prosecutors, we will be in serious trouble indeed. People sitting on juries (and everywhere else) should be hostile to crime and to criminals, and should try to use the crude mechanism of criminal justice to convict the guilty—regardless of how they may disapprove of this cop's character or that lab's sloppy procedure. Prosecutors and jurors are—and rightly should be—on the same side when the day is done. I hope prosecutors still enjoy their traditional edge of favorable public predisposition—but always with the stipulation that in any particular case, an alert and skeptical jury will hold the prosecutor to a high level of persuasion.

Though the prosecution case still comes into court draped in the mantle of rectitude, the prosecutor may not invoke that mantle. The law is quite stern on the point. The prosecutor may say nothing that can be taken as a personal endorsement of the credibility of his witnesses or as a personal belief in the guilt of the accused on trial. The prosecutor must be wary of putting the authority and integrity of her office behind the case, of hinting that she knows something damaging that the jury doesn't know.

These lessons have been repeatedly taught in courts all around the country. While the Supreme Court has excused express vouchers where defense attacks "invited" such personal comment from the government lawyers, and courts have withheld reversals where they thought the prosecutor's lapse could not have affected the jury's evaluation of the evidence, the rule remains firmly in place: don't put your own virtue behind your case. Don't suggest that you, an honorable public officer, have made a thorough, expert, and detached examination of the case and it looks good to you—even though, if you've done your job, you have done exactly that.

There's a pretty good reason for the rule. The courts have instructed us that a juror who might be dubious about the motives or character of a prosecution witness, or the plausibility of his story, may happily take the earnest young assistant's endorsement as an easy release from the ultimate responsibility to decide the hard questions. Here's what one appellate court had to say about the prosecutor's putting his own stature behind his case: "It is fair to say that the average jury, in a greater or less degree, has confidence that these obligations [to prosecute fairly and according to the evidence], which so plainly rest upon the prosecuting attorney, will be faithfully observed. Consequently, improper suggestions, insinuations, and, especially, assertions of personal knowledge [by the prosecutor] are apt to carry much weight against the accused when they should properly carry none." Another court summarized the accumulated wisdom on the point thus: "Attempts to bolster a witness by vouching for his credibility are normally improper and error. The test for improper vouching is whether the jury could reasonably believe that the prosecutor was indicating a personal belief in the witness' credibility. This test may be satisfied in two ways. First, the prosecution may place the prestige of the government behind the witness, by making explicit personal assurances of the witness' veracity. Secondly, a prosecutor may implicitly vouch for the witness' veracity by indicating that information not presented to the jury supports the testimony."

It's duplicitous, in a way. Of course the prosecutor's office is behind the prosecution. They decided to bring it. They could have washed it out if they didn't believe their witnesses, or thought the evidence of guilt was equivocal. And, presumably, jurors know that. But they must not be told so explicitly. Not that prosecutors don't comport themselves as though they believed every word coming from their witnesses on the stand; woe betide the prosecutor who looks bored or skeptical as prosecution testimony comes in. But acting convinced, in the wonderful naivete of the law, is different from speaking the line: "I am convinced."

It's tempting, damn tempting. Just to say something—in summation for example—after your adversary has ridiculed your witnesses and suggested that you were prosecuting this piece of garbage only because it was your duty (or worse, out of malice). To his regret, one prosecutor yielded in a federal fraud prosecution and found himself chastised, along with defense counsel who precipitated the intemperance, by the United States Supreme Court in a 1985 decision. Summing up to the jury in *United States v. Billy Young,* defense counsel started out with a blistering attack on the prosecutor's integrity. Here is Chief Justice Warren Burger's description:

> Defense counsel began his own summation by arguing that the case against respondent "has been presented unfairly by the prosecution," and that "[f]rom the beginning" to "this very moment the [prosecution's] statements have been made to poison your minds unfairly." He intimated that the prosecution deliberately withheld exculpatory evidence, and proceeded to charge the prosecution with "reprehensible" conduct in purportedly attempting to cast a false light on respondent's activi-

ties. Defense counsel also pointed directly at the prosecutor's table and stated: "I submit to you that there's not a person in this courtroom including those sitting at this table who think that Billy Young intended to defraud Apco [the victim]."

Although he did not object, when he got up to rebut the defense summation, the prosecutor said, as the Court retells it,

> "I think [defense counsel] said that not anyone sitting at this table thinks that Mr. Young intended to defraud Apco. Well, I was sitting there and I think he was. . . . So, I think he did. If we are allowed to give our personal impressions since it was asked of me."

Continuing with a review of portions of the evidence against respondent, the prosecutor responded to defense counsel's statement that Apco was not defrauded:

> "I don't know what you call that, I call it fraud."

That odd little aside, "If we are allowed . . . since it was asked of me" is significant. It reflects the prosecutor's underlying misgivings about his personal avowals. And it is an attempt to justify what he is saying as responsive. It turned out that he was right on both counts. The Court, deeply split on other aspects of the case, was united in condemning the "improper" and unnecessary "expression of personal opinion" by the prosecutor. But by the application of two oddly juxtaposed doctrines (causing four of the nine to split off), the Chief Justice managed to reverse the Circuit Court of Appeals and reinstate the conviction.

First is the so-called invited response doctrine. While the improper voucher is not excused by the attack that provoked it (even the Supreme Court knows that two wrongs don't make a right), it is thought that the otherwise harmful effect on the jury is mitigated by the obvious purpose of reply. Like several members of the Court, I am somewhat baffled by the logic of this doctrine; why should the jury's reception of the prosecutor's assurances of personal credence be any less influential because they were provoked? Perhaps the Court felt that failure to accept such a bold invitation to respond might be construed by the jury as inability to respond convincingly.

Anyway, that idea is coupled with a major boon to errant prosecutors, an idea that is really at the center of this decision. The prosecutor at trial, hearing defense counsel's initial salvo, did not object to it and obtain a judicial remonstrance, and perhaps corrective instruction to the jury, that would have obviated the improper rejoinder. (Everybody agreed that is what he should have done, but no matter.) More to the point, defense counsel did not object at the time to the prosecutor's improper comments in reply.

Now that omission is important because, without an objection and a ruling on it, there is no issue preserved for appellate review. I am anticipating a chapter that lies ahead, but I must note that there is one and only one circumstance where a federal appellate court may consider an error sans contemporary objection, and that is where the error was so blatant and indisputably damaging that it is "plain." Meaning that the error was so gross that even a nodding trial judge should have caught it without having his attention called to it by a timely objection. An objection is not necessary to preserve plain error for review. But the prosecutor's wrongly voiced personal opinion, the Supreme Court held, did not rise to the status of plain error.

A considerably diluted version of the plain error doctrine saves many convictions from reversal even when the prosecutor's wrongful comments to the jury have been preserved by objection. Embraced by all courts as a realistic doctrine that looks beyond narrow questions of isolated impropriety to broader considerations of justice, the "harmless error" doctrine holds that a conviction will not be reversed for errors that could not have affected the outcome. As Justice Frankfurter once said, "In reviewing criminal cases, it is particularly important for appellate courts to relive the whole trial imaginatively and not to extract from episodes in isolation abstract questions of evidence and procedure. To turn a criminal trial into a quest for error no more promotes the ends of justice than to acquiesce in low standards of criminal prosecution." The Chief Justice's description of the case against Billy Young made it sound as though, even had the defense objected, the conviction would have been affirmed on the harmless error dodge.

So (I can hear the cynics chortling) what it all comes down to is that the lofty principles about the seemly detachment of the prosecutor have no clout. Let the A.D.A.s and the A.U.S.A.s say what they please, vouch for their witnesses, lay the honor of their offices on the line, what they will, the worst they need fear is a lame scolding; if the case is strong—or especially if they got away without an objection—the conviction will be affirmed anyway. The great advantage of the white hat, the supposed virtue of their office, their detached discretion, and their client-free dedication to justice may be asserted after all to reinforce a case and assist the jury across some rough spots in credibility or coherence. Do you call that fair?

There is more than a modicum of truth in the chortle. Whatever the virtues of the harmless error doctrine, it surely does mitigate the impact of appellate disapproval and, to that extent, encourage government lawlessness. Yet even with the shelter of the context, even knowing they can shield their error if the provocation was vivid and the supporting evidence thickly layered, the government can rarely be completely confident of how the case will scan to an appellate tribunal. What seemed like a pretty rich fabric going into the jury may look distressingly pale and frayed crossing the appellate bench. Not all cases are overwhelming, not even those that convince a jury beyond a reasonable doubt, and the sensibility of the appellate judge is a well-known wild card. Thus it would be a reckless prosecutor indeed who would consciously inject a clearly inappropriate personal voucher into a case, relying on the harmless error doctrine to bail him out on review.

It is far more likely to be defense counsel who falls back on personal endorsement or asserts personal opinion to denigrate the proof against him. These heroes are not supposed to vouch on their personal chit for the credibility of their witnesses or the innocence of their clients either. The Model Rules of Professional Conduct (the law in some states) apply equally to lawyers for both sides: "A lawyer shall not," Rule 3.4(e) enjoins, "in trial . . . assert personal knowledge of facts in issue, . . . or state a personal opinion as to the justness of a cause, the credibility of a witness, . . . or the guilt or innocence of an accused." But for defense counsel there is no dire consequence pendant—even remotely. No acquittal is reversible. And the worst counsel need fear—in addition to a possible light reprimand—is that on the invited-response doctrine, the prosecution may be excused from replying in kind. But this disparity is probably less a result of a policy preference than the by-product of the appealability gap—a matter I get into farther along.

What is the basis for the law's long-standing and unyielding opposition to expressed opinion from counsel on the reliability of proof? Even in the many cases in which courts cannot or will not do anything about it, they never tire of preaching the lawyers' ethical obligations to refrain from putting their personal integrity behind their cases. I think that the ethical rule against personal vouching derives from an ancient British tradition. It's an odd little atavistic trace that has somehow survived major American transformations of seventeenth- and eighteenth-century English practice.

In our great country we not only permit, we encourage lawyers to become involved with their clients, witnesses, experts, and investigators. In the sports metaphor, we think of them as a team, a group working together toward a common, competitive object. The theatrical trope is also useful. The lawyer—prosecutor as well as defense counsel—often directs the efforts of the others in their respective companies, managing the assembly of the elements of the production, marshaling the legal support, and even supervising the staging of evidence in the courtroom. The most dramatic example of this theatrical image is a small feature of our trial system that goes virtually unnoticed among domestic practitioners but shocks our British and European colleagues: American lawyers rehearse their witnesses. And thoroughly.

Another comparison of note. In the United States, it would smack of malpractice for a lawyer to go to trial without full and continuing consultation with her client; in Great Britain, it would be malpractice for a barrister to talk at any time directly to the accused person he represents; they don't sit together in court, they don't confer beforehand or in the breaks, they do not enter or leave the courtroom together, and the barrister deals with the accused only indirectly through the solicitor who retained him. To call the berobed and bewigged English trial lawyer a teammate of the person whose case he has agreed to plead would strike him as little short of ludicrous.

Were we Americans consistent in eradicating old-world barriers between counsel and client, we would have no scruples about lawyers stating their personal convictions in support of their cause. We would allow the legal voice of the defense team to do in court what many now do on the courthouse steps, tell the world that they believe in their client's innocence. And more important, we would allow prosecutors to say openly what they are forever hinting, that they have put their official honor behind their decision to prosecute. What we find so deeply offensive about this notion must be its collision with the precept that lawyers are professional assistants, not the alter egos of their clients. We members of the ancient guild offer service, not immersion; we counsel and represent our clients, we do not become them. And the key to this role, thus defined, is detachment. Even we

American lawyers understand that our progenitors were right: there must be limits on our personal involvement with our causes or we will lose all claim to professional integrity.

The interests of professional stature, then, explain the ethical command to the bar to offer no personal endorsement of a client's or the government's case. To be sure, the principle of detachment loses much of its energy when we speak of government lawyers. They have no client as such, and there is little loss of dignity risked by a government lawyer's statement of personal belief in the government's position. After all, throughout the ranks, attorneys in government service are freely offering their own opinions on the justice of their official proposals without casting any ethical shadows on their professional detachment. Nonetheless, we take the government lawyers in the criminal prosecution trades out of the general category of government lawyers and, for ethical purposes, put them in the same league as their defense counterparts. So be it.

That line may get us closer to an understanding of the roots of the ethical injunction. But not every breach of ethical obligations infects a verdict. So somewhat more problematic is the basis for the rule that the prosecutor's voucher can fatally pollute a verdict of conviction. The prosecutor is not supposed to converse with a represented defendant in the absence of his counsel (even if the defendant wishes it), but if she does so, and later uses that defendant as a witness against an accomplice, a resulting conviction will not be overturned on that account. There is obviously something particularly toxic, beyond mere ethical transgression, when a prosecutor voices his own opinion on matters given to the jury to decide.

The only theory I can come up with is the one that courts have recited: the white-hat factor. In the prevailing doctrine, the government's voucher comes with an official imprimatur that instills undue deference in the ordinary jury. Touching faith in the majesty of government. It's a small point, but I cannot help but wonder whether the government's assurances still carry that sort of weight with our juries. Is it still true that the subtlest, gentlest reminder of the evident truth that the government believes in its case will carry the day, despite unsteady proof, dicey questions of credibility, or gaps in the evidence wide enough to leak plausibility?

The rule against putting the integrity of the lawyer (or his office) behind the credibility of testifying witnesses lived for many years in perfect harmony with a curious little contradictory doctrine at common law. (And by "common law," remember, I don't mean the ancient laws of merrie England; I mean the laws of any state, including my own, founded on a long case-law tradition, relatively untouched by statutory rules of evidence and the like.) Known as the voucher rule, this universal principle of evidence law simply demanded that parties not impeach the credibility of their own witnesses, witnesses they themselves had chosen to call to the stand. Once you have called a witness, offering the witness's testimony as worthy of consideration by the fact finder, you implicitly vouch that the witness is credible. There is no point, so this rule holds, in having parties call witnesses they don't trust just to show them up as liars.

Commentators thought the voucher rule was stupid. The world is not divided into your witnesses and my witnesses, they reminded us. Neither side makes its witnesses to specification. We both take our witnesses as we find them without any implicit endorsement of their laudable character or scrupulous veracity. The coup de grace was administered by the Supreme Court, which found the voucher rule to be a denial of due process—at least in the peculiar facts of the peculiar case before them, *Chambers v. Mississippi.*

On a warm Saturday evening in June 1969, two police officers entered a pool hall in the small town of Woodville in southern Mississippi. James Forman and Aaron "Sonny" Liberty had a warrant for the arrest of a young man named C. C. Jackson. Let Justice Lewis Powell, writing for the Court, take over the retelling of this dramatic story:

Jackson resisted and a hostile crowd of some 50 or 60 persons gathered. The officers' first attempt to handcuff Jackson was frustrated when 20 or 25 men in the crowd intervened and wrestled him free. Forman then radioed for assistance and Liberty removed his riot gun, a 12-gauge sawed-off shotgun, from the car. Three deputy sheriffs arrived shortly thereafter and the officers again attempted to make their arrest. Once more, the officers were attacked by the onlookers and during the commotion five or six pistol shots were fired. Forman was looking in a different direction when the shooting began, but immediately saw that Liberty had been shot several times in the back. Before Liberty died, he turned around and fired both barrels of his riot gun into an alley in the area from which the shots appeared to have come. The first shot was wild and high and scattered the crowd standing at the face of the alley. Liberty appeared, however, to take more deliberate aim before the second shot and hit one of the men in the crowd in the back of the head and neck as he ran down the alley. That man was Leon Chambers.

Officer Forman could not see from his vantage point who shot Liberty or whether Liberty's shots hit anyone. One of the deputy sheriffs testified at trial that he was standing several feet from Liberty and that he saw Chambers shoot him. Another deputy sheriff stated that, although he could not see whether Chambers had a gun in his hand, he did see Chambers "break his arm down" shortly before the shots were fired. The officers who saw Chambers fall testified that they thought he was dead but they made no effort at that time either to examine him or to search for the murder weapon. Instead, they attended to Liberty, who was placed in the police car and taken to a hospital where he was declared dead on arrival. A subsequent autopsy showed that he had been hit with four bullets from a .22-caliber revolver.

Shortly after the shooting, three of Chambers' friends discovered that he was not yet dead. James Williams, Berkley Turner, and Gable McDonald loaded him into a car and transported him to the same hospital. Later that night, when the county sheriff discovered that Chambers was still alive, a guard was placed outside his room. Chambers was subsequently charged with Liberty's murder. He pleaded not guilty and has asserted his innocence throughout.

The story of Leon Chambers is intertwined with the story of another man, Gable McDonald. McDonald, a lifelong resident of Woodville, was in the crowd on the evening of Liberty's death. Sometime shortly after that day, he left his wife in Woodville and moved to Louisiana and found a job at a sugar mill. In November of that same year, he returned to Woodville when his wife informed him that an acquaintance of his, known as Reverend Stokes, wanted to see him. Stokes owned a gas station in Natchez, Mississippi, several miles north of Woodville, and upon his return McDonald went to see him. After talking to Stokes, McDonald agreed to make a statement to Chambers' attorneys, who maintained offices in Natchez. Two days later, he appeared at the attorneys' offices and gave a sworn confession that he shot Officer Liberty. He also stated that he had already told a friend of his, James Williams, that he shot Liberty. He said that he used his own pistol, a nine-shot .22-caliber revolver, which he had discarded shortly after the shooting. In response to questions from Chambers' attorneys, McDonald affirmed that his confession was voluntary and that no one had compelled him to come to them. Once the confession had been transcribed, signed, and witnessed,

McDonald was turned over to the local police authorities and was placed in jail.

One month later, at a preliminary hearing, McDonald repudiated his prior sworn confession. He testified that Stokes had persuaded him to confess that he shot Liberty. He claimed that Stokes had promised that he would not go to jail and that he would share in the proceeds of a lawsuit that Chambers would bring against the town of Woodville. On examination by his own attorney and on cross-examination by the State, McDonald swore that he had not been at the scene when Liberty was shot but had been down the street drinking beer in a cafe with a friend, Berkley Turner. When he and Turner heard the shooting, he testified, they walked up the street and found Chambers lying in the alley. He, Turner, and Williams took Chambers to the hospital. McDonald further testified at the preliminary hearing that he did not know what had happened, that there was no discussion about the shooting either going to or coming back from the hospital, and that it was not until the next day that he learned that Chambers had been felled by a blast from Liberty's riot gun. In addition, McDonald stated that while he once owned a .22-caliber pistol he had lost it many months before the shooting and did not own or possess a weapon at that time. The local justice of the peace accepted McDonald's repudiation and released him from custody. The local authorities undertook no further investigation of his possible involvement.

When the case against Chambers came to trial, he produced an alibi witness. The witness testified that he had been looking at Chambers at the time the shots were fired that killed Sonny Liberty and that Chambers did not fire them. Chambers also tried to prove that the killer was McDonald. He called an old friend of McDonald's, who said he saw McDonald shoot Liberty. Chambers also had a witness who testified that he saw McDonald shortly afterward with a pistol in his hand.

In addition, Chambers tried to show that McDonald had repeatedly admitted killing Liberty. He had McDonald subpoenaed to court and put him on the stand when the prosecution failed to call him. The defense then elicited from McDonald the fact that he had confessed to Stokes. On cross-examination, the state brought out the repudiation and the whole story of why McDonald had given a false confession. Defense counsel rose to impeach the repudiation. Just how the defense hoped to do it does not appear because the trial judge cut him off. Chambers had called McDonald; he was a defense witness and could not be discredited by the party calling him. The ruling was upheld on appeal.

The Supreme Court had only scorn for the voucher rule in general and, in its application to Chambers's case, they found it inconsistent with due process: denying the defendant the opportunity to develop critical evidence. "Whatever validity the 'voucher' rule may have once enjoyed," they wrote, "and apart from whatever usefulness it retains today in the civil trial process, it bears little present relationship to the realities of the criminal process." For good measure, citing three heavy hitters among evidence scholars, the Court added, by way of footnote, "The 'voucher' rule has been condemned as archaic, irrational, and potentially destructive of the truth-gathering process."

When Congress got around to enacting a federal code of evidence, effective in 1975, it contained a provision (Rule 607) that says simply, "The credibility of a witness may be attacked by any party, including the party calling the witness." Many states have subsequently enacted their own evidence laws—many of which closely track the language of the federal code—and the abolition of the voucher rule is now all but complete.

But not quite. There is still something appealing about the rule.

Of course, parties do not really vouch for the honesty of their witnesses, nor do they have much choice in whom they call. But the prosecutor has some. However you might wish it, you can't erase that criminal record hanging on your only eyewitness, can't tidy up your arresting officer's paper trail, can't redo your victim's first description of her assailant. You must call these witnesses with all their impediments to credence hanging out. But at root, you call them because you believe that they are telling the truth about the critical facts. If you didn't believe that—or at least if you had some good reason to doubt that they were telling the truth—you wouldn't have called them. And if the case went down without them, so be it. The best reason in the world for a prosecutor to dismiss a case: insufficient credible evidence to support the charge.

So in a sense, the prosecutor—unlike defense counsel—does still vouch for his witnesses. And there is still no good reason why he should be allowed to call someone from whom no helpful evidence is expected just to impeach her—and perhaps thereby put before the jury data that could not otherwise come in. And despite Rule 607, federal courts still see it this way. For example, in 1984 Judge Posner, writing for the Seventh Circuit Court of Appeals, considered a case where the government, trying a man named Webster as an accomplice to a bank robbery, called as a witness the robber himself, one King, who had pleaded guilty and received a long sentence. The prosecutor, forced to put King on the stand cold, heard him testify that Webster was clean. She then sought to impeach King with his prior statement to the FBI in which he had implicated Webster. That statement by King to the FBI would not have been otherwise admissible on the government's case against Webster. It's hearsay. Webster complained that the government was using Rule 607 as a means of circumventing the prohibition against hearsay evidence.

Judge Posner's court agreed that the abolition of the voucher rule did not mean that a witness could be called by the government simply as a subterfuge to introduce otherwise inadmissible impeachment evidence. Having taken that view (as have all Circuits that have thought about it at all), the Court of Appeals went on to affirm the conviction since there was no reason to believe that the prosecutor had put King on the stand knowing he would exculpate his cohort. And, the court thought, good faith is the crux of the issue.

So what that leaves of the antivoucher rule is that the prosecutor may not impeach his own witness unless, when the witness was called, the prosecutor had no reason to think that the witness would betray him on the stand. That is pretty close to the common-law rule before Rule 607 was born. In common-law voucher jurisdictions, if the witness unexpectedly turns hostile, the party calling him may treat him as an adverse witness and try to impeach him by any means that might have been employed had the witness been called by the other side.

I think Judge Posner could have gone an inch farther in *Webster.* The court could have resolved ignorance against the prosecution. He could have held that the government should not have put King on without some reason to think he would inculpate Webster. In fact, in this case the prosecutor had good reason, based on the FBI report, to believe that King would inculpate Webster. But if the prosecutor had put her witness on without knowing what the witness would say, or believing the witness might be hostile, the court should have held that the risk belongs to the prosecutor who called the witness. Fairness, it seems to me, dictates that the prosecutor be stuck with the unfavorable testimony she should never have elicited, bound by the voucher rule not to impeach the witness with otherwise inadmissible evidence. It is fully consistent with the special discretion of the prosecution to require that the prosecutor not call witnesses unless she has some good reason to think the evidence will further the government's case.

Calling witnesses blind—and then impeaching those whose testimony you don't like—is not my idea of a good, orderly campaign.

However we may long for the beautiful world of naive lawyers and spontaneous witnesses—remember, English and European lawyers still bring their witnesses fresh to the stand—our system expects that witnesses will be selected and prepared by the lawyer producing the show. So the injunction on this side of the Atlantic is: if you can't find out what the witness will say before you call him, don't call him. Of course, if you have every reason to expect support and suddenly find yourself taking hostile fire, then (as under the old voucher rule) you can surely impeach him (or try) to undo the surprising harm. So what I am saying is, despite the broad generosity of Rule 607, the voucher rule still makes a lot of sense and should be applied against the prosecutor—and against the prosecutor only.

Is this an unfair imbalance? Don't both sides deserve due process? If Chambers was unfairly deprived of the opportunity to make his case, why can't the same be said for the prosecutor in *Webster* if she were not allowed to impeach King?

Imbalance, yes; unfair, no. Because the prosecutor chooses to go forward and carries the interests-of-justice discretion to dismiss at any time, the prosecutor does vouch for the evidence in the sense of offering it as worthy of belief in its critical particulars. And for that reason the prosecutor should not be allowed to undermine his own case—unless caught by genuine surprise.

Defendants, by contrast, must play the cards they are dealt. True, they needn't call witnesses they think will harm them, but denied pre-trial subpoena power (to say nothing of authority to compel answers by grant of immunity), lawyers for the defense may not be able to learn a witness's version before he goes under oath on the stand. They must be permitted to make their defense by whatever the means at hand. If the prosecutor fails to call a witness, the defense must be permitted to call him—blindly, if necessary—and impeach him if he must.

Even the sinister cast Judge Posner gave the canny prosecutor, who deliberately used the license of Rule 607 to subvert the rule against hearsay, pales somewhat on the countenance of the defense. Suppose the defense actually knows that a witness will be unhelpful (and the witness is, for some reason, ignored by the prosecutor), and the defense has in hand a prior statement of the witness that would be decidedly helpful on the merits—if only it weren't barred by the hearsay rule. How bad do we feel about allowing the defense to call the witness and use the prior statement to impeach?

It's true that Chambers called McDonald to give *helpful* testimony on direct: that he had previously confessed to the murder. What the defense was trying to impeach was the recantation, elicited on cross-examination. But let's just suppose for a moment that in calling McDonald—a central figure—the defense could not be certain which of his conflicting accounts he would render from the stand, though it seemed likely that he would stick to the recantation. It's hard medicine to tell the defense, don't call him. And harder still to preclude impeachment by the prior confession if McDonald takes the stand and proclaims his innocence. (We are stipulating here, of course, that the confession would have been—as it well might have been under Mississippi law—inadmissible hearsay otherwise.) How would Justice Powell, even Judge Posner, have felt about that one? Is impeaching a recantation elicited on cross so different from impeaching exculpatory evidence adduced on direct?

Imagine a case, for example, where a prosecutor fails to call a second police officer, knowing that the officer, a dumb rookie, had made out an interim investigatory report listing all the evidence that might exonerate the suspect, evidence that was never pursued in the subsequent investigation. The rookie's savvy partner testifies that all evidence was thoroughly investigated. The report was of course turned over as *Brady* material in discovery but is inadmissible in evidence (let us suppose). Is there any good reason why the defense should not be allowed to call the dumb rookie even if there is every reason to expect that, on the stand, he will corroborate his colleague? I can find no such reason. I think that is what a defense is, at best: an urgent effort to get the missing pieces into the picture, and to challenge the prosecution by whatever honest evidence they can come by. And along with the Supreme Court, I would not allow any voucher rule to get in the way.

This brings us around to where we started: Is the prosecution entitled to wear the white hat? Should juries—though not prompted by the trial assistant—listen more receptively to the prosecution case than to the defense?

As I've said, skepticism is healthy. Juries should not sit simply to applaud the work of law enforcement agents. The presumption of innocence should be translated in the jury room to a willingness to entertain the possibility that this prosecution witness is mistaken, or that one is embroidering or enhancing his recollection; that these cops or experts are less than fully forthcoming, or that some among the prosecution parade are tailoring the evidence to facilitate what they deem to be the just outcome. In every case, the intelligent juror should examine the evidence with these possibilities in mind.

But at the same time, jurors should know that the advantage of credibility belongs with the prosecution. Not so the government can send more people to prison, but because the prosecution case is generally entitled to a presumption of credence simply as a matter of justice. Not all criminal defendants are guilty, but most are and all, the guilty along with the innocent, will do everything in their power to convince the jury of their innocence, or at least their minimal culpability. Lawyers for defendants have no compunction concerning dissimulation. They might scruple to lie outright, but they believe they have the ethical obligation to make the true look false and the false appear true. Unlike the prosecutor (who may be wrong, but has tried to figure out what really happened), defense counsel is no arbiter of probable truth. On the defense side, there will be a reading of the portents, omens, and odds of conviction by verdict, but that is hardly the same thing.

To find the true innocents among all the pretenders seems to me an overwhelming task. But jurors do it all the time—or think they do. While I would lay no bets on their accuracy rates, I am confident that the impossible task is no more effectively accomplished by starting with the assumption that all testimony is false, all exhibits are faked. I do not think the skepticism enjoined by the presumption of innocence translates into that working assumption. I realize I am on a tight wire here, but I am urging that the appropriate level of skepticism lives comfortably with a recognition that the prosecutor's evidence has survived a critical review that the defense evidence has not.

Prosecutors good and bad—and doubtless many conscientious field officers as well—earn their entitlement to the presumption of rectitude. It's only a presumption. And they earn it not by high moral character or superior dedication to truth and justice. Let's face facts: many of them are unworthy servants. They deserve the presumption simply because they enjoy the discretion to choose, to choose which cases to prosecute and which to dismiss. They may not invariably select wisely—there are surely more mistakes than we would like—but they do exercise judgment. The vast majority of them take the responsibility seriously, and consult their conscience along with their common sense. This unique aspect of the public prosecutor alone entitles the office to the advantage of the credible advocate. The power of choice plus the attribution of goodwill adds up to a deserved claim on the mantle of virtue. Of course (I hasten to append), it is what lawyers call a readily rebuttable presumption. Government claims on the white hat are precarious. Wherever one can conscientiously doubt the attribution of goodwill, the entitlement collapses—as it should.

In arguing for a retention of the white hat on the government's brow, in urging all you future jurors to remember that, in most cases, most of the time, the prosecution forces deserve greater credence than the defense, am I validating the old bootleg presumption of guilt? Am I saying that—contrary to what the judge instructs the jury—a presumption of validity accompanies the accusation? I cannot deny that I have confirmed the heretical transposition. Still, paradoxically, I think that the traditional presumption of innocence is not wholly displaced.

The jury should commence deliberation with the instruction firmly in mind: the burden of persuasion rests on the prosecutor; if you have a reasonable doubt, you must acquit. But moving on from there to sort the persuasive fragments from the dubious, to make the delicate assessments of veracity and plausibility, the jury should keep in mind that cops, agents, government lab technicians—to say nothing of happenstance witnesses—do not have their careers riding on the jury's verdict. The prosecutor will live to try another case whatever the outcome. The law enforcement officers will get neither a medal if the jury convicts nor a reprimand if it acquits. The most likely reason they are testifying as they are is that what they are saying is the best reconstruction of the truth they can make. And the prosecutor is arguing to you that it all adds up to guilt because that is what he or she really believes. As I keep saying, they could all be wrong; mistakes are made. But in judging whether the prosecution has met its burden of proof, I submit, it would not be amiss for you, the jury, to appraise the evidence presented to you with a fair and realistic sense of where it comes from, how it got to your attention, and the respective stakes of the advocates who propound and challenge it.

$$\left(5\right)$$

BURDENS AND PRESUMPTIONS

Rescue from the Quandary of Perhaps

SOME PEOPLE APPEAR TO BE clear and certain about everything they know and believe. They seem to have the unerring faculty of separating truth from falsehood and mistake in whatever people tell them. It is a wonder and a mystery to me. I am suspended in perpetual perplexity about what really happened. Especially when I must rely on the reports of others—which covers just about everything—I find it very difficult to reach a confident conclusion about a past event. And things have gotten worse since I learned to discount my own gullibility. I know from experience that I tend to believe the most recent account, or the story told by the most sympathetic person. Suspecting my inclination to credence, I find there's not much to go on.

Empirical studies have reassured me that my shaky grip on the historical truth is not a peculiar fault in my own wiring. Experiments have shown that what is believed to be true has more to do with the projected personality of the teller than with the actual truth of the tale told. Psychologists have found that certain subtle, superficial traits project a aura of honesty; people endowed with those attributes tend to be believed whether they are fabricating or not. It's not a surprising datum, really. Swindlers and confidence men—along with their victims—know it well. So, too, there are shady types, studies confirm, whose accounts are suspect even when they are meticulously truthful. Other studies have shown that all the behavioral tics that people rely on in assigning credibility—hesitation, stammering, sweating, dry mouth, eyeball focus and movement, shifting body position, touching the face with the fingers, and the rest—have no correlation whatever with veracity.

Jurors are regularly called upon to sort fact from fiction. From the stories of conflicting witnesses, they must put together an accurate version of past events, sifting through fragments of physical evidence and the uncertain, incomplete, inconsistent recollections of strangers. They must evaluate the comparative credibility of the professional police witness, the casual bystander, the highly trained expert in hematology, the previously convicted criminal, the defendant's teenage lover, and an assortment of other exotics. As I have said, I consider fact finding to be a daunting task. I sometimes wonder: if I were ever selected to sit on a jury (which I have not yet been), would I be able to come to a conclusion at all, or would I be forever mired in the world of maybe, maybe not?

A criminal trial is not a philosophic inquiry; it does not favor Cartesian skepticism, existential doubt, and epistemological ambiguity. The law wants verdicts, conclusions. Matters in legal dispute must be resolved; that's why courthouses were built. If jurors are still not persuaded after they have squeezed the testimony through whatever credibility filters they have at hand, if they have done their best to put together the shards of physical evidence and found that the reality still has gaping holes, if they have reasoned from one plausible hypothesis to a contrary and equally plausible conjecture without discarding either, if they have labored mightily and still find the solution elusive, the law must step in to bring the conflict to a conclusion. So the mission at hand is to find a way to lead the jury from the rational quandary to a decision on the facts.

To the rescue: burdens and presumptions. When lawyers say "presumption," they are using the word in a slightly different way than Stanley did when he said, "Dr. Livingston, I presume?" If Stanley had been a lawyer, he would probably have said, "Dr. Livingston, I assume," meaning, "From what I observe, I will adopt the working hypothesis that you are Dr. Livingston." A lawyer would translate Stanley's presumption thus, "Never having met you, I cannot know, but I shall take it as a fact that you are Dr. Livingston until the contrary is established to my satisfaction." To a lawyer, in other words, a presumption is a means for transferring to another the burden of establishing the contrary of the presumed fact. Which means in the absence of proof one way or the other, or mired in a state of uncertainty where a conscientious decision on the evidence is impossible, the burdened party loses.

Many of these useful little creatures simply make proof easier, in accordance with generally observed connections. A person is presumed to intend the natural and foreseeable consequences of her actions. Prove that she did the act, and you have proved that she intended the result, unless she can convince me otherwise. Some presumptions have more to do with social policy than observed reality. The mother's husband at the time of birth is the child's father, unless he can prove that he is not. In criminal cases, however, some of these garden-variety proof helpers must be approached with caution: the jury can never presume an elemental fact, though they may infer it. Thus the jury may infer from the multiple wounds an intent to kill, but they are not relieved, by virtue of any presumption, of the obligation to find that elemental fact to be true. Nor may they find the fact merely because the defendant failed to prove the contrary. That would be inconsistent with the presumption of innocence.

The famous presumption of innocence in criminal cases means only that the prosecution bears the burden of proof. And that means that if a juror, after wrestling with all the evidence, still can't conclude that the defendant did it, he must vote for acquittal—even if the juror can't honestly say the defendant didn't do it, either. The defendant always gets the benefit of the doubt, we sometimes say. Why? Because we have elected, as a matter of social policy, to place the burden of proof upon the prosecution.

I am talking about individual jurors, not the jury as a whole. If an individual juror is not fully convinced that the defendant is guilty, the defendant gets her vote. If the jury as a whole is not persuaded, however, though its members may all be convinced one way and the other, then we say the jury is undecided, or hung. We do not say the presumption of innocence dictates acquittal. When the judge accepts the hopelessness of the deadlock—which may not be when it is first reported by the struggling jury—a mistrial is declared and the matter will be tried all over again from the beginning with a new jury.

This rule may seem a bit odd. The prosecutor's burden is not merely to persuade each individual juror but to persuade the jury as a whole. Having failed to do so, the prosecutor—one might expect—should lose. Or to put it another way, a split jury is irrefutable evidence of a reasonable doubt. Yet we do not think of it that way. True, the defendant has a constitutional right to acquittal if the state fails to sustain its burden of proof beyond a reasonable doubt (such was the implication of *In re Winship,* a case argued to the Supreme Court by my wife). But so long as some jurors—even a solitary juror, in most jurisdictions—believe that guilt was proved, the doubts of the rest do not dictate acquittal.

Actually, the defendant may be convicted on a less-than-unanimous verdict; the dissent of some jurors does not infect the verdict of the jury as a whole with reasonable doubt. An argument to that effect was rejected by the Supreme Court in two cases decided in 1972:

Apodaca v. Oregon (upholding an Oregon statute that allowed conviction in noncapital cases by a vote of ten of twelve jurors) and *Johnson v. Louisiana* (upholding a conviction for robbery on a 9–3 verdict). Just as two or three doubters do not preclude conviction (in states where the statute allows it), so too eleven for acquittal does not preclude a retrial before a fresh jury. It is therefore clear that the right to acquittal on proof that leaves a reasonable doubt, though a due-process entitlement, does not mean that a defendant cannot be convicted by a partly dubious jury, or that a largely dubious jury will preclude retrial.

Curious as it is, I do not think this rule declining to construe the split jury as a jury in doubt need detain us longer. I've never heard it argued that the government's opportunity to take a second shot, despite its apparent conflict with the principle forbidding double jeopardy, amounts to an unfair advantage. We'll have a closer look at the idea of double jeopardy a few chapters ahead. For the moment, suffice it to say that we don't consider successive prosecutions unfairly burdensome when the first effort fails—through no fault of the state—to reach a conclusive conclusion. The idea, I suppose, is that the state, too, is entitled to a resolution of the matter, and may, therefore, press on until the end is reached, even if it means empaneling a new jury and starting again.

On the other hand, the rule requiring individual jurors to vote for the defendant so long as they remain in doubt gives the defense an advantage. In fact, some would say, in view of the difficulty of proving anything with the evidence that happens to be available—and especially proving it beyond reasonable doubt—the allocation of burden is a very significant advantage indeed. Gaps in prosecution evidence, weakness in their witness's character, forgetfulness or unpleasant demeanor all work as well for the defendant as evidence of his innocence.

It's meant to be a great advantage. We boast that in our society we do not punish even the likely malefactor unless the state can demonstrate guilt to the neutral fact finder with a relatively high degree of certainty. Not scientific certainty, of course, but considerably greater confidence than the more-likely-than-not standard that governs civil cases. Both the burden and the degree are axiomatic in this great nation. And we profess, at least, to embrace happily the intended consequence that many guilty people will be turned loose to assure that a single innocent person does not suffer a wrongful conviction.

The abstract proposition is an article of cultural faith: better 100 guilty people go free than one innocent be condemned. Do we actually believe it? Try to summon to mind one vivid example, and ask yourself: are you comforted by the proposition that your guilty predator and 99 others like him are cruising freely in society in order that one single hypothetical innocent will not be locked up?

Even if you think this is a fair exchange—100 criminals and one innocent at liberty rather than all 101 in jail—you may wonder, does it really work this way? Is it really necessary to release the 100 guilty to protect the one innocent? Just how does the acquittal of anyone on failure of proof assure that someone else will not be convicted on flawed evidence? Different cases, different juries. One jury is highly demanding, scrupulously applying the burden even against their strong suspicions. Will that acquittal caution the next jury not to believe the believable but mistaken eyewitness? To discount the custodial confession by the weak and suggestible defendant? To see the gaps in the seemingly seamless web of circumstances?

The answer, of course, is that the maxim provides no assurances in this imperfect world. While one jury is conscientiously acquitting a guilty defendant because the proof didn't measure up, another down the hall is dutifully convicting an innocent person on an erroneous reading of the honesty of a critical witness. Tell every juror to acquit the probably guilty but possibly innocent, and you will secure the release of some people who were falsely accused—not all, but some— along with an unknown number of the truly guilty. How these numbers and proportions play out in real life is anyone's guess. And the utilitarian stature of the proposition is therefore unknowable. Unless you subscribe to the credo that virtually any number of acquitted felons is preferable to a single convicted innocent, I do not see how you can judge the moral value of the presumption of innocence.

The question is—I hate to bring great theorems of social policy down to questions like this—which sort of error is it harder to live with? Injustice is surely done both by false conviction and by false acquittal. And count on it: we're going to get both sorts of error. Simultaneously. Because there will surely be innocent people convicted no matter how many guilty ones are acquitted. It's very hard to know the proportion of false positives to false negatives. I've given up trying, though others have offered estimates. Some few false convictions in particular cases can be identified with some degree of assurance, but how can we possibly know how all the other verdicts comport with absolute truth?

In view of the cost of the somewhat dubious equation (100 guilty freed for one innocent spared), I would like to focus instead on the things that enhance the likelihood of acquittal of the innocent apart from the release of guilty people. There are some. Relaxation of some rules of evidence that exclude evidence of innocence; provision for enhanced pretrial investigation by the defense; emphasis on the prosecutor's obligation, ethical and professional, to pursue leads inconsistent with the hypothesis of guilt; provision for conviction by a vote of ten or more and acquittal by a vote of eight or more; relaxation of the rule forbidding defense challenge to internal misconduct, misunderstanding, and disqualification of a jury following a verdict of conviction. I'm sure I can think of some others. My interest in exploring these more promising modifications does not imply that I am losing faith in the presumption of innocence. Although I find it hard to justify in terms of the conventional cost-benefit calculation, I recognize a fundamental tenet when I see one.

The prosecutor's burden of proof, and the high standard of proof beyond reasonable doubt, are so fundamental as to be carved in immutable law. Beyond fairness; the presumption seems to embody basic notions of the relation between individuals and their government, bedrock ideas of personal dignity on which a liberal democracy like ours is built. One hates to admit to idealistic inclinations in these enlightened times, but inescapably there are some principles so deeply etched that they deserve a place in our understanding of due process of law. And the presumption of innocence seems to me one of them.

Descending from the patriotic rhetoric, parking the gleaming theoretical chariot, we should slip into the nearest courtroom and see how the great presumption is working. If it functions as designed, the presumption of innocence in a criminal case should go a long way to offset many of the prosecution's supposed advantages in gathering evidence, choosing a target, and summoning the angels to bear witness to the rectitude of the government's cause.

Reports from the front lines, however, tell us that the dominant presumption of innocence—though solemnly and faithfully announced by judges to their juries in all cases—does not really carry much weight in most trials. Jurors are not often in that state of hopeless irresolution in which the presumption directs an acquittal. Jurors tend to believe the prosecution case, the lawyers tell us, and once they choose to believe the government's witness, or endorse the prosecutor's version of the events, the presumption does nothing to influence the outcome.

Plus, defense lawyers often assert that there is a silent presumption of guilt in the minds of most jurors from the moment they are sworn. "Why would this bozo be here unless someone—perhaps someone who knows a lot more about it than we will ever know—thinks there is good reason to believe he is the culprit?" they are thinking. "Where there's smoke, you know." This "smoke presumption," it is said, is a far more potent factor in jury deliberation than the official burden laid on the prosecution.

It's hard to tell. There is certainly some truth in this perception. The smoke presumption is a natural inference, and a powerful one to many jurors, I am sure. Earnest prosecutors have doubtless won lots of weak cases largely on the strength of it. Still, there are many acquittals coming down, and all prosecutors can tell stories of jurors walking over to them in the hallway after rendering a *not guilty* verdict and blurting out something like, "I just wanted you to know we all thought the defendant was probably guilty, but we just weren't satisfied that you *proved* it—not beyond a reasonable doubt anyway." What are we to make of this common comment? It drives prosecutors mad. "How could you acquit if you thought he was guilty!" they feel like shouting as they smile at the juror and murmur, "Thank you so much for sharing that with me." One fair interpretation is that, at least somewhere, some of the time, the presumption of innocence is working, and dictating a verdict in spite of the jurors' heavy suspicion. Reports of the demise of the presumption of innocence, then, are probably exaggerated.

It might be worth a brief digression to explore one of the finer points in the life and vigor of this basic and definitive presumption in the American adversary model of criminal justice. As usually framed, the presumption of innocence is monumental and immutable as granite: the full burden of proof rests upon the prosecution as to every material element of the charge, from the first moment of the trial to the last, never shifting to the defense. But there is a soft spot in the formulation: just what is a "material element"?

The Supreme Court has spoken. One day in the mid-sixties, in the great state of Maine, a man named Stillman E. Wilbur Jr. attacked one Claude Hebert and beat him to death in his hotel room.

Although for some unfathomable reason Wilbur introduced no evidence in his defense, he argued that he was not guilty because he did not intend to kill Hebert or, at most, he was guilty only of manslaughter because he had acted in a frenzy induced by Hebert's homosexual advances. The jury convicted him of murder.

Murder was defined by statute in Maine in the old common-law terms: the intentional and unjustified killing of a human being "with malice aforethought." In ancient times, the element of malice aforethought distinguished the secular crime of murder, a capital offense, from the crime of manslaughter, which might be punished in ecclesiastical court by imprisonment for one year. Manslaughter, Maine held in accord with long tradition, was a killing without malice aforethought and in "the heat of passion on sudden provocation." The trial judge charged the jury in Wilbur's case that the prosecution need not prove the element of malice since malice is presumed in the absence of persuasive evidence from the defense that he acted in the heat of passion. The defense challenged the use of this burden-shifting presumption on the distinguishing element of malice aforethought.

In 1975 the United States Supreme Court got the case. Though Maine is the judge of its own law, the defense claimed that under *Winship* (then recently decided), a criminal defendant had a federal constitutional right, by virtue of the due-process clause of the Fourteenth Amendment, to have the state prove every material element of a criminal charge beyond a reasonable doubt. In *Mullaney v. Wilbur,* the Supreme Court agreed. Having chosen malice as the defining element of murder, Maine could not place on the defendant the burden of disproving it by showing heat of passion in order to qualify for the lesser crime of manslaughter.

At about the time of Wilbur's crime, New York adopted a new and advanced penal code. Among other things, in defining the crime of murder, the New York law abandoned as obsolete the old terms:

"deliberate and premeditated" and "with malice aforethought." As currently interpreted, those phrases add nothing, New York realized, to the concept of intention. So New York provided that a person was guilty of the highest degree of homicide when he "intentionally" killed another human being. In New York, too, the grade of murder was reduced if the killing was done in a state of "extreme emotional disturbance." Not much difference between "heat of passion" and "extreme emotional disturbance" except the words. New York also put the burden upon the defense to prove the mitigating factor and again, only two years after *Mullaney v. Wilbur,* the Supreme Court got the issue.

After a brief and unstable marriage, as Justice Byron White recounted the story of the New York case, Gordon Patterson Jr. became estranged from his wife, Roberta. Roberta resumed an association with John Northrup, a neighbor to whom she had been engaged before her marriage to Patterson. Two days after Christmas 1970, Patterson borrowed a rifle and went to the residence of his father-in-law. There, he observed his wife through a window in a state of "semi-undress" in the presence of John Northrup. Patterson entered the house and killed Northrup by shooting him twice in the head. Patterson defended against the charge of murder by asserting that he had acted in a state of extreme emotional disturbance, but the jury was not persuaded.

This time, in *Patterson v. New York,* the Court said the burden shift was okay. The burden imposed by the New York law on the defendant—to prove that he acted under extreme emotional disturbance— did not require him to prove the converse of a "material element." Unlike Maine, New York had not defined the crime of murder with an element that amounts to the state of mind incompatible with extreme disturbance. Intentionality, they held, is not like "malice aforethought." One cannot act maliciously in the heat of passion, but one can act intentionally under extreme emotional disturbance. Sounds suspiciously like wordplay to me.

This somewhat baffling *Wilbur-Patterson* split in the Court has led to the reconsideration of a number of other aspects of a criminal case where matters long thought part of the prosecutor's burden have been shifted to the defense. In the wake of the assassination attempt on President Reagan's life in 1983 and the subsequent acquittal of his assailant, John Hinckley, on grounds of insanity, many jurisdictions took a long, hard look at their insanity defenses. Why, they asked themselves, should the prosecution have to prove beyond a reasonable doubt that the defendant was not insane? It's hard to prove a double negative and, after all, sanity is not a material element. So most jurisdictions switched the burden, in effect presuming sanity. And the Supreme Court approved.

The next ripe candidate was the defense of self-defense. Ohio and South Carolina had reassigned what was traditionally among the prosecution's burdens: upon the allegation of self-defense, to prove that the defendant did not act in the belief that he was in imminent and inescapable deadly peril. Ten years after *Patterson,* Ohio's shift in the burden of proof was on the Supreme Court's docket. A woman named Earline Martin, after an argument with her husband, Walter, over grocery money, went upstairs and returned with Walter's gun, which she emptied into him at close range. She was convicted of "aggravated murder" after she failed in her burden to persuade the jury that she fired in self-defense. In *Martin v. Ohio,* a closely divided Supreme Court found that the Ohio law did not offend due process by shifting to the defendant the burden of disproving a material element. As in *Patterson,* the majority held, the state retained the burden of proving all of the elements of murder; the self-defense defense was, in effect, a claim that despite the proof of guilt, the defendant's conduct was justified as imperative self-preservation. Presumably, in virtually all jurisdictions—where the elements of murder do not include the absence of self-defense—*Martin* would allow a shift of the burden to prove the defense.

The Supreme Court also relied on *Patterson* to decide, in 1986, that a state may define a crime without some factor that might have been included as an aggravating element ("visible possession" of a gun in the case before them, *Dynel McMillan v. Pennsylvania*) and transfer that factor to a mandatory sentencing provision where it need be established by a mere preponderance of the evidence only. Not a burden shift, but a lightening of the prosecutor's burden to prove every element beyond a reasonable doubt—a constitutional entitlement of all defendants (as my wife helped establish).

Obviously, there must be some limit to this elemental shuffle. A legislature could not define robbery or rape as pointing anything at anyone for any purpose, and then constitute as affirmative defenses—for which the defense has the burden of proof—that the object was not a weapon, that it was not pointed to induce fear, and that no theft or sexual contact followed. The Supreme Court has alluded to the "core definition" of a crime as containing the unshiftable material elements. Maybe there are core elements of old common-law crimes like murder, arson, rape, and robbery. But in today's world, we have many crimes without common-law antecedents or so evolved from their ancestors that the core may have lost its clear definition. What are the core elements of insider trading? Racketeering? Money laundering? Hacking or cybertheft?

The point is that what we call a crime is actually composed of a bundle of behavioral and cognitive features with strong consequential aspects. What that means is simply that, to be guilty of a crime (murder, let us say, which in turn must be designated and defined with considerable particularity in enacted law), a person must perform certain actions (like pointing a loaded gun at someone and pulling the trigger) in a certain state of mind (like intending to produce the death of the person in line with the muzzle) and with certain consequences (like a bullet, ejected from the gun, striking and killing the intended target or some other human being). These are said to be the "elements" of the crime.

There are a host of other factors which might aggravate, mitigate, excuse, or justify the crime. To reel off a random few of these, the crime of murder may be aggravated by the fact that the victim was a police officer in the performance of duty; or that the killing took place during the commission of some other serious crime like robbery or rape; or that the killing was preceded by physical torture; or by any other fact you deem significant: the victim was a child; the killer and victim were strangers to each other; the defendant had a prior conviction for aggressive violence; the defendant was assisted by others; more than one victim perished in the slaughter; et cetera.

Then there are the defenses: the defendant was mentally deranged, unable to comprehend the lethal quality of his action; or he fired under the plausible belief that the deceased had placed him or another person in imminent mortal peril; or a third person had a gun pointed at his head and ordered him to shoot; or the defendant was a police officer preventing the escape of a person who had just committed a crime of violence; et cetera.

Anyway, these supplementary ingredients of the crime, aggravating or mitigating culpability, may be distributed in various ways. They might be appended to the definitional elements and included in the prosecutor's burden of proof; they might be inscribed as affirmative defenses, on which the defendant bears the burden of proof to some lesser standard of certainty (like "by a preponderance of the evidence" or "by clear and convincing evidence"), or they may be taken into consideration by the judge in sentencing. Which factors are appropriate in assessing gravity, and how they are to be distributed is largely a matter of legislative choice. Subject, of course, to the overriding principle that, as a matter of constitutional due process, the prosecutor bears the burden of proving all material elements beyond a reasonable doubt.

Let's illustrate. Here we are in a mythical American jurisdiction, and we want to pass a law writing a new crime onto the books. We want to call it "sexual harassment." The essence of the crime should be that sexual harassment is committed whenever any person, of either sex and any age (over the age of criminal responsibility, of course), makes unwanted sexual overtures—including verbal—to a person of either sex and any age or, by word or act, makes sexually specific references that are intended to, or are likely to, induce a feeling of sexual discomfort in that person. As we think about our new crime, we recognize that we are covering a wide spectrum of conduct, over a broad range of gravity. Obviously, we need some differentiations.

Our differentiating factors, we realize, are several. There is, first, the nature of the conduct. A lewd remark is hardly in the same category as a physical assault involving forced disrobing or sexual contact. Then, we might consider the age of the victim, or perhaps the disparity in age between aggressor and victim. There might be several other factors—the number of aggressors against a single victim, the repetition of the conduct, the disparity in positions of authority between the aggressor and the victim, a previous relationship of intimacy between the parties, provocation or acquiescence—that also weigh in the seriousness of the crime.

We have various options. We could divide the crime into several degrees—three, four, or five, say—and take the most aggravating features and put them in the definition of harassment in the first degree, then subtract them one at a time as the degrees were reduced. Or we could define the generic, least aggravated elements of the crime and then add aggravating factors as we climbed our degree structure. As we ascend, each degree would call for a sentence of escalating severity.

Thus, if we choose the latter (a better, though less conventional) structure, we might define sexual harassment in the fifth degree as any sexually suggestive, demeaning, or aggressive comment or conduct, done with the intent or likely consequence of inducing discomfort, anger, or shame. So defined, it would include everything, down to a lewd or sexually teasing remark between adults. This lowest degree would be a low-level misdemeanor.

Then we would work our way up till we reached the first degree of the crime, which we might define as conduct directed to a person under the age of sixteen by a person at least ten years older that involved unwanted and unprovoked sexual contact or disrobing. This could be a five-year felony. Maybe we would decide to lodge in some intermediate degree consensual sexual behavior between persons of power and those in their control: teachers and students, employers or workplace supervisors and employees, coaches and athletes, and so on. We are aware that we are creating definitional elements on which the prosecution will bear the unshiftable burden of proof.

At the same time, we might decide that certain mitigating factors should be available as defenses. Among these might be a prior relationship of intimacy between the parties, or some good reason for the defendant to believe that the conduct would be welcome—or at least not offensive. Proof of these we might allocate to the defense to prove by a preponderance of the evidence. Then we might put some of the factors in the judge's sentencing chart. So we might provide, for instance, that the punishment should be increased by 50 percent upon a showing, by clear and convincing evidence (a lower standard than beyond a reasonable doubt), of similar behavior on prior occasions, between the defendant and the same victim, at which time the victim had clearly indicated she or he found the conduct offensive. And the sentence would double if the actor was joined by two or more others in the harassment.

I'm not saying such a statute would be well drawn, or even that the crime of sexual harassment would be a good addition to the criminal code. I mean only to demonstrate that, by these choices of draftsmanship, we are distributing burdens, as well as allowing certain factors to be proved to a reduced level of certainty. Or, to put it another way, we are relieving the prosecution of the full obligation to prove the case charged, in all its particulars, to a degree of certainty beyond reasonable doubt.

The point of this digression is a demonstration that the major defense advantage of a firmly implanted prosecutorial burden of proof is not quite as monolithic and immovable as advertised. For many of the ingredients of culpability, the presumption runs against the defendant. My state of New York, for example, has a relatively modern and well-framed code (comprehensively revised by intelligent, politically independent drafters in the latter half of the twentieth century— the virtues don't get much better than that). The law of New York presumes that crimes are committed by sane people, that they were not induced to commit them against their disposition, that they were not acting under threat of physical harm, and that, if accessories, they persisted, unswerving, in their efforts to accomplish the crime. To justify his crime on any of these grounds (insanity, entrapment, duress, or renunciation), the defendant must not only raise the issue but prove the justifying facts. Though a prior criminal record occasionally makes an appearance in the substantive definition of crimes in New York (it raises the degree of the crime of unlawfully possessing a weapon, for example), it is a major and pervasive factor in sentencing. We have already seen how some shifts in these and other burdens, traditionally shouldered by the prosecution, have met with Supreme Court approval.

Sobered by the realization that the great presumption of innocence may be slimmed down to basic ingredients, that the assertion of a defense does not necessarily enlarge the elements falling within the prosecutor's burden, we ask two questions: First, is there any principled way to tell the shiftable defenses from the immutable material elements? Or is this just an arbitrary legislative shuffle, a political response to unacceptable acquittals like John Hinckley's? And second, does the burden, in its trimmer configuration, still serve to take unsure jurors to a verdict of acquittal with regularity adequate to the task of protecting the innocent?

Defenses come in many shapes and sizes. A defense is any response to an accusation that, if true, would cancel or reduce culpability. They may be purely responsive, denying a fact the prosecution submits as true: "I didn't do it." "I wasn't there." "I didn't mean to hurt anyone." "The witness is lying." "The lab test doesn't show what they say it shows." "This document has been altered." When any defense of this sort is made, the defendant assumes no burden of proving it. Never has and never will. Because all he is asserting is the negative of something the prosecutor must show to prove his case in any event. The defense of alibi also falls in this category. To defend on the grounds that you were elsewhere is, in essence, nothing other than a denial that the perpetrator was you. While identity is not technically an "element" of a crime, it is a fact that the prosecutor must prove in every case beyond a reasonable doubt. And there is no way courts are going to relieve the prosecution of that burden merely because the defendant asserts, affirmatively, that she was in Beloit at the time the crime went down in Detroit.

Then there is another category of defenses, defenses in which the defendant asserts a fact that would not otherwise be part of the case. If it hadn't been raised by the defendant, no evidence would have been submitted on the question by the prosecution. So you might say the negative of the defense is not a part of the prosecutor's normal burden of proof. But if raised, it must be answered. Here's where the legislative option comes in. The law could provide (as it does in New York) that once self-defense is asserted, the prosecutor assumes the burden of proving that the defendant was not acting to defend himself or another from attack. Or (as elsewhere) the law could state that the defendant who claims such an exculpatory circumstance should bear the burden of proving it.

The prime characteristic, then, by which these optional burden shifters can be recognized is that the guilt of the defendant may be fully established without evidence negating the defense. Homicide may be proved without a word being spoken concerning peril to the killer. A second feature—pragmatically, if not theoretically, important—is that the data by which the defense may be proved is peculiarly within the knowledge or control of the defendant. Insanity fills the bill nicely. It is not inappropriate to ask the defendant who claims to have been insane to take his mind and medical records to a doctor and assemble the proof of his claim. Self-defense and entrapment, too. "I thought I would be killed if I didn't shoot first," or "I never would have done a thing like that if I hadn't been persuaded by the undercover agent," are both propositions on which we might fairly expect the proof to be forthcoming from the person who makes the assertion.

Aggravating factors are a harder question. We could pass a law, say, providing that first-degree rape is nonconsensual intercourse involving the infliction of physical injury or by the use of a deadly weapon; second-degree is nonconsensual intercourse by any force or by reason of the intoxication or incompetence of the victim. The Constitution demands that to prove the first degree under such a statutory scheme, the state bears the burden of proving the injury or the weapon beyond reasonable doubt. But in capital punishment statutes, the aggravating factors can be relegated to the sentencing decision and, as such, removed from the beyond-reasonable-doubt standard of proof. If this may be done in homicide cases, it is hard to maintain that the same facilitation is prohibited in lesser felonies. That means we could simply define rape as nonconsensual intercourse and leave it to the sentencing authority (usually the judge in noncapital cases) to decide whether it is more likely than not that a weapon was used or serious injury inflicted. Such a modification doesn't shift the state's burden on these definitional elements, but it does lighten it, and that comes to much the same thing doctrinally.

Traditionally these decisions—how to define crimes, what defenses to assign to defense proof—are a precious responsibility of state legislatures. Many people don't want the federal courts poking their noses into the democratic choices of local constituencies. But burdens and standards of criminal proof are a constitutional concern—and rightly should be—so transfer or dilution of those burdens cannot be immune from scrutiny. Still, the hard question remains. Has the transfer of burdens reduced the protection afforded by the great presumption to the point of triviality?

I guess the question is better put thus: do we have any assurance that the cluster of "material elements," guarded by the presumption, is erosion-resistant, and will these elemental features, standing alone in their demand for high proof, sufficiently caution the jury against hasty conviction on weak evidence? As I said, I am pretty confident that when it comes to the basic definitional elements of a crime, no shift of burden will be tolerated (or attempted). And as long as those elements (plus identity) must be overwhelmingly proved by the prosecution, I take it that the danger of convicting the innocent will be, to some degree, reduced. And insofar as we all agree that that is an indisputable social good, we can rest content with the fairness of the arrangement.

At the same time, there is no question that some "innocent" defendants will lose out by the trimming of the great presumption. If I am innocent because, although I was in on the early planning of the bombing, I changed my mind, renounced the project, and did what I could to dissuade the others from going through with it—but I can't prove it—I will be convicted if the burden of proving the defense of renunciation is placed on me (even though the prosecution cannot prove that I did not renounce). So there is no blinking the fact that burden shifts amount to presumptions of guilt insofar as they presume the contrary of certain defenses. Put another way, with a burden shift, I will be presumed guilty of not renouncing the plot.

How that sits with you depends, I suppose, on your compassion for those who have recourse to these affirmative defenses, and how far you believe the announced burden actually serves to avert the conviction of those truly entitled to the defense. For me, burdening the prosecution with proof of the negative of these defenses—that the defendant was not insane, not acting under duress, and so on—is unfair, and I see no unfairness in requiring the defendant to demonstrate special circumstances, within his ken, claimed to relieve him of culpability, culpability fully demonstrated by the prosecution's proof of the material elements of the crime. And these remain rather exotic cases. In most cases, cases in which common defenses like mendacity, mistaken identity, lack of criminal intent, or simple denial are asserted, the traditional burden still frees the defendant whose defense has not been fully disproved.

And in any case, the presumption still rides to the rescue of the irresolute juror from the quandary of perhaps.

6

THE BLESSING OF BANKROLL

Financial Disparity and the Riddle of Bail

SOME PEOPLE, I KNOW, believe that the entire American criminal justice system is just another institutional example of the grievous economic disparities that afflict us. We've all heard the refrain: the quality of justice you get depends upon the heft of your wallet. The argument is often voiced to compare the rich and the poor defendants—one well armed for the conflict and therefore likely to triumph, the other mustering only a few, weak, and hungry troops and therefore doomed to defeat. And the unequal protection point is frequently coupled with the ugly cry of racism, a claim that differential justice is meted out according to the differing pigmentation of the defendants.

Since I am not here concerned with the equal protection of defendants among themselves, I need not address these pernicious disparities, if such there be. But as I have already noted, the asserted link between wealth and justice also has it that only the financially fortunate have the resources to match and meet the legions of the government. And thus, in this scheme, while the playing field may be more or less level between the prosecutor and some few rich defendants, for the many poor it is woefully out of kilter, forcing them to play against the government at an irreparable disadvantage.

As I may have indicated, I am not persuaded. Primarily because I think the metaphor of the playing field is inapt. And stripped of its imagery, little remains of the point. Those who so hold must explain to me just what it is that wealth on either side can do to tip the scales of justice. I need to know just where and how defense dollars might be spent to match or balance government resources. Does the supposedly plentiful well of prosecutorial funds (a supposition that never fails to elicit a rueful smile from perennially budget-cramped prosecutors) bring a more skillful, experienced lawyer to the government's side, outmaneuvering, outsmarting the meager talent that the grudging allowance from public funds will muster to the defense of the indigent? Even outplaying the retained champion of the occasional solvent defendant?

The balance of lawyering skills is, indeed, often tilted, sometimes one way, sometimes the other. But the defendants favored or disfavored by the imbalance cannot be readily distinguished in bankbook terms. Many of the ablest trial lawyers work for public defense agencies or are available for assignment. And the skill of prosecutors varies widely. Even in the best local offices, the scrupulously non-political, quality shops, many assistants are young, inexperienced, poorly trained, weak, ignorant of the rules of evidence, and inept. It's easy to be overwhelmed in your first few years at the bar (if not, indeed, perpetually). Effectively presenting a case for the prosecution demands energy, dedication, sensitive judgment, confident knowledge of law, special skills of articulation, and just the right personality. Some few have it, but not even the most determined recruitment or rigorous hiring process can assure a staff of first-rate trial lawyers. The blessed, the few United States Attorneys who attract an exceptionally well qualified applicant pool, can probably boast that, by and large, they have the finest young lawyers at the bar. But these are a rare breed and even among them, courtroom grace is far from universal, and often proficiency lags behind their more experienced adversaries.

The fact may be (though I doubt it) that, across the board, prosecutors are a more impressive lot than the members of the defense bar. If so, it is not the disparity of wealth between the U.S. government (or the county treasury) and the population of criminal defendants that accounts for the disparity between the performance of government and defense attorneys. A simple comparison of the wages of the average public prosecutor and the average lawyer standing up against him should dispel that fiction. Not that most defense lawyers are rich, far from it, but among them are many in private practice who are bringing home considerably more bacon than our lean young trial assistant.

What accounts for the talent gap is the indisputable (and, to me, understandable) truth that, to the best law graduates of the best law schools, to the ex–judicial clerks, probably to any graduating law student interested in public law or courtrooms, the prosecutor's side is more attractive than the defense. Not for all, of course. There are many graduates, and good young lawyers among them, who, for idealistic or other reasons, want to champion defendants against the government. At least in my experience, though, fewer of the best are drawn to this starting point of their careers. Doing justice—and doing it in a highly principled way—is more likely to be the work of the prosecutors' offices.

But that is just the entry level. Most young prosecutors see their public service as a limited term, a few years of exciting work, to be followed by a long career in the private sector. Not all, of course, perhaps not even most trade their white Stetsons for the Mark Cross briefcases and Paul Stuart pinstripes of the criminal defense bar. Many—maybe most—of the best young prosecutors find themselves "litigators" in a brand of private practice that never touches a criminal case. But a substantial number can never shake the sawdust of the criminal arena from between their toes. To many young lawyers, the trial of criminal cases is the most challenging, most gratifying—indeed the only way to practice law that matters. And the only way to make any money doing it is to convert to the defense side. So many of the graduates of great prosecutors' offices populate the elite defense bar—and acquire seasoning as the years pass. Gray is not always a match for green, but in the courtroom, a talented junior can only improve with age.

This is not to say that all defense counsel are the mature versions of the best of the prosecutors' lawyers. Gray hair alone is not a badge of superior knowledge and skill. Many defense lawyers are simply old gray mares, going through the motions, who ain't what they used to be, but in fact never were the promising colts who once embellished the government herd. There's a wide spread of ability in this line of work. But it cannot be denied that even the brightest young prosecutors are often matched against their more mature, and no less formidable predecessors.

Incidentally, I am not even so sure that, as between defendants, the one who can afford to retain private counsel will come out better than the one who, by reason of indigence, must accept assigned counsel. I read a careful study by the National Commission on State Courts that found no significant difference in promptness of disposition, likelihood of conviction, or length of a prison sentence for those convicted after a publicly or a privately financed defense. And I frequently hear or read of verdicts won by assigned lawyers for impecunious clients that any high-priced attorney would be proud of. In the summer of 1996 in New York, for example, a jury acquitted an indigent defendant of an arson-murder of a hero firefighter despite the defendant's several confessions and the sense of the jury that he was probably guilty.

It's not troops, or their well-fed bulk, that win trials; it's evidence. And I have already written at some length on how wealth may affect the production of evidence. I concluded that, while some extra bucks might turn up a lucky find, or even an extra—and extra-convincing— expert, we have probably gone as far as fairness demands in according all defendants the resources to develop helpful data. The advantage remaining with the prosecutor is entirely consistent with the responsibilities of prosecution.

But even I must concede that there is one aspect of our criminal justice system where financial disparities are manifest and deeply troublesome. Bail. A nasty, miserable business that defies all pretense of reason and good judgment. And a commonplace feature of the criminal justice enterprise that risks gross injustice for some—the incarceration of the innocent—while carrying dire consequences for all. I hate even to think about it, let alone to try to write fairly and dispassionately on the subject. It's worse even than sentencing, where there is also no rational way to know what is right. At least when it comes to sentencing, judges get some statutory guidance (tight control in the federal courts) and can learn the collegial lessons of custom. The decision on bail is casual, impulsive, largely idiosyncratic, totally arbitrary, wildly variable, and without any possibility of objective verification. It's a wonder to me that trial judges don't show their palms in despair every time a bail call is presented to them. I guess one of the reasons these people are judges is that they not only make bail decisions, they make them routinely and easily. I know a judge who finds it harder to decide what to order for lunch than to set bail.

Bail is our answer to the imponderable dilemma of what to do with a person between the time of his arrest and the final judgment of the court. Once he has been taken into custody and that apprehension has been validated by a judge's finding some good cause to think that the defendant committed a crime, he is no longer free, like the rest of us, to move about at will. Though presumptively innocent—in the sense that he has not yet been proven guilty—he is not entitled to be treated as though innocent. The government has an interest in seeing the case through to a conclusion, and having the defendant on hand is the best way to do it. The prosecution also has a fair interest in neutralizing the dangerous proclivities of the person it has arrested during what may be a fairly long stretch between arrest and conviction. At the same time, the defendant has a strong interest in being out where he can most effectively participate in preparing his defense —to say nothing of carrying on with his life. And, especially if the prosecution case is strong and the crime grave, the defendant has an interest in avoiding judgment—or at least (as Woody Allen said about dying) not being there when it happens.

I do not mean to say that a defendant may not be tried in his absence. If fully warned that by absenting himself he would be waiving his right to be present at his own trial, a defendant who flees during trial does not precipitate an automatic mistrial. The trial may continue and the fugitive, if convicted (I know of more than one case where the empty chair was acquitted), will be subject to incarceration when and if later captured.

I've often thought that courts should take advantage of this invitation to efficiency. When bail is set, the defendant should be fully advised that he is responsible for knowing when his case is on the calendar (the next date is always announced whenever the case is adjourned). The defendant, in other words, must be given full and fair opportunity to avail himself of the right to presence. Then set a bail you know he can make. If he shows, we have avoided needless incarceration and consequent disadvantage. And if he chooses flight, let him go. It will (usually) be that much easier and faster to convict him in his absence. Then all we have to do is catch him (or wait till he gets collared again on a new transgression—not likely to be too long a wait), and straight to jail without all the bother of a trial first. In fact, if the defendant is so ill-advised as to vanish, and the trial of his empty chair should unaccountably fail, the prosecutor gets a second bite on a charge of bail jumping—the easiest case in the world to prove. So if conscious flight waives the right to presence, I don't see what all the fuss is about.

But everyone hates these trials. Fairness and efficiency are not everything. My idea does not stand a chance. There's something unseemly about the trial in absentia. It smacks, somehow, of the totalitarian state. It's one of those rare points on which all parties seem to agree: the live, breathing body of the defendant prominently seated in the courtroom immeasurably enhances the proceedings. Most judges will not start a case if the defendant has skipped, regardless of how vigorously the warning was previously administered.

It's not just that we want the witnesses, and the jurors, to see the person they are talking, or hearing, about. We also want the defendant to hear the evidence that might condemn him. That's one of the reasons we refuse to try a defendant who is mentally absent by reason of defect or derangement. We provide an interpreter, at considerable expense, for the same reason. We are simply unable to deal with defendants as disembodied abstractions. At the same time, we will not allow the bailed defendant to pull the plug on his own trial, well under way, by an unscheduled departure. The empty chair being tried as the case resolutely continues still holds the imprint of its recent occupant.

Let's put aside for the moment the urgent question of prophylactic custody: preventing the dangerous captive from going out and adding counts to his own indictment. Let's first focus on the problem of how to keep the flight-prone defendant available without locking him up before he is convicted. Even the most peaceable sort of embezzler must dream of growing a beard, dying his hair, and finding a friendly, extradition-proof South Pacific island on which to do a Gaugin while the government gnashes its big teeth and that terrifying indictment just molders away. To discourage consulting travel agents in lieu of legal counsel, to keep conferences with counsel focused on defensive tactics rather than pursuing offhand queries concerning which nations of the world still have no criminal extradition treaties with the United States, the best move is doubtless confinement in some quasi-prison. Locked up but not imprisoned, these preconvicts must be jailed in special quarters separate from the convicted population, they may not be forced to work and are given certain liberties within the facility— little things to suggest that, though easily mistaken for sentenced felons, they are in fact presumptively innocent citizens, temporarily and unfortunately deprived of their locomotive liberty for the convenience of the court.

Actually, one of two reasons explains why most of the prejudgment crowd are sitting in jail, contemplating their future from its most dismal perspective, taking solace and bad advice from other losers. Either the judge has intentionally set terms for their preconviction release that are beyond their reach, or they are simply unable to come up with the sort of monetary security that others ordinarily manage. The going rate in the jurisdiction for robbery, first offense, no injuries, averages out at $2,500, let us say. Second felony, $5,000; recovered weapon, $7,500; injuries inflicted, $10,000; some combination of the above, fifty to a hundred grand. That is bail. A financial bond to assure appearance. There is no such standard scale, of course, individual judges consciously or unconsciously set their own rates. And, as I said, they vary widely. But my hypothesis is not unrealistic. Bail, on a crude monetary scale, is supposed to reflect the gravity of the offense, the strength of the prosecution case, and the familial and other roots of the defendant in the community. Factors that supposedly influence the strength of the temptation to flee.

The old, the traditional, the primary hold that we put upon the accused to counterbalance the urge for liberty preservation is financial incentive. Would you book a flight for Bali (which I select only because it is an anagram for bail) if it would wipe out your savings and impoverish your wife and children? How about if it meant your folks would forfeit the house they had lived in all their lives? This is the conventional calculus of bail.

There are several wrappings in which this financial commitment may be packaged, some of them having little to do with incentive. A defendant who is required to post his own bank balance or a bond backed by his own property, or to pledge the home of a loved one may be motivated to avoid forfeiture. But it is hard to find any such motivation where some popular figure raises his bail money by public subscription; neither the defendant nor his backers expect to get a penny back and, I suppose, the contributors would be perfectly satisfied if they had collectively purchased their hero's freedom, albeit as a fugitive. Only his lawyer has an interest in preserving the bail fund as some assurance that the fee will be paid.

The judge to whom the bail application is made does not have to set bail at all. Defendants may be released on their "own recognizance," as we say, giving only their word that they will be present when needed. These are generally folk who are accused of minor crimes, have clean records, strong roots in the community, and good reason to think they may be vindicated. Your average second-strike rapist, with neither funds nor regular lawful employment, does not stand a chance, while the middle-class woman in therapy, with a doting family behind her, accused of a minor shoplift, is an excellent candidate for pretrial release on her word alone. The reason for the disparity is plain, but the invidious result begins to show through. Wealth—especially when coupled with a solid middle-class background—counts.

Or the judge may deny the application for bail outright, ordering that the defendant be held in custody. There are some few nonbailable state offenses, crimes so serious that the legislature has determined that any person accused of one would likely flee no matter what the stake posted. The federal list is growing. Capital crimes have been traditionally deemed nonbailable. In addition, a judge may decide, after hearing, that a particular person is simply too great a risk at any price—someone, perhaps, accused of a serious crime on strong evidence, with no fixed address, no employment, who has been arrested as a fugitive after a previous flight. Unfortunately, such high-risk cases are not rare.

In addition to the fear of flight, the judge may deny release on bail, either openly (by denying bail) or covertly (by setting it way beyond the defendant's means), because of a belief that the defendant at large poses a grave threat of violence. Exploration of this factor I have reserved for later in the chapter. I will say here, however, that much of the discussion that follows pertains only to state courts. In 1984, Congress enacted the Bail Reform Act, which enables federal judges openly to deny release to the dangerous or irresponsible—and prohibits them from doing it covertly by setting unreachable bail.

Today, technology offers a third option. New devices for maintaining control of a person's vagrant impulses without incarceration are promising. The electronic monitor, an ankle band that broadcasts your presence where you are supposed to be, offers a more meaningful "house arrest" plan. But there are still many tracking problems, to say nothing of the difficulties of maintaining surveillance of a large population of ambulatory prisoners. A rogue former prosecutor of Sommerset County, New Jersey, named Nicholas Bissell Jr., convicted of thirty-three federal felonies and awaiting sentence under virtual house arrest and a $300,000 bond (including his mother's condo), demonstrated another shortcoming of the device. He simply cut it off his ankle and disappeared for a while before, facing recapture in Nevada, he put a bullet through his head. Still, this outpatient approach to preconviction custody may turn out to be the best answer and, off in the future, the prevalent device of choice.

Meanwhile (we pragmatists love that word), people are released or detained according to their ability to ante up the cash or property called for by the terms of the bail set. And whether they can afford to purchase their own release must have a significant bearing on how well they meet the charges against them. Here I could really use some good numbers. I would just love to see a chart neatly lining up the released defendants against the jailed and comparing the outcomes in terms of plea and conviction rates, and maybe sentence time for comparable felonies. Not that we don't have numbers. Several hearty souls have ventured forth to do some counting. But the net harvest illustrates why many legal scholars are skeptical about the contribution of the social scientists to the understanding of our problems.

It's easy enough—given adequate funding—simply to go out there and add up the conviction and acquittal rates of the jailed and the bailed, and maybe even tote up the mean jail time per crime category awarded to those residing within and those without bars. But the result would be meaningless. In setting high bail or refusing bail, the judge takes into consideration the very factors that are likely to result in conviction and long-term incarceration: a serious crime, a strong case, and a bad criminal history. So it would be hardly surprising to discover that those tried from jail fared badly on verdicts and sentences. The trick is to hold all other critical factors equal, to compare bailed and jailed defendants in comparable cases.

That is a trick to challenge even the most resourceful empiricist. Take a street robbery as an example. We have, let us suppose, an aggravated instance (weapon used, injuries inflicted), a strong case (good eyewitness identification, rapid apprehension, proceeds on the defendant's person), and a bad actor (prior crimes of violence). Our researcher will have a difficult job holding those critical factors constant across the bail/jail divide for the simple reason that she will discover few if any cases with those features among the bailed population.

That does not mean there are none of the intrepid band who do not claim their "regression analysis" method has held all other critical factors constant. They all do. Unfortunately, however, their conclusions differ. In the early sixties, Anne Rankin, then a member of the Vera Foundation, published a study of defendants arraigned in Manhattan's felony court over a period of almost one year. She carefully analyzed those factors associated with both detention and disposition and concluded that even when such factors were equalized, "defendants who were held in jail continuously between arrest and final adjudication received unfavorable dispositions much more often than those who were free on bail during all or part of that period."

About a decade later, Eric W. Single conducted another study in New York, again examining other factors such as those I have alluded to. He reported: "The study demonstrate[d] that neither independently nor in combination do any of these factors account for the disparity in outcome and in severity of sentence between those detained and those released. The inescapable conclusion, is that the fact of detention itself causes those detained to be convicted far more often and sentenced far more severely that those who are released."

In 1980, Professor John S. Goldkamp published a reexamination of the hypothesis that "pretrial detention exerts a strong negative bias against the defendant's prospects at adjudication and sentencing." He sifted through a three-month intake from Philadelphia during 1975. Claiming superior methods, Goldkamp is (to me) insolubly incoherent in his result. He says at one point that a "noticeably larger proportion" of those in jail get convicted at trial and, at another, that "a weak relationship of little consequence was found between pretrial custody and findings of guilt or innocence" by trial.

Then in 1982, a pair of researchers, Gerald R. Wheeler and Carol L. Wheeler, looked back over a number of studies by several researchers and found that eight out of thirteen (including Goldkamp) "found no statistically significant differences between detained and bonded defendants on conviction rate." The Wheelers did, however, detect agreement that release status affects sentencing.

This last bit I find counterintuitive. There are, to be sure, some few minor cases in which a defendant who has spent time in pretrial detention is sentenced to "time served," obviously a disposition unavailable for his counterpart on bail who, in similar circumstances, would just get a suspended sentence. Too, there are compassionate judges who are reluctant to imprison a person who is, other than the crime in question, living a responsible life. Imagine for example a person convicted of driving while intoxicated—perhaps injuring someone in an accident—working, in AA, supporting a family, never arrested before. The decision to impose a prison sentence on such a person might be easier if he is already locked up in default of bail. But other than these relatively rare cases, I can imagine no reason why a judge would sentence a jailed defendant to a longer term than she would pronounce upon a similarly situated defendant at liberty.

So you can see why for people like me, thirsting for hard data, the work of those who toil in the empirical fields is so often disappointing. In this fix, we tend to rely on personal experience and courthouse anecdote (of which there is always an ample supply). It almost doesn't matter what the numbers really are. We know what we know. And every defense lawyer will tell you it's harder to defend a jailed client. Just the basic matter of communication is a hassle. How many times can a lawyer, busy in court all day, take herself out to the local lockup to interview a client? For many, the hurried conversations in the cramped and public holding pens behind the courtroom are the main chance to talk about the case.

In addition, lawyers rely in large measure upon the defendants themselves to produce some evidence to back up their stories. "You say your aunt will remember serving you supper that night, followed by TV? Maybe you should pay her a visit and see if she really does remember that particular evening. If so, bring her around to see me." Even lawyers mounting a gold-plated defense frequently depend upon the accused to point their investigators toward exculpatory fact bearers. "I want you to go over your plant records for last year and bring me the documentation regarding inventory so I can have our accountants verify your claims in that loan application." While not totally disabled, the jailed defendant is severely handicapped in this sort of endeavor. And others may not be as knowledgeable or motivated to assist. So, regardless of the score among the empiricists, I take it as established that imprisonment in default of bail is a severe disadvantage.

We have, I should note, completely erased the disadvantage jailed defendants once suffered when they were tried in prison garb, or when the jury could see them led by court officers to and from the holding pen at the open and close of each day's work. Jurors, it was thought, would quickly surmise that someone thought this bloke was a dangerous character, or that they would be less reluctant to convict a person already lodged behind bars. So today—everywhere, so far as I know—we make sure the defendant dresses for trial in street clothes. We scrupulously allow the jury to file out of the courtroom before the defendant is escorted back to his cell, and we do not allow them into the courtroom until the defendant is seated at counsel table, his handcuffs removed. Cosmetic, perhaps, but it neutralizes one of the encumbrances of confinement.

Is the remaining disadvantage of custodial incapacity unfair? It is unfair insofar as the bail decision is itself irrational. If there is a good and substantial reason to keep the accused behind bars awaiting and during trial, then the handicap is only one of the several unfortunate disabilities of being in that position. No more or less unfair than being on trial at all—paying lawyers' fees, spending sleepless nights, and the whole ordeal. Burdensome but tolerable. But if the defendant is clawing at the walls of a cell because some judge took a fast look at the papers and said, "Hmmm, a carjacking, eh? Gun used. Driver held hostage. Shots fired at pursuing police. Nobody hurt. Defendant nineteen years old. Lives at home occasionally, works sometimes. Prior robbery. $50,000 cash or $150,000 bond," I would call it unfair. And more likely than not, under our present system, the bail was set by a calculation very much like that. How can any human judge possibly calculate the correlation of any of these factors with the prospect of flight or the likelihood of recidivistic behavior? Surely, you scoff, I must be exaggerating; this couldn't be the way it works. I wish I could reassure you.

The judge could as easily have fixed the bail at $5,000 or $500,000; it was a number pulled out of the air. If the judge gave it any thought at all, what flashed across his mind was, "There's no way this mope is going to come up with that kind of cash or the security for a bond of that dimension—which is just fine with me." Not: what level of inducement will assure his return? but: he ain't goin' nowhere. Now, how has this judge arrived at his conclusion that this particular individual cannot be trusted at liberty under some financial arrangement that was within his means?

From long experience, the judge has concluded that a bail of say, $100 cash or $500 bond could probably be posted by a defendant in this fellow's situation. His family could probably scrape it up, even if it meant putting the kids on a peanut butter and jelly diet for a week. But once posted, it could be readily sacrificed. A cheap price for freedom, particularly if the defendant is facing five to ten years and thinks he can slip out of town and live invisibly as a fugitive forever. And few carjackers would feel any moral compunction about ducking the law's punch.

But other than "experience" in other cases (which is probably more repeated conjecture than actual, verified experience), whence does His Honor derive the notion that the particular person before him is irresponsible? Has he inquired of the man's occasional employers concerning his punctuality? Has he taken evidence concerning how this person meets his other obligations, including his previous court appearances? The inference from probable criminal conduct, the carjacking, to truancy is not as strong as one might imagine; all judges know that many really bad criminals are meticulous about keeping court dates.

Perhaps the infamous Judges' Nightmare flashed before our judge's eyes. Every trial-level judge and magistrate, everyone who has ever set bail, knows it well. You set a bail, the defendant posts it, then a couple of weeks later you pick up the morning paper and read that your defendant has killed someone. The papers are screaming, Why did you release this predator when you had him in the palm of your judicial hand? In vain you murmur, I thought the risk of flight was negligible. What everyone is talking about is not the risk of flight, dummy, it is the risk that the defendant, if released, will commit another crime, especially a crime of violence. Never mind that he has not yet been convicted of the crime charged, no sane person, the newshawks screech, knowing what you knew of this defendant's character and history, would trust him out in the community of potential victims.

It has always seemed remarkable to me that the law actually takes account of the risk-of-predation factor—at least in some jurisdictions. The constitutions of nine states specifically authorize judges in setting bail to consider whether release of the defendant poses a danger to potential victims, and many other states allow it by implication or by statute. And the Bail Reform Act of 1984, covering the small fraction of crimes prosecuted in the federal courts, includes a provision for denial of bail on the grounds that the defendant would pose a danger if released at liberty pending judgment. The act allows a federal judge to detain an arrested person pending trial if the government, in an adversary hearing, demonstrates by clear and convincing evidence that no release conditions "will reasonably assure . . . the safety of any other person and the community." On paper, the Bail Reform Act seems to require a careful, case-by-case inquiry before ordering detention, but in practice, hearings in the federal courts are a lot more casual (and expedited by congressional presumptions for the wholesale detention of defendants accused of crimes involving violence or drugs).

Many were skeptical. This preventive detention feature of the Bail Reform Act—and the state laws to the same effect—faced at least two constitutional hurdles that seemed formidable. First, to lock someone up because he poses a potential threat is anathema to cardinal principles of Anglo-American jurisprudence. Our criminal laws are founded on the proposition that punishment follows only from what you do, not who you are, what you think, or what you might do. We imprison people because they are bad actors, not because they are dangerous people. And odd as this philosophy may seem to some, I am on safe ground in saying it is an immutable, foundation principle of a liberal democracy like ours. So we have a major due-process scowl against a law allowing incarceration of unconvicted citizens because there is reason to think they are dangerous.

Even more to the point was the language in the Constitution's Eighth Amendment that "excessive bail" shall not be required. Coupled with the "cruel and unusual punishment" proscription, this bare injunction is somewhat mysterious. It doesn't say that the defendant has a right to have bail fixed, much less that he has the right to be released on bail before conviction. Still, *excessive* had generally been thought to mean: more than the amount necessary to assure the defendant's future appearances in court. The Supreme Court confirmed this understanding of the term almost fifty years ago in a case called *Stack v. Boyle*. On this reading, bail set in an amount designed to preclude release would be clearly "excessive." And many believed that the denial of bail, particularly without regard to the likelihood of flight, is tantamount to prohibitive—or excessive—bail.

Anthony Salerno, or Fat Tony as he was known to the press, was thought to be a major underworld character back in the seventies and eighties. The government indicted him and a bunch of cronies on thirty counts of racketeering, fraud, extortion, and gambling. On his arraignment, the government applied to the court to hold Salerno without bail. Prosecutors provided evidence that he had participated in a number of conspiracies to use violence—including murder—in furtherance of the criminal enterprises of the underworld "family" of which he was "boss." The government argued that, if he was released, he would resume his gangster activities, with consequent danger of violence to others. Tony was ordered detained, but on appeal the Court of Appeals for the Second Circuit held the Bail Reform Act unconstitutional insofar as it allowed his detention on dangerousness alone. When the case got to the United States Supreme Court in 1987, the Solicitor General defended Congress and the idea that release could be denied on a prediction of future harm.

The Court bought it. They held that the Constitution does not establish a right to bail. "No excessive bail" does not imply that defendants are entitled to be at liberty on bail. And detention pending judgment is not, the Court said, the sort of "punishment" that is offensive to due process. "As an initial matter," Chief Justice Rehnquist wrote for the Court, "the mere fact that a person is detained does not inexorably lead to the conclusion that the government has imposed punishment."

In an exercise that some cynics might be tempted to label judicial sophistry, the chief found that the purpose of pretrial detention is "regulatory," not "punitive," a response to the social problem of acts of violence committed by indicted people awaiting trial. And housing those who might contribute to the problem in a secure facility is only a means for regulating their behavior. And the Court recited a wad of precedent showing that the due-process clause had been construed to tolerate regulation in the interests of community safety though personal liberties were thereby curtailed.

Call it what you will, we are all glad to hear from the Court that crime prevention is a legitimate concern of the legislature. And the preventive detention provision of the Bail Reform Act, circumscribed as it is, serves that end. "When the Government proves by clear and convincing evidence that an arrestee presents an identified and articulable threat to an individual or the community," the opinion of the Court goes on, "we believe that, consistent with the Due Process Clause, a court may disable the arrestee from executing that threat." Nor does the Eighth Amendment require (as the Court had implied thirty-six years earlier in *Stack v. Boyle*) that bail be set for the exclusive purpose of encouraging presence in court. "Nothing in the text of the Bail Clause," Chief Justice Rehnquist instructs us, "limits permissible Government considerations solely to questions of flight."

So the Court has approved of prejudgment detention both where no feasible incentive for reappearance seems adequate to deter flight and for those cases where release would appear to imperil the physical safety of others. And since prediction is a risky business, the *Salerno* decision seems willing to tolerate a fair number of false positives in the interest of community safety. If federal judges, by exaggerated apprehension of public outcry or otherwise, misread the harbingers of danger, their orders of detention, conforming in procedural particulars with the demands of the statute, will not find disfavor with the appellate courts.

Outside the federal beltway, the decision has firmly closed the door to those who see a remedy for the disabilities of the jailed preconvict in universal release. The due-process concept in the Constitution accords no right to be free on bail. If anyone beyond the reach of the Bail Reform Act is tempted to argue that "excessive bail" in the Eighth Amendment means bail that exceeds the means of a particular defendant, forget it. If anyone harbors any lingering feeling that equal protection implies that all should enjoy equal opportunity to assist in preparing their defense regardless of the funds at their disposal, sorry, that cause is lost.

Is there any hope to rectify the unfairness of a defendant wrongly deprived of the opportunity fully to participate in his own defense?

There is, of course, review of the bail decision available to the defendant by writ of habeas corpus. But a second judge, looking at the same constellation as influenced her brother, is not likely to substitute her own equally ill-informed judgment and come up with a different number. They are both pretending to go through a rational process to arrive at a figure that seems consistent with a nonexistent standard and is heavy enough to deter flight. Or, covertly, they are trying to pick a number that will either allow release or (more likely) prevent it. If permitted by statute, in special cases, they might be openly imposing preventive detention. As I have said, bail as currently administered is hardly a system to inspire confidence in the rationality of the judicial process, or in our commitment to a system in which disparities of wealth do not distort fairness. But, taking my cue from Tony Salerno's case and having the federal model in mind, I think I see a way to right the wrong by making the detention decision more rational and financially neutral.

Here's the idea. It's not very original; it has been around long enough to be ignored in the federal courts. But it is still a radical proposal on the state side, where reform is most urgently needed. The idea is really very simple. In every case, the judge would be presented with two decisions. The first would be whether this particular person should await and endure his trial from inside or outside. This decision has nothing whatever to do with wealth. A careful inquiry must be made into factors affecting the likelihood of flight.

I know someone will leap up at this point and say, hold on! Likelihood of flight has a lot to do with wealth—it depends, in part at least, on the financial stake that deters it. Do you mean the judge should evaluate the likelihood of flight of a person released without bail? On that standard, a lot of people will look like potential fugitives. No, I mean the judge should assess the likelihood of flight of the defendant released under financial conditions which he will be able to meet. I'm not proposing abolition of monetary bail, only scaling it to the financial capabilities of the person standing before the bench.

Thorough and serious consideration must also be given to the defendant's violent propensities. (Don't you love the reformers who write "we must" do this or that, and something else "must be" done? Never a thought to whether it will be or can be done; no regard for whether it has been done—and if not, why not? In fact, I am told that federal experience has been discouraging with regard to these "must be"s. The "thorough and careful consideration" I call for suggests commitment of resources as well as judicial will. If federal bail hearings have been perfunctory, I can only say, lamely, we must do better.) This might be an easier call than discerning dreams of Bali. At least when it comes to violence, there's a rap sheet to offer hints. Though the law of evidence insists propensity means nothing, for these purposes it can be taken as predictive. And though the defendant is presumed innocent of the crime described in the indictment, the judge may presume guilt in making the release decision. No dispositive presumptions, please, like those imposed on federal judges by a foolish Congress. Just every case on its own peculiar facts, and the best guess a conscientious judge can make. It's a vast improvement already.

If the judge decides, on good evidence, that the defendant should be in, he denies bail. He doesn't set high bail; he denies release altogether. The decision should be subject to immediate appellate review, and the case should be automatically routed to an expedited track for trial. (Again, federal expedition of detained pretrialers does not inspire confidence. We must do better.)

If the court decides the person should be out, the second effort is to set terms and conditions of release, including monetary inducements, that the judge is assured the defendant can meet. If it turns out the defendant cannot post the security set, the judge must reconsider and reduce it. Did I already say, federal bail law has just such a provision? These people must be out, and the court may set appropriate terms. No one, under such a regime, would be required to defend himself from a disadvantaged position merely because he lacked the financial means to secure his liberty.

The reform is radical in one respect: it shifts the issue. Focusing on the question "Is there any good reason why this person should await judgment on the inside?" it turns judges from their traditional concern: just how much money is likely to deter disappearance? I am, of course, delighted to see the ancient query wither. And my enthusiasm is due only in part to the inevitable result of the traditional formula that the better heeled are more likely to be bailed. I am pleased, too, to see the demise of the pretense of a sensible judgment on a foolish question. How can any judge, even the most scrupulous and the best informed, possibly predict just what sort of financial inducement, within the financial capability of a particular defendant, is also a stake that he would not forfeit for the status of fugitive? Just try to imagine the number of variables that go into a choice like that: hopes for the future built on existing externalities, readiness to change identity, confidence in a remade life, the importance to self and others of a financial asset, optimism/pessimism concerning the likely outcome of the trial, a hundred other unknowables. The freedom of the pre-convict should not depend upon a judge's hasty effort to weigh such imponderables.

Equally gratifying is the federal allowance of frank concern for interim danger. Only slightly less imponderable than the prediction of flight, perhaps, the propensity of the defendant awaiting trial to resume a criminal pattern nevertheless should be openly addressed, and expressly considered in the decision.

Obviously, this scheme does nothing to liberate the person erroneously adjudicated—or presumed—to be violence- or escape-prone. It does nothing to invigorate the defense by freeing the accused bearing those apparent propensities. But properly administered, the determination of who waits on the inside and who on the outside would have more to do with the purposes of detention than with the comparative wealth of the defendants. And unless we succumb to doleful assumptions that most people accused of crime are disposed either to flee or to resume a career of violent crime, we must believe that under the proposed regime those disabled by pretrial incarceration will be a relatively small group of people—at best, far fewer than those now held in default of bail. And as to them, I am ready to swallow the claims of disadvantage in the interests of promoting community safety and the integrity of the process.

That, then, is the idea, simple and beautiful. Only two problems. But they are major, all-but-disheartening problems. The first, a matter of design, the second, of experience. Number one: have I really taken my judges out of the tea leaf–reading game, as I claim, or have I just shifted the propensity prediction from likely-to-forfeit to likely-to-flee (or recidivate)? And while I urge a "serious inquiry" and "careful consideration" after a thorough investigation, I must know that—even with the best will in the world—the law of courtroom economy will inevitably bring the release inquiry back to the perfunctory. Besides, by what occult equipment do I imagine that my judges are any better equipped to make the enlightened prediction than they were to do the old fashioned stake-setting?

In defense, I reply. For one thing, I have removed the catch-22: the only bail high enough to assure his reappearance is too high for him to make. Appearance and disappearance are to be predicted by factors other than financial motivation. I recognize—nay, insist—that the decision of the bail jumpers is rarely the consequence of the size of the stake they were required to post. Do I have empirical evidence to support this certainty? Of course not, only observations and common sense. And those data lead me to conclude that, whatever the defendant's station, if he can afford to put up the bail, he can afford to lose it—if he wants badly enough to exchange his prospects at trial for the life of a fugitive. Are there some, perhaps middle-class defendants, on a million dollars' bail representing their family's future security, who are influenced to stick around by the desire to keep their families solvent? I'm sure there are, but I strongly suspect that those are the same folks we would count as good bets to show up anyway. And I certainly do not disparage some added financial encouragement of the otherwise qualified.

I cannot claim that the new prediction is fortune-free. Wealth-free, maybe; but not fortune-free. In any system short of everybody in or everybody out, social stability counts. By any rational method of differentiation, on any operative standard, those on the outside will tend to be those with a greater stake in the law-abiding world and a more secure place in it, while those behind bars will be the socially marginal. Thus, with the exception of a few successful but highly dangerous felons, the insurmountable fact is that the disadvantage of pretrial incarceration will always fall more heavily on those disadvantaged in other ways as well. All I have proposed is a broader—and I think more realistic—basis for prediction. As such, I think the plan offers, too, some reason to hope that peaceable people, not otherwise prone to escape, will not be held in custody solely for lack of funds.

I would also defend the plan by offering some assistance to judges in their expanded inquiry. While in no way directing their choice or curtailing the discretion to differentiate between similar cases, I might try to formulate a set of guidelines simply to introduce them to the range of operative factors. It might be compiled by consultation with the judges themselves, drawing on their supposed experience with shows and no-shows under the old system. In this way, we might come up with biographical factors like geographic and work history, family associations and friendships, prior lawbreaking, and hopes and plans for the future; we might add case-specific considerations like the seriousness of the crime charged and the strength of the prosecutor's proof (the optimism factor); we might also look for other evidence of reliability with respect to solemn obligations. History, character, and optimism: it's not a formula, but it is certainly a far more sophisticated approach to prediction than our customary voodoo.

So much for design. On the experience front, the news is deeply discouraging. Remember the federal Bail Reform Act, which enacted many of the major features of the idea I have sponsored here? We have some data on the federal experience with that act since 1984. Data not on whether pretrial release helps in the conduct of a defense but on whether the revised standards for detention have altered the size or composition of the slice of federal prisoners pacing their cells. Judge Thomas E. Scott has published a compilation of several federal studies, reaching the conclusion that—contrary to expectations, perhaps contrary to legislative intention—a large and growing proportion of federal prisoners are detained, and detention procedures are becoming cursory and routine.

True enough, the experience is with a federal law, applied in federal courts to federal prisoners. Perhaps the statistics instruct only on the federal failure and say little about how a similar model would work in state courts. For one thing, case numbers vary widely from federal district to district, and there's no telling where a state would fit into the range. Then, too, federal and state defendants are dissimilar in critical respects. People involved in commercial frauds, underworld conspiracies and racketeering, financial crime, counterfeiting and currency offenses, and international drug smuggling (which describes the bulk of the criminal business of the federal courts) are a different bunch from the murderers, rapists, robbers, burglars, thieves, and assorted street predators who find themselves accused of state crimes. A good idea that decays in one climate may flourish in another.

More than that, we should be instructed by the federal experiment. Perhaps we can avoid a major cause of the discouraging news from the federal courts. To a large extent, the discretion accorded judges by the 1984 act was withdrawn by Congress in another section of the law. Intended, no doubt, as aid to judicial decision, the provision specifies a number of "rebuttable presumptions"—cases in which the court, in the absence of evidence to the contrary, may find that no conditions of release will assure the future appearance of the defendant or secure the safety of the public. These include crimes "of violence," serious drug offenses, and crimes for which the penalty is death or life imprisonment. In practice, the presumptions rule, and in this significant portion of the federal docket, release is routinely denied.

Discretion is a fragile creature, always vulnerable to legislative second thoughts, never wholly eradicable. It's an old story. Initially, enlightened legislation recognizes the obvious truths that (1) every case is different, and (2) judges are mostly well-intentioned, reasonably diligent, and generally not stupid, and (3) the judge in any given case is in a better position to select the best disposition in those particular circumstances than a bunch of legislators thinking of the problem abstractly. So the law gets into the courtroom, and judges start applying it variously, according to the demands of the case at hand and their own best judgment, and soon the press and the politicians get wind of the fact that some defendants are being treated leniently. It's more than the political image makers will allow. Soon the legislators are outdoing each other to repair the law to drain any discretion that judges might put to good use. We've seen it in sentencing, we've seen it in plea bargaining, anywhere the pols think they can come off as "tough on crime" without having to give too much thought to where reform is really needed. Don't get me started.

So, to hope for a sane state bail policy we must write it well, urge our judges (accustomed to Ouija boards) to think sensibly and realistically about who should be where, help them by reminding them of the sorts of considerations their peers deem relevant, and then fight to preserve the precious discretion that we accord them against the predictable predatory raids of the political branches. On the barricades, our banner will proclaim: "An informed, discriminating, broad-based discretion is still the only hope of approaching a fair bail regime."

And keep the faith. Cynicism is an attractive alternative. It's easy to swerve down the road to "Why bother, nothing works." I know that rationality is a long shot, unfairness ineradicable. But a more rational system is a good thing in itself. And there is more than esthetics to recommend a program calling for well-founded decisions toward a well-formulated objective. Even as a pragmatist, I harbor some hope that function will follow form, that with a superior design in place, the operation of the system may come in time, and to some extent, to conform. But I know that, especially in the explosive capsule of the process we call bail, the struggle persists between good intentions and enlightened prescriptions on one side and, on the other, the practical realities of courtrooms and legislative chambers. And as we watch that familiar spectacle, optimism does not flourish. It is only one of the reasons I hate the subject of bail.

EXCLUDING ADVERSE EVIDENCE

Truth or Justice?

WOULD IT NOT BE AMUSING if the exclusionary rule of evidence cut both ways? Truly to vindicate the core rights of personal privacy and individual autonomy, courts should reject evidence obtained by intrusive search and seizure or by cognitive coercion whether the oppressive acquisition was by the government or by some private agent. A private detective, doing the private defendant's bidding, forcing his way into someone's personal space or sneaking through boundaries of civility to snatch a document of interest to the defense, is offending notions of individual integrity to the same extent as a public officer on a government mission. The insertion of the muzzle of a gun into the ear of a reluctant witness violates cognitive sovereignty whether the finger on the trigger belongs to a private investigator seeking a statement that exonerates the defendant or to a state police officer trying to induce self-inculpation. And to deter such investigative methods, we should exclude the product regardless of whether it is offered against or by the defendant in the prosecution.

Yet it is indisputable that our Constitution is less a declaration of personal rights—security in space, sovereignty in mind—than a set of constraints upon government conduct. So searches and seizures, interrogations, and other intrusions are noticed by the Constitution only when they are conducted by the government, state or federal. The Fourth Amendment does not say as much—indeed, it implies the contrary (it provides simply that "the right of the people to be secure against unreasonable searches and seizures shall not be violated"), but that's what it means. And evidence, otherwise relevant and reliable, is excluded from consideration only when the method of its acquisition violates the Constitution. So only the defendant in a criminal case may keep from jurors' eyes and ears evidence they might find helpful in deciding the issue of guilt. Is this advantage fair or unfair?

First, let me say again, it is neither fair nor unfair because it is one-sided. Even were we to rewrite the Constitution (and necessarily reconceptualize the Bill of Rights) to put the matter in terms of the rights of all to be secure against the invasions of all others, even were we to apply the exclusionary rule in those few instances in which the defense had aggressively wrung evidence from uncooperative sources, we would still have to ask: is the exclusionary rule unfair? For in any given instance in which probative prosecution evidence is barred, fairness depends on the values served by the exclusion rather than whether defense evidence could also be suppressed in some other unrelated case.

Moreover, the unilateral character of the rule is not itself unfair when we consider the real and urgent concerns of the Founders (and their latter-day heirs) about the danger of government power. The great contribution of the Anti-Federalists at the end of the eighteenth century was to empower the individual citizens against the government, a potential source of oppression far more ominous than their fellow private citizens. Insofar as the exclusionary rule today serves these core values of a liberal democracy, it should be honored as a potent modern echo of the individual's warning to his government at its creation: "Don't tread on me!"

So to do justice to the question, I must once more try to discern the demands of fairness in the values of the system. Does the defendant's control of inculpatory evidence, illegally acquired, serve the interests of individual freedom? Or does the frustration of truth disserve justice and public confidence in law, all to the detriment of collective liberty? These are not easy questions. I am not confident that I have answers any better than yours (and, wrestling with these questions over many years, I have come to distrust those who peddle neat answers, however heartfelt).

One way to begin is to attempt to locate the primary purpose of the system of criminal justice. Aside from the obvious goal of sorting the innocent from the guilty as accurately as possible, other important purposes are served. The two that are most often cited are reaffirming public confidence in the process and keeping the government forces duly respectful of the precincts of personal autonomy. These two are sometimes opposed as faith in the system can be shaken by an outcome that enforces the commands of individual security enjoyed by the accused lawbreaker along with the rest of us. Or they may be seen as interwoven for, as many have argued, confidence is generated not only by a result conforming to the inclinations of the general public but by assurances that the result was achieved without threat to their own individual security against government abuse.

Indeed, some muster powerful arguments to support the claim that the latter functions of the criminal justice system—confirmation of confidence and security enhancement—are more important than the truth-seeking aspect. The way a nation adjudicates punishment for its malefactors, they say, is the most visible and reliable litmus of the level of virtue in the government as a whole. We can live with some false verdicts, but we are deeply imperiled by police impunity. Just imagine yourself in a position where your private spaces were subject to sudden and arbitrary intrusion by police unaccountable for their invasion, where personal records and confidential communications were available to government "intelligence" surveillance for any reason the executive agencies thought appropriate to their purposes, where citizens, reluctant to "cooperate" in furnishing the government with information that might destroy them, could be put under coercive pressure, physical or psychological. The fact that such government powers were commonplace in our own history, and are not rare in many parts of the world as we prepare to enter a new millennium, brings the imagined horror of such a society onto the plane of reality. And to those who are most sensitive to the large and small oppressions of the race-conscious, poverty-plagued, multilayered society in America today, the threat of unbridled police power presents a real and frightening prospect.

How does the exclusionary rule of evidence advance the cause of true justice in the criminal process? Can a court's decision not to let a jury hear some piece of inculpatory evidence because the police who seized it had no good reason to search the car from which it was taken really modify the license that law enforcement enjoys to gather evidence and place handcuffs on suspects? To put it bluntly: does what judges do in court really affect what cops do in the streets?

I sense that we are approaching the heart of the matter. But (as so often happens to me) just as I begin to hear the throb of the vital organ, confusion overwhelms the question and I begin to feel the quiver of panic. What has happened, I think, is that we have discovered that our ethical-social-political problem rests on some questionable empirical assumptions. It's all very comfortable to muse upon or debate issues of juro-political preference as abstractions: should the criminal go free because the constable blunders? Are we all more secure with our criminals in jail or with our houses impervious to search without court-ordered warrant? Does the promise of freedom from coercion in police interrogation imply a right of silence when asked in scrupulously noncoercive circumstances for an account of one's conduct? But the discovery that the question of how rules actually affect behavior is a factual question puts the matter in a different light altogether.

It's like the awful realization that most decisions in life are founded on predictions and nothing is predictable. We just don't know the critical facts, and probably never will. In the vacuum of knowledge, we resort to myth and faith. And it is a critical article of faith in our governing mythology that what happens in court has a major effect on the street. We are too wise to say that we can control crime—or police lawlessness—by what we decide in the courtrooms of the nation. But we must believe that we can influence it in a significant way. It is reminiscent of the old chestnut, Does law enforcement actually reduce criminal conduct? Don't we have a secret suspicion that for every drug dealer we convict, rather than deterring another from entering the trade, we simply open a place in the labor market that is quickly filled by an eager replacement criminal? On the other hand, tight enforcement of the Internal Revenue Code has a distinctly negative effect on most of those tempted to try to keep a bit more for themselves.

How much more difficult it is to know the extent to which any given police officer, out there gathering evidence, is affected by what happened in some courtroom in some other case on somewhat different facts sometime last year. The theory of social control is, of course, that depriving the prosecution of the spoils which might otherwise produce a conviction at trial will deter the troops from the next illegal raid. But do we even know with any degree of certainty whether police officers really care whether the case survives in court when they are hot on the discovery of the factum that will close their file? And even if they do, can we say with any assurance that they understand the effect their next move will have on the eventual outcome of the case?

In the light of the existential uncertainty of these empirical predicates, it is easy to retreat to the prescriptive mode. Whatever their effect, we need an authoritative source of propriety in law enforcement. But should the adjudication of guilt be the means for instructing police concerning the limits of their authority in future encounters? Aren't there administrative alternatives? The police forces are, after all, quasi-military structures; don't they respond to orders from the command tier? And how about the civil alternative? If the feds or the local cops trespass on the citizen's protected preserves, sue the bastards.

The facile reply is: the prescriptive alternatives don't work. Can you picture any jury returning a verdict for plaintiff after police break in and find a cache of illegal arms under the plaintiff's bed? And even in lawsuits from those incursions that win a verdict, what kind of damages can be proved as the result of a fruitless and nondestructive search? The cost of replacing a broken lock on the front door? And even if the law provided some sort of standard penalty–type of award, it's not coming from the cop's paycheck. "Let the boss pay" is a powerful disincentive to scrupulous care.

On the other hand, if civil fines or other penalties were to be exacted from the offending police officer's wallet, vacation time, promotion eligibility, we would encounter the other half of this perplexing behavioral puzzle. At what point does the penalty mode of instruction become counterproductive? For we can be pretty certain that the prospect of a really painful consequence of excessive zeal will induce lethargy. We do want our police to be aggressive, as well as respectful of the rights of their targets. The job can be dirty and dangerous. We do not motivate these young people to go out and take chances in ugly situations by telling them that their conduct will be reviewed with suspicion—if not hostility—by their superiors, the courts, and the community. And they will suffer personally if their field decisions are thought, in the cool light of Monday morning, to have overstepped some vaguely defined boundary of authority. Such a prospect does not make for an active corps.

So the bitter truth is that in order to maintain a desirable level of initiative in the troops, adverse consequences must be remote to some degree. Exclusion of the evidence at trial may be the most ingenious consequence of going too far precisely because it does not deter too much.

In the empirical wilderness, not knowing just what effect judicial response to police illegality has on other cops in other, different, and future situations, I am dubious about the underlying premises of the exclusionary rules. I am unconvinced that a judicial suppression of a piece of good, probative evidence is necessary or effective to instruct officers in future situations not to go in without a warrant.

My wife, who sits as a judge in the felony part of our state court, had a case just the other day where police responded to a call of "burglary in progress" at a multiple-dwelling house. As the police arrived, two men were descending the stairs, looking around in what the cops described as a "suspicious manner." The officers stopped them (as they are legally entitled to do) and asked them their business. Receiving a mumbled response, one of the officers gave the men a "frisk," a superficial pat-down of the outer surfaces of clothing. On one of the men, the cop felt an object that he said felt like it might be a knife. He reached into the man's pocket and withdrew a plastic strip of the sort frequently used by burglars to open latches. Meanwhile, the other officer went upstairs looking for the person who had phoned in the burglary. On the landing, he found a duffle bag which, when opened, revealed a more elaborate assortment of burglar's tools—wrenches, hacksaw blades, and such.

The narrow issue before my wife was the suppression of the plastic strip. (The duffle bag was admissible as "abandoned property," but more difficult to tie to the individuals under arrest.) Taking the police officers at their word, the question comes down to this: could this plastic strip, felt through the fabric covering the pocket, be mistaken for a weapon? If so, under a famous Supreme Court case called *Terry v. Ohio* and the law of every state in the country, the reach into the pocket was lawful and the object withdrawn would be admissible in evidence, though it turned out to be something other than a weapon. If not, the search of the pocket was unlawful and the evidence discovered would have to be suppressed (with potentially dire consequences to the prosecution). On mere suspicion, *Terry* held, a search is allowed only to neutralize physical danger. My wife denied suppression, but it is hard for me to believe that had she ruled otherwise, the conduct of future teams of police in first encounters with possibly dangerous suspects would be altered one tittle.

And this implies no disrespect for the concerns of those who place the value of a law-abiding police force above the value of convicting the guilty. I simply doubt the continuing effectiveness of the remedy of suppression to achieve the worthy goal of police restraint. Nor do I venture to say that the law requiring suppression has had no impact. It has. Judges may not instruct the ground troops, but they have been instructing those who train them. Search warrants, almost wholly unknown before 1961 in states with no exclusionary rule, have become standard procedure since *Mapp v. Ohio* burst on the scene, requiring exclusion in state trials. Well, maybe not *standard* procedure, but at least all cadets are taught the essentials of the lawful search, and the field manuals do not ignore the Fourth Amendment as in days of yore. And, by and large (most observers agree), the ethic of police license has dramatically changed. Police threat and brutality, once a common feature of interrogation, has all but disappeared— replaced with disputes over whether Miranda warnings were timely administered, or whether the defendant's damaging remarks were spontaneous or "deliberately elicited." And the heedless intrusions into personal space have been largely replaced by a warrant culture, pleasing to the Fourth Amendment.

The program of automatic exclusion, it seems to me, has largely done its job. The marginal deterrence we can expect from excluding evidence is now, I believe, greatly exceeded by the social cost of depriving fact finders of relevant and probative data on which to make the difficult determination of guilt. Moreover, our judicial instructors have knit themselves into such a snarl that it is difficult for even the most sophisticated to discern the clear shape of doctrine. The law of search and seizure has become such a dense web of special cases, exceptions, allowances, and rigid precepts with flexible applications (all with sizable state, federal, and local variances) that we can only sympathize with those charged with unknotting the judicial output and weaving it into intelligible rules for the guidance of law enforcement officers.

Approach, chase, capture, immediate search, deferred search, of person, containers, automobiles, and premises residential and commercial are all events mined with hazards of illegality. And the state of interrogation law is not much better. The pretense that cops guide their behavior—or could even if they tried conscientiously to do so— by the illumination provided by the courts is becoming untenable even for the faithful.

In addition to the goal of social engineering—making cops more law abiding—the exclusionary rules still exert one powerful hold on the social conscience. The precept used to be called the interest of "judicial integrity." What it means is that we do not want our courts to become indifferent to lawlessness in the cause of law enforcement. I call it the "dignitary interest." It commands that, of all our official organs, courts must remain alert to and fundamentally intolerant of any incursion on the precious—and precarious—liberties of the citizens. Whether it be insistence on the racial integration of public facilities, the recognition of rights to engage in repugnant expression, assurance of a fair trial for despicable criminals, or any of the countless other things that the political branches would shun, we insist that our courts be principled and free of goal-oriented sentiment.

As our priestly class, judges must also condemn instances of official abuse that come before them. And it is not enough just to profess shock and dismay. Judicial displeasure should have some teeth in it. Rejection of evidence come at by arrogance in disregard of the right of personal integrity seems the appropriate judicial response in a free society such as ours. To preserve the dignitary interest, if for no other reason, there is much to commend the proposition that we must be prepared to reject evidence obtained by abuse, unwarranted by the circumstances.

So it is not easy to discern the demands of fairness when it comes to the indisputable advantage the defendant enjoys by his power to suppress relevant and probative evidence. Even for those (like me) who believe that the dominant value in any criminal justice system is to produce verdicts based, as far as humanly possible, on all the reliable evidence bearing on the issue of guilt, even for us unrepentant formalists the countervailing values deserve serious consideration.

I think if I had to start from scratch and construct a fair system that most closely served the best of the competing values now crudely approximated by the jerry-built catacomb we call the exclusionary rules, I would sit down and write a code, a coherent, comprehensive, and simple document that would govern the quest for evidence and the impunities of those who might harbor it. My mouth fairly waters at the prospect. A document where any fool could go and look up what is legal and what is not. To replace the dozens of big cases, little cases, opinions, dicta; all those various circumstance-driven outcomes; along with the few isolated statutes governing this corner of the endeavor or that.

Somewhere I have probably said that the evolution of the common law is tidal. It starts with a few isolated decisions, each based on the right thing to do in the narrow and particular circumstances presented by the case. Something the judge just knows, feels in his bones (can this be transcendental idealism?). Then lawyers begin to notice that, as a rule, in this sort of case, with these pertinent factors, courts tend to go this way—and a generalization is born. As the generalizations accumulate, we get what we call the common law, a set of predictions of the behavior of future courts based on what other courts have done in the past in similar cases. Not just the notion that judges think alike, but of collegial continuity, deference to wisdom of one's predecessors. *Stare decisis* we call it, the power of the decided case over the undecided.

But as decisions build up, situations multiply, subtleties abound, and anomalies accrete, people begin to cry for simplicity. This is precisely where we are today with regard to Fourth, Fifth, and Sixth Amendment law. So when the call is heard in the legislative chambers, codes are written to try to rationalize and harmonize the cacophony of case law. Next, of course, courts begin to realize the limits of a code. Of necessity, they expand on the simple language of the statute and engraft exceptions and extensions as required to do what is right in the particular case at hand. All of which gradually turns into a new phase of common law, the law of interpretation—or "gloss," as lawyers call it. When this gets too complicated and arcane even for lawyers to deal with, the next stage is revision, and new codes are born. And so it goes.

So in writing my shiny new code, I would allow myself some license with decided cases. I would not simply try to codify whatever the Supreme Court has bequeathed to the new millennium. In my dreamworld, I could write on a clean slate, faithful only to a reasonable reading of basic constitutional tenets and to some personal notion of efficiency and fairness. By efficient, I mean likely to promote the primary purposes of the enterprise with the least extrinsic friction in the moving parts. By fairness? Well, that's what this book is about. Trying to figure it out—picking a fight, it's called in some circles.

So here we go. First, I would throw out the Miranda rules requiring an incantation of "rights" to exorcise the coercive atmosphere of "custodial interrogation," and along with it the affiliated doctrine based on the Sixth Amendment that a suspect is entitled to the "assistance" of counsel at lineups and interrogation after some mystical point in the process known as "formal accusation" has passed. I have elsewhere expounded on my dissatisfaction with the evolved constitutional constraints on government access to the mind of a suspect or accused person. Suffice it to say that I think we might dispense with Chief Justice Earl Warren's magic incantation—"You have the right to remain silent, anything you say may be used against you, you have the right to counsel with you during this interrogation, if you do not have funds to retain a lawyer, one will be provided for you free of charge, do you understand what I have said?" I, for one, do not understand what you have said, officer. Do you mean that if I say the word, you will go out in the dead of night in this godforsaken neighborhood and bring back a lawyer to sit here and give me free advice as I answer your questions? Just what I always suspected: cops are either liars or damn fools.

And speaking of cops, the so-called Miranda warnings were a cop-out at the time they were invented, born of the Court's suspicion of isolated interrogation and its unwillingness to outlaw all confessions produced by it. The effect of the famous advisory will always be un-knowable (despite the serious efforts of several scholars to figure out whether the litany actually deters confessions, and if so with what effect upon convictions). But it probably had a good effect indirectly on interrogation procedure, keeping the cops mindful of the fact that a court was looking over their shoulders. It also probably had a bad effect insofar as it taught cops that a little white lie in the right place could save a good case, otherwise doomed by a tardy or incomplete warning. But today, the Miranda ritual is a meaningless little joke having virtually no curative or prophylactic effect on the initial condition that prompted it, oppressive and coercive inquisition.

In place of Miranda, I would deem all deferred and extended police interrogation after arrest to be inherently coercive, and the coercion of custody could not be magically dispelled by the recitation of some formulaic litany. (Calling for the presence of a lawyer at these sessions is plainly disingenuous; with a lawyer present there simply would be no interrogation—questions, maybe, but no answers.) I would, however, allow police freely to ask questions immediately on capture and to listen to anything the captive decided to tell them at any time. Such uncounseled conversations—uninhibited by any artificial advice concerning the "right to silence," "right to counsel," and all that—would be limited in time and occasion to the natural exchange attendant on the initial encounter or the unprovoked initiative of the defendant himself. And, of course, these conversations must be free of any "true" coercion—physical force or the threat of it.

Is this an impossible standard for a reviewing court to apply on a motion to exclude? I don't think so. Was the conversation immediately and briefly associated with the initial encounter between police and suspect? Did the suspect, unbidden, initiate the exchange? Was any threat or manifestation of physical force the precipitating cause of the suspect's statement? Hard as they may be for thee and me, these are just the sort of question trial judges are accustomed to answering.

I would substitute for deferred or extensive police questioning intensive interrogation by the examining magistrate at arraignment when the case first gets to court. At that time, the judge, prompted by counsel, should obtain a full account from the person accused. The accused person may decline to answer questions at this examination, of course, but if he does so, the judge may draw—and allow the jury who eventually hears the case to draw—the appropriate inference from the choice of silence under the circumstances.

The first objection to this idea is that it violates the "right to silence" embodied in the Fifth Amendment. Closer inspection reveals, however, that that right is nowhere in the provision. It is a Court-engrafted interpretation of the right not to be forced to be a witness against oneself. And it was the Supreme Court, in a decision that still sits uncomfortably on some scholars, *Griffin v. California,* that said that drawing the natural and logical inference flowing from the assertion of the privilege to decline to answer questions was itself a violation of the Fifth Amendment privilege. My proposal would beg for a recision of old *Griffin.* To play this clean-slate game, I must ask for some erasures.

The accused would be represented by counsel at this judge-conducted inquiry, and the lawyer could counsel replies as well as help the judge elicit details or clarification of the story. But in giving this good advice, the lawyer for the defendant would, of course, know the damaging inference that could be drawn from reticence, and would know that if her client subsequently deviated from that initial account—testifying differently at the trial, for example—he would be subject to impeachment by the discrepancies.

I am unapologetic about this drastic reconfiguration of the interrogation scenario. The great Justice Benjamin Cardozo wrote in 1937, in a case called *Palko v. Connecticut,* words from which I take my inspiration (though the holding in *Palko* has not survived). Writing about the Fifth Amendment immunity against coercion, Cardozo said, "Justice . . . would not perish if the accused were subject to a duty to respond to orderly inquiry." I think that an open-court inquiry by a judge of a counseled defendant is just what Cardozo meant by "orderly" and is fully consistent with the Framers' injunction against compelled self-incrimination. It goes considerably further than the foolish Miranda charade to protect against hidden, subtly coercive probes of the isolated suspect's mind. At the same time, it allows fair access to the mind of the person who is most likely to know something about the events at issue—or at least about his own removal from them.

Along with support from Cardozo, I draw assurance from the wise scholarship of Professor Albert Alschuler of the University of Chicago Law School. In an important article published in 1996, Alschuler takes the so-called privilege against self-incrimination back to its doctrinal origins. He demonstrates that today's formulation of the privilege as a "right of silence" is the result of a linguistic shuffle, derived neither from the text nor the history of our Fifth Amendment. As written, the provision guaranteed freedom from physical torture and from the implicit coercion of being required to answer potentially inculpatory questions under oath.

The inquisitorial oath was, historically, the precipitating device of today's constitutional entitlement. The oath ex-officio, as it was called, was employed in the early seventeenth century by Elizabeth I's High Commission investigating suspected religious deviation (Roman Catholicism, principally). On neither formal accusation nor the evidence of a known accuser, suspected heretics were called and sworn to reply to all questions bearing on their faith. The threat of eternal damnation implicit in the oath was taken seriously in those days, and was regarded as the equivalent of torture. Two Puritans, Munsell and Ladd, challenged the procedure by habeas corpus in 1607 and lost. Then, in 1637, John Lilburne stood before the Star Chamber and declared that "no man's conscience ought to be racked by oaths imposed." *Nemo tenetur seipsum accusare.* No person may be required to accuse himself. Or sometimes *nemo tenetur prodere seipsum*, no one should be held to betray (produce) himself. By the middle of the seventeenth century the principle was well established in England and in the new colonies across the Atlantic.

Why should any system of laws utterly disavow noncoercive access to the mind of the criminal suspect? Alschuler writes: "The virtues of an 'accusatorial' system in which defendants are privileged to remain passive are far from obvious. The person who knows the most about the guilt or innocence of a criminal defendant is ordinarily the defendant herself. Unless expecting her to respond to inquiry is immoral or inhuman . . . renouncing all claim to her evidence is costly and foolish."

Thus, Alschuler argues, in history as well as text, our descendant of the *nemo tenetur* maxim was intended only to shield suspects from interrogation under torture or its functional equivalent. The constitutional precept was never intended to forbid questioning in threat-free circumstances, nor to prohibit the reasonable inferences that might be drawn from a failure to answer truthfully. Never intended, in other words, to establish a right of silence. Nor does freedom from compulsion imply freedom from persuasion.

Miranda stalwarts will reply, That's just the point: persuasion from a police officer in a police-dominated place is never threat-free. Well, say I, I don't know about the "never," but whenever such circumstance-induced fear is detected, the confession should be excluded. In any case, the solution for this atmospheric coercion is not a verbal incantation. Nor is it the creation of an artificial right to withhold information in all circumstances. The solution is to take the interrogation out of the polluted precincts and into an open and coercion-free environment—namely, the courthouse.

To those who say, "A courtroom is hardly coercion free, especially with that negative inference in prospect," I say, the perception that one is expected, even encouraged, to speak the truth in court is not what I call coercion. The open courtroom—on the record, the accusation stated, the judge and counsel actively present—is the very antithesis of the devices for compelled self-damnation that the Fifth Amendment forswore.

Considering where to go from here, how to preserve the essence of the privilege as conceived by the Framers in a modern context, Professor Alschuler associates himself with a list of heavy hitters in the profession who for decades have been advocating a return to something like the procedure of the mid–sixteenth century: a pretrial interrogation before a magistrate, after a finding of good reason for suspicion, unsworn, and subject to the appropriate adverse inference from failure to answer fully and truthfully. Add a few modern accoutrements like the presence of counsel, and I could make a comfortable berth aboard that Marian vessel.

The plan forces no one to bear witness against himself, only taxing the suspect with the natural and fair implications of a failure to respond in a noncoercive setting. Does this impose an obligation to divulge cerebral evidence that might be used against him? Assuredly, it does. But obligation, Alschuler asserts (with my enthusiastic concurrence), is not compulsion in the constitutional sense.

It is not an easy position to maintain without cutting loose from a good deal of well-worn doctrine that surrounds the subject. The Supreme Court has gone pretty far in insulating from adverse use any statements obtained from a citizen by force of law. *Griffin v. California* is only one of my obstacles. For example, everyone is under an obligation to file a tax return, which might contain some inculpatory information. But any individual retains the right to leave the potentially damaging lines blank (and let the IRS fill them in as well as possible from what they know). So on a theoretical map, since we lost *Palko,* Cardozo, Alschuler, and I are stranded pretty far out here in lonely territory without a friendly authority in sight. The mantra I repeat is: the right not to be compelled to be a witness against oneself does not mean being immune from inquiry. And that implies being subject to the ordinary inducements to candor and implications of silence, freely elected after full advice of the consequences.

On a practical level, many law enforcement people will howl that my model would deprive them of important confessions procured by patient, protracted, and skillful interrogation of the suspect alone—not forced from the suspect's lips, but eased from his guilty mind by the studious employment of a variety of personal, one-on-one techniques that can convert a confident denial into a detailed confession in a matter of hours. I'm sure they're right. But many of these late-night confessions are questionable. In the lengthy, unsupervised, unrecorded interaction of cops and suspect confined on police turf, free choice becomes a rather murky element. Yet it remains the qualifying feature of a jury-bound confession. Plus, daylight examination of the manner in which the confession was elicited is always muddled by questions of police credibility. In short, though valid confessions would surely be lost, a dark corner of sequestered police practice would also be closed. And that is good for public faith, I think.

In exchange (if not in full compensation) for the loss, my model offers the important (and perfectly reasonable) inference of guilt from the silent suspect. In addition, I imagine that in many major cases the investigation would continue after the initial arrest and arraignment of the suspect. If that investigation turns up anything new or contrary to the suspect's story, I see no reason why he shouldn't be brought back to court and interrogated further. Indeed, this process—unlike today's station house opportunity—could continue for days, even weeks, until the court decides that there is nothing new to go on. Having been arraigned, the defendant would have no basis for urging the process forward and cutting off the interrogation component. Today, the suspect's right to a prompt arraignment, along with his "right" to the presence of counsel after arraignment and to refuse to cooperate without adverse inference, puts tight temporal constraints on interrogation. So while putting a somewhat dark and dubious process into the open light of the courtroom, I am not (I hope) sacrificing good and valid evidence of guilt drawn, without coercion, from the mind of the suspect, including the fair inference from the suspicious failure to answer pertinent questions.

Exclusions emanating from the Sixth Amendment right to help from an attorney is an easy fix: I would simply restore that right to the courtroom setting where it belongs. The right to the assistance of counsel does not imply (as the Supreme Court has erroneously read it) assistance in blocking the government's access to damaging evidence. It means help in courtroom proceedings where the special qualifications of a lawyer as such come into play. So no otherwise admissible evidence would be excluded simply because it was obtained in the absence of counsel at some stage deemed critical—other than the court proceedings themselves.

Dismissive as it may seem, I actually believe my proposal accords with the secret agenda of the Supreme Court. I think the Court has put the Sixth Amendment right to counsel to foolish uses simply as a way of limiting the inquisitorial access police have to the mind of the defendant in their control. This purpose I achieve directly by simply limiting police inquiry of an uncounseled suspect to a brief initial exchange.

As to the exclusionary rule applied to the acquisitions by search and seizure unlawful under the Fourth Amendment, I would retain all instruction to the ground troops on the simplest, core essence of the provision: make your intrusions only by warrant bearing the sanction of the court. In fact, I would beef up the warrant, requiring that where the search may entail lengthy, destructive, or deeply intrusive probes, special need must be shown and special authorization given. I would also require advance judicial authorization for the use of spies and covert agents insinuated into the private councils of suspected conspirators, an area of privacy that the Supreme Court has deemed outside the concern of the Fourth Amendment.

At the same time, I would greatly simplify the mechanics by which warrants could be obtained, so that—aided by minimal technology and planning—the search warrant could become (as the Supreme Court has demanded for years) the normal, ordinary protocol of search. Electronics today accord the means by which warrants can be instantly issued on the radio-transmitted, sworn allegations of the field officer. Laws are in place allowing the oral search warrant. As I preached in an earlier book, *Virtual Justice* (Yale University Press, 1996), all that is required is the will of the law enforcement people and a roster of judges and prosecutors to provide twenty-four-hour coverage of the hookup.

Today, the product of search-by-warrant is all but exempt from exclusion. I would relax the exemption so that warrants could be challenged if issued on false allegations or inadequate grounds, or if they contained vague specifications of the place to be searched and the things to be seized. I would exclude also evidence gained in the course of abusive or needlessly destructive execution. Where it is likely that the object of your quest will be lost by reason of the detour necessary to obtain the warrant, I would assure the troops, a search without warrant may be lawful, but beware, each case will be judged on its own circumstances, by a test of reasonableness. Exigency and circumstantial reasonableness are not, of course, unknown to the law as it stands.

For these seizures without warrant (few, we hope, under my electronically enhanced regime), I would depart from the current dogma of automatic exclusion of the product of an unlawful search and seizure. Even today, exclusion is not, in reality, quite so automatic as it may seem. Yes, unlawfully acquired evidence must be excluded. But in finding the unlawfulness of the search or seizure, even today, there is plenty of room for discretion in the determination of reasonableness. I would enlarge that discretion. To the extent judges may find that law enforcement officers acted illegally, and yet be reluctant to deprive the jury of the evidence recovered, I would allow them a means to save the product. I would follow the lead of our siblings in the common-law tradition, as well as many of our cousins in the

European school, and leave the question of exclusion to the sound discretion of the trial judge to determine on a case-specific basis.

The standard would be something like this: in all the particular circumstances of this acquisition, are the interests of justice advanced more by admission or exclusion? I would expect that judges applying this standard would take into consideration such factors as:

(1) the gravity of the matter under investigation;
(2) the depth or destructiveness of the search;
(3) the importance of the evidence sought in the light of other evidence available;
(4) the availability of less intrusive means to acquire it;
(5) the degree of privacy that should be accorded the person, place, or container searched or the property interests infringed by its seizure.

Surprisingly, many of these considerations—which I would have thought central to the idea of a "reasonable" search—are ignored in the current understanding of that term. With statutory stylus in hand, I could comfortably inject them in my instruction to the judges to consider carefully the demands of justice in each particular case.

It would surely be objected that as I increased the discretion of the presiding judge, I would weaken the prescriptive virtues of the exclusionary rule. And so it is wherever flexibility is called for. But I would protest that today we have only the illusion of a set of rules by which future police conduct can be guided. Prescriptions and proscriptions are unclear, hedged by terms like *reasonable* and *in the circumstances*. Courts divide, and every case is different. Even the illusion of settled directives is difficult to maintain. So little is lost.

But more fundamentally, it should be acknowledged that the vagaries of this highly complex system are such, the opportunities for slippage are so hidden and numerous, that we depend for guidance on only the crudest inferences from past adjudication. Accustomed to these shifting currents, courts would hardly be out of their element if asked to decide an issue according to the fluid dictates of justice in the particular circumstances.

In the last analysis, that is what law is: a compendium of resolutions of particular—and in many ways unique—patterns of fact, mostly blurred and conflicting. To say right out that these delicate decisions should be made "in the exercise of discretion," according to "the interests of justice in the particular case," is really saying no more than what we regularly say by other formulae. Discretion is not a dirty word. Indeed, in the last days of 1997, the United States Supreme Court reversed an intermediate court of appeal for insufficient deference to the discretion of the trial court. In *General Electric v. Joiner,* the trial judge had held that plaintiff's scientific experts were basing their opinions on conjecture, and threw out the lawsuit. The Supreme Court took a look at the case and decided: no abuse of discretion. Though scientific standards of reliability were scarce, though legal standards for the qualification of experts were virtually nonexistent, the trial judge could be trusted to do what's right—and, within generous limits, the appellate courts should defer to the discretion of the trial court.

So let us not be reluctant to declare what we do, banish dissimulation, and write out what are the appropriate considerations of sound, case by case, resolution of this difficult issue.

Overall, am I advocating abolition of the controversial "exclusionary rule"? Certainly not. Confessions obtained by brute force, the threat of it, or its equivalent should not be used in evidence. That has been the root meaning of the Fifth Amendment since the beginning, and the exclusionary consequence is so plain that we have not required a case to prescribe it. Nor should confessions that were obtained in delayed or protracted police interrogation be introduced in evidence or their indirect leads used. That proscription, I know, will produce a sizable increase in excluded evidence of autoinculpation.

As to the product of searches by search warrant, my proposal would be, if anything, slightly more inclined to exclusion than current federal law (states deviate somewhat on this). Notably, I would bar the harvest of a search by warrant unsupported by probable cause or lacking a particular description of the mission. What is sometimes called the "good faith exception" to the exclusionary rule exempts from review the judgment of a magistrate expressed in a facially adequate, nonfraudulent warrant. Thus, in effect, seizures by warrant are not subject to exclusion. I would have it otherwise.

When it comes to illegal searches and seizures without warrant, I do replace "automatic" exclusion (if that's what we really have today) with discretionary exclusion. And that means illegally seized evidence would be admitted in some cases where, today, it would be excluded. To those who mourn the slimming of the exclusionary rule (and there are surely some who would), I say two things. First, as I have noted, the idea that current law presents a rigid, automatic response is illusory; the exclusionary rule is already punctured by multiple, discretionary escapes. But second, and I hope more reassuring, these warrantless searches, which today draw most of the fire, will become the exceptions rather than the common practice. If I can persuade law enforcement agencies to use the electronic "oral search warrant" procedures they already have approved, and use them as a matter of course for virtually all field searches, the warrant will supplant the officer's impulse, and the Fourth Amendment will, at last, be content.

Would such a plan deprive the defense of the significant advantage today enjoyed by blocking damaging evidence because of the means of its acquisition? Largely, perhaps, but not entirely. If the electronic warrant catches on, the bases for excluding physical evidence would be reduced (though not erased), and judicial discretion might be somewhat more receptive to the occasional acquisition without benefit of warrant. But the plan would have the contrary effect on the admissibility of police station unburdenings. And as between intrusions on the privacy of property and invasion of the autonomy of the mind, it seems to me we should be more severe about the latter.

Notwithstanding the loss to the defense in search-and-seizure cases, I believe that the design would enhance fairness and justice. Reduction of the grounds for challenge would serve the interests of fairness because it would, to some unknowable extent, improve the factual picture presented to juries charged with the difficult task of deciding what actually happened. This would promote truth in verdicts, a goal I consider important in itself and for the uplift it might have on the public's respect for the processes of law in general (a feature of a successful justice system that could use some repair in today's world). And the resort to discretion and the case-by-case judgment of a judge is fair because it cuts through what appears (not without reason) to be a senseless morass of "technicalities" in the law of search and seizure.

Of course these technicalities encumbering Fourth Amendment jurisprudence are themselves the product of case-by-case decision making. Calling on discretion is, perhaps, no more than a temporary respite from the lawyerly pursuit of rule making. But it does tend to focus judicial attention more on the particular demands of justice in the case at hand than on the disposition of another case something like it last year. More important, perhaps, the discretionary rule of exclusion is fair because it returns exclusion to where it should be: a device for the enhancement of the dignity of the judicial process, reserved for those situations in which the dignitary interest demands it.

Perhaps I can claim a final paragraph or two to say an additional word about *discretion,* a concept at the heart of my radical proposal. The word carries connotations of both good and evil—both richly deserved. In common parlance, the word can mean anything from diplomatic circumspection to sophisticated discernment. As a term in juro-speak, the definition I favor (of the many around) is the unreviewable authority of a decision maker. Meaning that, within generous limits, whoever the empowered authority may be, anything goes. Whether the cop on the beat, the prosecutor, defense counsel, or the trial judge, discretion means that final authority rests with him or her. Or to put it bluntly, there is no law on the matter, only someone's best judgment.

How offensive you find this sort of lawlessness depends on your craving for predictability, your expectations from structured institutions, and perhaps your experience with tyranny. For there is no blinking the fact that, insofar as law inhibits the tyranny of arbitrary, vindictive, or self-serving exercises of power, grants of discretion are worrisome retreats. Discretion is anathema in a society built on the principle of legality. And the principle of legality (or the rule of law, as it is sometimes called) is central in the design of our liberal democracy. This principle insists that the government take no action injurious to any citizen's legitimate interests without a prior law, democratically or constitutionally generated, specifically authorizing the exercise of authority.

At the same time, postmodern Realists (like me) see the law riddled with discretionary choices, all living happily under the rule of law. The principle of legality, as we see it, defines basic structures of our domain, providing the roof and walls of the habitation. But no just society can thrive on beams and joists alone. Furnishings are the essential, discretionary embellishments. In the selection and arrangement of these features of daily activity, living within the constraints of law becomes possible. When judges are bound to adhere to rigid prescriptions of sentences, for example, adding up the aggravating and mitigating factors according to a set formula, injustices are bound to result. When you leave the computation of each sentence, within a prescribed range, to the sound discretion of each judge, disparities may be expected, but (unless some judge suffers an unfortunate distortion of judgment) the results are likely to be closer to the fair demands of each individual case.

So I am basically inclined to celebrate discretion as the mark of a mature and responsible system. Since faith must be lodged somewhere in an open system of justice, I choose (with appropriate misgivings) to trust judges. Not because I have complete confidence in them as people. Wisdom and sagacity are in about as short supply among them as among the rest of humankind. And we may rightly tremble as they each turn inward to consult personal proclivity on the pivotal question of exclusion. But they are studied in the feat of detachment. And by and large, I think the robe bestows a genuine sense of professional honor. Most of the many judges I have met consider it important, terribly important, to be cautious, conscientious, and objective. These are not noteworthy features of the job descriptions of the other players in the theater of criminal justice.

Lest I be called naive, I would add that my inclination toward discretion spurs urgent attention to the processes of appointment and removal of those empowered. Improvement in the woeful American political appointment process, however, will come not from reducing the scope of judicial license but, paradoxically, from increasing it. As we recognize the scope of discretion with which we empower our judges, perhaps we will strive more earnestly to select the best qualified for the role. We will eventually come to realize (as the British have) that people should not be thus empowered by virtue of party service, or racial, sexual, or ethnic fit.

But in the final count, it is the people, not their backgrounds or training, who sit on the benches. And the lore of the courthouse is packed with cases of the most unlikely people turning out to be the best judges—along with some grievously disappointed expectations. In an uncertain world, we rely most heavily on the power of judicial responsibility itself to imbue the trait of scruple essential to its virtuous discharge. Then we need to take more seriously, and use more readily, the power of peer review in this profession as we do in others.

And finally, in this as in so many things, we cannot hope to reduce the complexity of life and the difficulty of choice by artificially imposed constraints on options, or the pretense of dictated resolutions. About all we can fairly expect from the collective experience is a set of generous—though carefully drawn—outer limits, borders within which we must improvise according to our thoughtful judgment—and hope for the best.

APPEALABILITY AND THE ORDEAL OF JEOPARDY

Capitalization of Error

NOBODY IS PERFECT. People make mistakes. When those people are in a courtroom, conducting a trial in the trappings of lawyers and judges, we say they commit error, as though it were some sort of crime. And they do it pretty persistently—with nary an apology or excuse. Like old sinners, they stumble through the complex tangle of trial rules, inadvertently snapping one here, breaking another there with only a fleeting backward glance, and deliberately bending a third out of their way. Nothing to be too concerned about; it's not like a surgeon's mistake, after all, or even a violinist's. No one expects a trial to be perfect.

Still, one thing that makes the trial business exciting to professionals is the lurking possibility that one of the many errors that poke out of the record may suddenly sprout into a lethal giant that can obliterate all else laboriously constructed at trial. Fear of the formidable *reversible errors,* as they are known in the courts, is what drives trial judges to perspiration in the effort—never wholly successful—to avoid or cure errors of any magnitude. Judges, only slightly less fervently than prosecutors, hate a retrial.

Error management—the adroit provocation of error, the deliberate acceptance of the risk of error, and the alert circumvention of error—is one of the great skills of a good trial lawyer. And after the dust has settled, the special talent of the appellate lawyer is to cull the trial record meticulously to identify, categorize, and magnify the stray error into a judgment killer.

Trial judges regularly have to rule on the potency of an error. There are many occasions when the trial judge is presented with a sort of appellate error question: has such clear reversible error been committed that it is useless to continue the trial? Will any conviction that may result surely be overturned on appeal? Defense counsel, opting for efficiency at the cost of a possible final acquittal, makes the motion for mistrial. Actually, rather than reflecting a shrewd if hasty calculation of odds and advantages, the motion for mistrial is almost reflexive with most defense counsel, usually voiced simply to underscore the urgency of an objection. Ninety-nine percent receive the scant judicial attention they deserve—though I remember one case where the judge, sick of the lawyer's face, weary of his ceaseless caviling, suddenly granted one of counsel's rote motions for mistrial, and for the first time enjoyed the sight of the lawyer stunned into speechlessness.

The motions are not always empty; sometimes the trial judge must seriously consider whether the error has irremediably polluted the proceedings, requiring a fresh start. If the prosecutor blurts out his personal conviction of the defendant's guilt, based on matters he cannot disclose to the jury, a motion will immediately be made to the trial judge to cancel the trial and start again. Or a prosecution witness, notwithstanding careful coaching, answers a question about his identification of the man who stuck a gun in his face and emptied his cash register by saying, "I recognized him from the time he came into the store, drunk, and assaulted a customer." The immediate objection is coupled with an insistent motion for a mistrial. And the trial judge will have to rule on the error. For the most part, however, the job of the trial judge is to prevent error (by ruling on objections), and to avoid committing any herself. The remedial approach to error is the prime business of appeals courts.

But in the appealability of error lies one of the major inequalities between the prosecution and the defense. Harmful errors committed by the prosecutor and the trial judge are appealable by the defense, but defense errors or judicial rulings wrongly favoring the defendant are not appealable by the prosecution. There is no such thing as a reversible error that will nullify an acquittal. Even the most blatant error, an error of law that indisputably affected the outcome, cannot be raised by the prosecution on appeal.

Let us say that the defense witness, Gamma, testifies that he saw the incident through the window of his store across the way, and that it was definitely not the defendant, Delta, who fired the fatal shot. He is then asked by defense counsel why he is so sure, expecting (let us assume) an answer about the size or appearance of the shooter. Oh, says Gamma, because my nephew, Beta, told me that Omega was boasting that he had done it. Motion to strike, granted; motion to instruct the jury to disregard, so instructed. Omega's in the wind and neither side can—or may—call Beta (whose uncorroborated testimony about what Omega said would be hearsay). But if some jurors take Gamma's blurt into consideration in finding a reasonable doubt (and who can ever know?), the resulting acquittal will stand for all time immune to challenge. While the defense may always seek cancellation of an adverse judgment, the prosecutor may never seek a second chance.

The reason for this peculiarly American inequality lies in the concept of double jeopardy. I used to teach the subject, and I can attest that the concept of double jeopardy, while easily stated, is so subtle and complex that it baffles veteran law professors—to say nothing of their students and former students, including many who now wear robes. Here it is in plain English: No government, state or federal, may try the same person more than once for the same crime. Unless, of course, the defendant waives the exemption. We have to tack on the waiver exception not only because most entitlements are waivable but because otherwise there would be no retrial allowed following the defendant's successful motion to cancel a trial by mistrial, or her victorious appeal from a conviction. And we do allow a second trial where the defendant herself seeks to abort or nullify the first.

For the sticklers, I should insert that double jeopardy will bar a retrial even if the first trial was halted on a defense motion for a mistrial if the prosecutorial error that provoked it was intended to procure a fresh trial. Not just egregious prosecutorial error, but devious tactics. Cases like these are collector's items; appellate courts are forever assuring us that such a thing could happen, but not in the case at hand. One can imagine a prosecutor, a likely acquittal looming before him, who makes an obvious, gross, and reversible error in the desperate hope that, rather than letting the case go to the expected dispositive verdict, his adversary will move for the mistrial. If he does so, the Supreme Court has said, the deliberately provoked mistrial constitutes no waiver of the double-jeopardy bar to retrial. I don't want to get too deeply into all this, and I will spare you the Supreme Court case and others discussing this wrinkle. You can see how it might make for some fun arguments: "The prosecutor was only trying to provoke me, he never would have made such a bonehead error otherwise." "Oh, no, the error is well within the range of my stupidity. Don't blame me for your ill-considered motion for mistrial." It is enough for my present purposes to note that in this department, even the waivers have exceptions.

We could, I suppose, enforce double jeopardy so strictly that an error toxic enough to require mistrial or reversal of a judgment of conviction would also preclude a second trial. Indeed, if the one-bite principle is so precious to the system, why should we give the offending state a second chomp merely because the harmed defendant chose to assert the error committed against him? So, you see right at the start, the rule seems to have become somewhat detached from its governing theory. It leads to the sneaking suspicion that maybe the whole concept of single exposure is not so critical after all. Or else that the almighty waiver overrides any plea for theoretical consistency.

The trouble with the latter explanation (attractive as it might otherwise seem) is this: what if something happens during the trial that makes it impossible to continue? No one's error, just an event. The judge, driven to hypertension by counsels' endless wrangling, has a heart attack. Or the last sworn alternate juror, replaying yesterday's testimony in her mind, is hit by a truck on the way to court. The defendant, though sympathetic, sees no reason why he should consent to starting over. He liked the way the case was going in; if the government can't see it through, he'd just as soon walk out a free man, thank you very much. Sorry, but no waiver this time. Nonetheless, the court will cancel the first trial and allow a new start because of *manifest necessity*. Neither the principle of double jeopardy nor the waiver rule will interfere with the interest of the state in these circumstances to bring the matter to a conclusion, even if that means starting again in a second trial. So we can begin ruminating on just what sort of event amounts to circumstances of manifest necessity.

There's another problem with the waiver theory as an explanation of allowing retrial after a successful defense appeal. Grinning behind this theory is the law's old nemesis, the logical flaw of circularity. The defendant may be said to agree to a new trial—indeed, to seek a new trial—by taking an appeal only so long as we postulate the power of the appellate court to order a new trial upon reversal. And the legitimacy of that power is the very thing we are attempting to validate. For certain types of error—errors like violation of the Sixth Amendment right to a speedy trial that cannot be corrected at a second trial—the appellate court will wash out the case. If we allowed them to dismiss with prejudice (precluding retrial) for all reversible errors, we could not say that the defendant waives his protection against double jeopardy by appealing.

But that's only the beginning of our troubles with the concept of double jeopardy. Let's meditate a moment on the rule: No second trial of the same person for the same crime. Okay, but what is one trial? What is the same crime? And how about retrial in the federal jurisdiction after a state trial? Or vice versa?

The first question—when does a trial end and a retrial begin—is really not hard. We just have to get it through our heads that a trial does not mean a completed trial. The first trial does not require a verdict in order to end; the retrial begins whenever a new jury is empaneled to start work from the beginning on the same issue.

Getting a mental grip on this idea may not be so easy because the concept of double jeopardy is the descendent of an older principle that was designed to preclude the oppression of repeated trials after one jury had spoken and declared the accused not guilty. The doctrine of *autrefois acquit* it was called in the Norman accents of old English law. It's an idea of fairness we can all embrace. It was only a small step from there to the preclusion of another trial following a conviction. If the state was unhappy with the verdict or the sentence, the prosecution was not allowed to put the accused to trial again in the hopes of winning a more severe judgment.

The leap came in the realization that it was not only respect for the judgment of the first jury nor the injustice of multiple punishment for a single misdeed that drove the double-jeopardy principle. It is the hazard of being on trial—the expense, risk, and anxiety of the adjudicative process—that should not be repeatedly imposed for a single criminal event. Beginning over and over without reaching a conclusion is just as debilitating, it was thought, as beginning again after a judgment in the first effort. So renouncing double jeopardy means not only no new beginning after a prior conclusion but also no new beginning after a prior beginning.

Now all we have to do is identify the moment when the trial begins—when jeopardy attaches, as lawyers say. Is it when the indictment comes down? When the defendant is arraigned (and becomes "the accused" for Sixth Amendment purposes)? When the case is called for trial? When the jury is sworn? When the first word is spoken thereafter? When the first witness is sworn? When the witness answers the first question? Any point might be selected. And in a few cases the choice may have consequences: the case has been called and the jury empaneled and sworn when the prosecutor discovers that her prime witness has disappeared. She seeks consent to a mistrial. The defendant—no fool—objects. The prosecutor, unready to proceed, is generally regarded as being in default, not a situation giving rise to manifest necessity. So whether the prosecutor can move to abort without losing the opportunity to try the case in the future depends on whether jeopardy has attached.

But this is a simple matter, too: all we need is a rule. And the Supreme Court has chosen one for us: jeopardy attaches when the jury is empaneled and sworn or, in a bench trial, when the first witness is sworn.

That was the easy part; are we ready for harder questions? The concept of double jeopardy was written into the Fifth Amendment of the Constitution: "nor shall any person be subject for the same offense to be twice put in jeopardy of life or limb." (The "life or limb" part is quaint but it may be read simply as "criminal conviction.") In 1969 the Supreme Court, reversing itself, decided that the double-jeopardy principle was of the essence of ordered liberty, and hence this clause applies fully to the states. In the decade following, the Court settled some of the basic questions. In addition to fixing the point at which jeopardy attaches, they established that the defendant who procures a reversal of a conviction (on grounds other than the insufficiency of the evidence) or the discontinuance of a trial may be tried again, but that the prosecution may never appeal from any adverse determination of the merits.

Not that the prosecution gets no appeals. Rulings by the trial judge before jeopardy has attached—rulings that dispose of the case, such as granting a motion to dismiss the indictment for any one of a number of reasons, or granting a motion to suppress evidence without which no prosecution is possible—these are appealable by the government. So, too, the state may appeal from a postverdict judgment of the trial court setting aside a jury verdict of conviction. This appeal is allowed because victory would bring not a second trial but only reinstatement of the verdict of the first trial. And on the defendant's appeal, the prosecutor may raise errors favoring the defendant and perhaps obtain either dictum (a statement of the appellate court without any effect on the case before them, but serving as instruction to judges in future trials) or, in the event of a reversal and order for a new trial, a direction that at the next trial the judge should rule differently. In some few jurisdictions (maybe only California), there is even a way for the prosecution to get a fast (and helpful) review of rulings on evidence while the trial is in progress. (California calls it "taking a writ," but they are called interlocutory appeals nearly everywhere else and rejected as such.) So some errors favoring the defense are not altogether sacrosanct. But any mistrial or acquittal, any outcome that cannot be corrected without a new trial, is final against the prosecution.

I am briefly tempted to tell the stories of some of these many cases, plucking, perhaps, a felicitous quotation from the tangled literature. But it would be a digression and, more important, this file is notoriously dull and confusing for all but the most dedicated aficionados. For our purposes, we already know enough to recognize that the Constitution itself has lodged an extraordinary advantage with the defense in criminal matters: if an error favoring the defense gets by the trial judge—or is committed by her, the defendant in jeopardy may bask in the benefit of the error without fear of cancellation on appeal.

Not that every error favoring the prosecution is a sure ticket to reversal. As we have noted, a doctrine—some would say, pernicious doctrine—allows appellate courts to overlook errors that it deems "harmless." What amounts to harm—and renders the error reversible—is, as you may imagine, debatable. Is an error harmful if, considered by itself, it is so pernicious that it is likely to influence the jury's thinking on the issue of guilt? Or is it harmful only if, in view of all the other evidence, it is likely to have had a determinative effect? And how "likely" is likely and how pernicious is determinative? Is an error harmless only when it is highly probable that not a single juror decided the issue on the basis of the datum? However these questions are resolved in the various jurisdictions, it is obvious that the doctrine affords considerable insulation for the prosecutor against reversal for errors they commit or induce. Still, convictions do get reversed; acquittals, never.

How the defense advantage of appealability plays out in court is difficult to describe with economy; the province of error is vast. Remember Gamma's volunteered testimony that Beta told him that Omega admitted firing the fatal shot? Even if Beta were available to testify, the admissibility of testimony by a witness who heard someone else admit to committing the crime for which the defendant is charged is dicey. You can see why: it's powerful evidence, evidence on which many conscientious people would readily repose a reasonable doubt of the defendant's guilt; yet it is easily fabricated. It is normally rejected as hearsay (after all, the alternate confessor is not even present to be cross-examined and evaluated for credibility) unless there is proof of unavailability of the confessor plus some reason to believe that his self-incrimination is true.

Suppose the trial judge takes the evidence without such assurances. Error. But if an acquittal results, that's the end of the case. In contrast, if the judge had erroneously attempted to cure the error in the robbery case when the prosecution witness blurted out the defendant's prior assault, any conviction would have been reversed, offering the defendant a second chance to try for an acquittal without the offending evidence. (The "cure," incidentally, would have been a soothing instruction to the jury to disregard the witness's unfortunate interjection; it's a remedy that the appellate court might well think inadequate to erase the prejudicial impression.)

Suppose a fleeing felon, pursued at high speeds from a bungled bank robbery, runs off the road and, when apprehended, claims to have been an innocent hostage of the robber, who took his car at gunpoint and fled from the crash site. The government brings in a police officer who inspected the wreck and is prepared to give his opinion that only one person was in the car at the time of the crash. Very important evidence for the government, which will have problems otherwise identifying the masked bandit. The judge (who has unaccountably overlooked a decision of the Supreme Court on the very question) excludes the evidence on the grounds that the witness is not a qualified expert because he does not belong to a recognized scientific specialty with its own peer standards of reliable judgment. And suppose the defense offers a witness to give an opinion as a counselor for a personality enhancement group that the defendant lacked the aggressive attributes of a bank robber, and our indolent judge sustains the prosecutor's objection. In a federal court, at least, these rulings on the experts may both be important errors. The first will never be reviewed; the second may become the basis for a reversal.

Or suppose the judge intervenes throughout the trial to question witnesses in a manifestly skeptical or hostile vein. If the witnesses are defense witnesses, the defendant might win a reversal; if they are government witnesses there's little the prosecutor can do besides begging the judge to lay off. Even errors of law, delivered to the jury in the customary papal tone, are the occasion for reversal only when they favor the prosecution. If the judge tells the jury that the defense of self-defense is sustained if the defendant believed she was in imminent danger but mistakenly omits the proviso that her belief must have been reasonably founded on the actions of the deceased, the resulting acquittal is immutable. But if the judge slips and tells the jury that a reasonable doubt is one for which a juror could supply a reason if asked, the resulting conviction will be overturned by an appellate court.

It remains to address the hard question, is this advantage unfair? I'll say this much: I can well imagine a different arrangement. I can imagine a different construction of our constitutional proscription of double jeopardy that would, without violence to the precept, allow government appeals and reversals of acquittals procured by error. We would need only to deem the first jeopardy to continue through appellate review—and retrial, if necessary—to an affirmed resolution, free of serious error. To quote again from the legendary Justice Cardozo, considering, more than sixty years ago in *Palko,* Connecticut's grant to the prosecution of a right to appeal:

> [The state] asks no more than this, that the case against [the defendant] shall go on until there shall be a trial free from the corrosion of substantial legal error. This is not cruelty at all, nor even vexation in any immoderate degree. If the trial had been infected with error adverse to the accused, there might have been review at his instance, and as often as necessary to purge the vicious taint. A reciprocal privilege, subject at all times to the discretion of the presiding judge, has now been granted to the state. There is here no seismic innovation. The edifice of justice stands, its symmetry, to many, greater than before.

The *Palko* decision has been overruled (by *Benton v. Maryland* in 1969) insofar as it declined to make binding on the states the double-jeopardy provision of the Fifth Amendment, but the words of the great justice still resonate with me. We (Cardozo and I) would, of course, couple such equalization with a stern prohibition of multiple trials for purposes of harassment or oppression. We could also limit their number and allow them only in cases of serious error—a variant of the manifest necessity exception. And I would reinforce Cardozo's opinion (which requires no reinforcement from me) by pointing out that other civilized countries allow government appeals in criminal cases.

It is difficult to see how the imbalance serves important values in the American system of criminal justice. Must one accept at face value the homily articulated in 1957, by Justice Hugo Black for the Supreme Court, in a case called *Green v. United States,* and quoted and reaffirmed many times since: "The underlying idea, one that is ingrained in at least the Anglo-American system of jurisprudence, is that the State with all its resources and power should not be allowed to make repeated attempts to convict an individual for an alleged offense, thereby subjecting him to embarrassment, expense and ordeal and compelling him to live in a continuing state of anxiety and insecurity, as well as enhancing the possibility that even though innocent he may be found guilty." Not only did Justice Black exclude the benighted State of Connecticut (which had allowed prosecution appeals for fifty years before the Supreme Court got the issue) from the Anglo-American system of jurisprudence, but he implied that Cardozo had somehow managed to miss the ingrained idea underlying the whole works—and this was still a dozen years before *Palko* was overruled.

The dual-sovereignty rule, for example, which allows multiple prosecutions in different jurisdictions for the same crime (albeit under different names) calls into question the centrality of the principle of one jeopardy. One may wonder how deeply ingrained this idea really is as we watch a row of former police officers, lately acquitted of assaulting a motorist, being tried and convicted in federal court of violating the motorist's civil rights by beating him senseless. A young black man was acquitted in New York state court of stabbing to death a young rabbinical student during a racial uprising in Queens; as I write, his trial is starting in federal court for the same killing. There are other examples. Most involve serious physical abuse by police officers or sheriffs; many have racial overtones; most arouse a disquieting sense that justice was not done on the state level. The cases are not common, but they are certainly not freakish.

The trouble with exceptions to a rule is that, while they allow the rule to live by giving it some breathing room, they cast doubt on the integrity of the underlying precept itself. From a rule of some importance, even constitutional stature, we expect some dominance. It should not buckle to too many other considerations. If it yields too often, we wonder whether the core principle is still worthy of respect.

If we now have the idea of *one trial* firmly under control, we look at the notion of *the same crime.* The Supreme Court has recently withdrawn a fairly liberal interpretation, sometimes called "the same-conduct test," of the idea of "the same offense." Justice Brennan had written for the Court in 1990, in a case called *Grady v. Corbin,* that two cases are the "same offense" when the prosecutor in proving one, must introduce evidence constituting the other. In the case before them, Corbin had pleaded guilty to driving while intoxicated and crossing the median of a divided highway. He was subsequently prosecuted for reckless manslaughter arising out of the same event. Affirming the New York Court of Appeals, Brennan sustained a claim of double jeopardy. To prove the reckless element of the manslaughter charge, the state had to prove the intoxication and reckless driving. This same-conduct test always seemed to me consistent with the theory of double jeopardy: it doesn't matter what the state calls the conduct, or what elements define it, multiple prosecutions arising from the same course of behavior offend the principle of single jeopardy.

Just three years after *Grady v. Corbin*, in 1993, the Court had another look at the problem and canceled the same-conduct test. In *United States v. Dixon*, Justice Scalia, writing for a fractured Court, returned to an earlier—and narrower—reading. In 1932, *Blockburger v. United States* had defined as the same offense two crimes neither of which has an element that the other does not. Under this same-elements test, Corbin's case would have come out the other way. Though reckless and intoxicated driving was the *conduct* by which the homicide was committed, it is not an *element* of the crime of homicide. Likewise, homicide has an element—causing a person's death—that drunken driving does not.

So, too, under *Blockburger*, a person prosecuted for a larceny committed during a burglary may be subsequently prosecuted for the burglary. Because larceny has the element of theft which burglary does not, and burglary has the element of breaking in which larceny does not, they are not the same offense, and sequential prosecution is allowed, even though both crimes arose from the same incident. Again, *Dixon*'s choice may be seen as evincing greater tolerance for multiple prosecution and hence further erodes the certainty that we are dealing with a crucial precept of American criminal justice.

But it is the dual-jurisdiction exception that I keep coming back to as the best evidence that the prohibition of multiple jeopardy is not a basic ingredient of a fair process. The Fifth Amendment, remember, says nothing about both jeopardies occurring in the same jurisdiction. To be sure, there wasn't much overlap between state and federal crimes at that time, but not every federal crime was exclusively in the federal jurisdiction; the founders might well have imagined that some aspect of the conduct falling into one of the few federal crimes could also be prosecuted at a state level. A stagecoach robbery might have been a theft from the U.S. Postal Service, but a private bank's funds might have been part of the booty. The framers didn't write: "nor shall any person be subject for the same offense to be twice put in jeopardy of life or limb in the same jurisdiction." Yet the Court has persistently read the clause as though it had the "same jurisdiction" stipulation tacked onto it. Then you embed the precept in the federal structure and you get the notorious liberality regarding multiple prosecutions. A person can be prosecuted as many times as there are jurisdictions, state or federal, that penalize some aspect of the conduct in question. One of the little, unanticipated blessings of the federal system.

Some states, like New York, have chosen as a matter of local policy to treat the United States as one big jurisdiction and decline to prosecute after jeopardy in any other place. That is, as they say, their prerogative. But the great federal court system has no such compunction. How often and when the feds should run a failed local prosecution through federal court is obviously a matter of some sensitivity. They do it only rarely, when in their best judgment there has been a miscarriage in a case of public importance. But even so, they do take a second swing occasionally. And who is to say that by subjecting the defendant to a second trial, the government is not vindicating a superior interest of the public to see justice done? An interest, Justice Black, that may even be more deeply ingrained in our social ethic than the avoidance of "embarrassment, expense, and ordeal."

Incidentally, I find it revealing that Justice Black's famous formulation in *Green* appears to be founded in his concern that *innocent* defendants not succumb finally to the exhausting effects of persistent prosecution. Is protection of the innocent a true predicate for the principle? Let us, for the moment, put aside as anomalous the dual-sovereignty exception and address the question: does the proscription of multiple prosecution protect the innocent defendant who might otherwise be convicted eventually?

There is surely in Black's idea an echo of the old idea of autrefois acquit. If we take a first acquittal to be the same as adjudicated innocence. But suppose we had a rule that said: no reprosecution after acquittal unless the verdict was very likely the result of the erroneous exclusion of evidence highly probative of guilt. Would we still say that a second trial of the acquitted defendant entailed a substantial risk of convicting the innocent? Or suppose we allowed the acquittal to be reopened upon subsequently discovered evidence raising a serious question whether the exculpatory defense evidence was perjured. The defendant's perfect alibi witness subsequently reveals to a friend that the testimony was concocted to disguise what the witness well knew was the truth. If we let a new jury hear the defense, subject to challenge, have we imperiled the innocent?

Besides, we have come a long way since the old common-law plea in bar called autrefois acquit. Surely, there is no special concern for the innocent in the second prosecution following conviction (the situation in *Palko*, incidentally)—though we might be worried that the latter effort was malicious or vindictive. And we should certainly have a provision that would disallow prosecutions—first as well as second—on that basis. Finally, consider the aborted trial. If a court calls a mistrial when a juror comes down with the flu (instead of suspending the trial for a few days), and an appellate court concludes there was no manifest necessity, is the retrial of the defendant before a fresh jury a particular threat to the innocent?

The Supreme Court has said that all defendants acquire the right to have the case adjudicated to conclusion by the first jury sworn. But what sort of right is that? With all due respect to the ghost of Hugo Black, it does not seem to be a right designed to shield innocent defendants from wrongful conviction. The first jury sworn, we must assume, is no more likely to acquit an innocent defendant than any other jury. Thus I find it hard to find in Black's comment a basic ingredient of fairness in the double-jeopardy rule as today constituted.

Let me be clear. I do not suggest that we accord the government a right to appeal from adverse trial errors so that we might level the playing field by equalizing remedies between prosecution and defense—despite Cardozo's appreciation of "symmetry." Rather, I note that our traditional disability may serve a lesser value than the one sacrificed. Sparing a defendant the hazard of retrial may be less vital to justice than allowing the state to reverse adverse rulings based on clear errors of law. The greater good may be the pursuit of a case to a resolution free of major, result-distorting errors.

I grant that this idea supposes that serious errors of law should not pass uncorrected, whichever side they favor. Can I defend that? What is so important about getting the law right? As I have said, trial errors are a regular feature of any trial, and usually pass all but unnoticed. I probably must admit that, to me, conducting a trial according to law is an important feature of the system, an entitlement of the community as important as the government's general commitment to governance by law. It is important that a defendant not walk away from a charge when his freedom is purchased by the disobedience or disregard of those procedural and substantive norms we have all agreed (theoretically) should govern a trial. It is also important that appellate courts have an opportunity to develop principles of law governing the conduct of a defense; without prosecution appeals they rarely see such errors, much less have the opportunity to instruct the trial bench and bar on their obligations to law.

At the same time, as a matter of regrettable prediction, I know full well that we will never allow the prosecutor to seek appellate review of trial rulings or the conduct of the defense. The influence, always and forever, of the ancient doctrine of autrefois acquit—reinforced by the sporting ethic of one shot—is immutable. Reprosecution after acquittal—or even a false start—will never be folded into a single jeopardy, and we cannot hope to correct errors against the prosecution by appeal to higher authority. Appeals courts can, of course, speak to them, instructing trial courts by admonition. And occasionally they do. In deciding appeals from judgments of conviction, in evaluating defendants' claims of reversible error, an appeals court may pronounce a dictum disapproving of some trial event that favored the defendant. It's hardly worth the trouble. But that's about as much as we can expect.

Prosecutors can control trial error in two other ways. First is by some sort of expanded and streamlined interlocutory appeal. Perhaps we should take California seriously. The "writ" they "take" (or more often threaten to take) they call a "writ of mandate" and is probably derived from the old common-law writ of mandamus, whose descendants populate the procedure codes of all jurisdictions. The mandamus—like its sibling, the writ of prohibition—is a device whereby a superior court orders the lower court to do what fundamental law requires, or to abstain from acting in excess of lawful authority. The writs are generally reserved for clear and obvious cases, often matters of basic jurisdiction. I can recall an instance, for example, in which I brought a writ on a trial judge who for some reason refused to impose judgment on a convicted man. Just let the case stand there on his docket, month after month, untouched, while the defendant roamed free on bail. In contrast to our understanding of the writ as an extraordinary remedy, California recently issued a writ to a trial judge prohibiting the judge from giving a simple trial instruction to the jury on a question of evidence.

I suppose we might take a page from the book of our innovative Pacific cousin and relax our ungenerous attitude toward the ancient writ; let the appellate court participate immediately in the trial decisions. It might slow things down a bit, and neither appellate nor trial judges will stand up and cheer the new arrangement. But it has some obvious advantages to both sides. Defendants would have a shot at correcting imminent minor errors, which are likely to end up in the "harmless error" dustbin on the appeal. And prosecutors would get their only chance to prevent the harmful errors that they could not even assert otherwise. Still, I think we can confidently predict, the idea does not stand a chance. The very thought that appellate courts might become involved in the quotidian errors of trials-in-progress would horrify policymakers on both sides of the appellate divide—at least on the East Coast. And they might well be right.

The other device to reduce the injury suffered by appeal-proof errors committed against the prosecution is far more casual, but no less potent. I used to think it was an unwritten axiom of practice, but I have since been steered to a couple of old state cases in which it actually appears in print as a legal tenet. It is nothing but the reasonable corollary of the unequal access to appellate review that I have been talking about. I would put it like this: at trial, while the defense is entitled to the benefit of the doubt on all questions of fact, the prosecution should have the benefit of the doubt on questions of law. This means that trial judges should not issue those unreviewable rulings in favor of the defense unless they are clearly entitled to them. On close questions, the trial judge should come down on the side of the prosecution so that the decision can be reviewed and corrected if wrong.

The only trouble with this salutary rule is that ego and professional caution incline many judges to the contrary: why tempt reversal; rule for the defense and you are secure against Monday morning quarterbacks on the appellate bench. Not that judges are unduly reversal-averse. In fact, many either express contempt for the intelligence of the judges who review their rulings or claim that they cannot possibly be guided by projected appellate response since the spectrum of likely reaction among the individual appellate judges is broad, and the composition of the appeals panel is random. Even so, no judge likes to be told by higher authority that his judgment is flawed. And in the ordinary interest of judicial economy, any trial judge would like to avoid the general anguish of a long-concluded case back on the docket for a new trial ordered by the appellate court. So on those important things that—if error—will likely be deemed reversible error, the understandable inclination of most trial judges is: close calls go to the defense. It won't kill the prosecution and it may avoid lots of trouble down the line.

Reversing this inclination and systematically calling the close ones for the prosecution would put the defense at a decided disadvantage. An imaginative defense strategy might be nipped in the bud; a dubious prosecutorial ploy might be tolerated. The general damage rulings such as these would do to defense interests might be substantial, pervasively skewing verdicts in favor of the government. And while appeals are important, verdicts are where it really counts.

On reflection, taking the point as seriously as it deserves (and insofar as I am offering a recommendation), I favor an adjustment in this "rule": on the close calls, judges should favor the proponent, whoever it might be. In other words, when in doubt, let it in. That way, we won't risk an erroneous preclusion of defense evidence, and we'll let the prosecutor risk reversal if he is sufficiently desperate or confident. Thus modified, I think the pernicious effect would be negligible. When it comes to allowing evidence, courts are already very generous to the defense. No one wants to think that a defendant was convicted because some judge wouldn't allow the jury to hear a piece of exculpatory evidence or a challenge to a prosecution witness. And although the presumption in favor of dubious prosecutorial offers may injure the defendant on trial, it is reviewable and, if the injury is really harmful, correctable.

It's a highly informal "rule of practice," if indeed it is that. But I think it goes a long way to compensate the government for its inability to reverse harmful adverse errors. At least the prosecution should not have to suffer the most harmful, the errors of preclusion. Cut off essential proof and you may disable the prosecution from carrying its burden of persuasion. It seems fair to me to allow the close calls to favor a full presentation. My feeling is, the more evidence the better. Let's make it a real rule and let it irrigate both fields.

TRUTH TELLING AND THE LIMITS OF ETHICAL LICENSE

Counsel's Tolerable Deceptions

AS DEFENSE COUNSEL IN A criminal case, I enjoy two options that no prosecutor has: tag them concealment and dissimulation. The first is to decide that some witness is not going to help our case so we just won't call him. I'll deep-six my notes on what he has told me and hope the prosecutor doesn't find him. I won't go so far as to tell him to get lost—that might be obstruction of justice, a crime—but I am surely not about to serve up his name and address to the prosecutor on the proverbial silver platter.

This first option derives from the defendant's diminished discovery obligations. Even in California, we have learned, the defendant does not have to divulge the identities and the stories of the witnesses he has decided not to call. The reduced disclosure duty in turn derives from the defendant's passive position in the confrontation in which he is required to prove nothing—much less to prove facts against himself, or provide the source of such evidence.

His stance—free of any burden of proof—is surely an advantage but hardly an unfair one. We all agree, do we not, that it is healthy for the criminal justice system to place upon the government, the party seeking the punishment of a free constituent, the entire obligation of proof? The deep-six prerogative, however, is not a hard-welded corollary. To say that, though he proves nothing, a person shall be acquitted if the prosecution fails in its burden of proof does not logically require us to say that nothing the defense learns in its investigation must be disclosed to the prosecution. As to discovery, then, fairness may require (I have already argued) a somewhat expanded obligation to share unprivileged material with the prosecution. And unprivileged material, I will here suggest, includes the products of a lawyer's investigation, though stimulated initially by the confidential communication of the client.

The secondary and equally troubling question that follows from this first defense option to withhold damaging evidence is this: to what extent may defense counsel argue from the lack of evidence that she herself has withheld? Having found a witness who told counsel that he had seen the defendant lurking about the scene shortly before the crime, and having decided to ignore the witness; having watched the prosecutor's trial evidence unfold without the appearance of that witness or any other to testify to the same effect, may counsel stand up and say to the jury: "Ladies and gentlemen, this case is purely circumstantial. No witness puts my client anywhere near the scene of this crime anytime close to its commission."

I know of trial judges who have frowned on such tactics after the evidence in question was excluded by law. "How can you believe the victim's identification of my client in this courtroom last week," a lawyer might argue to the jury, "when she hasn't seen the perpetrator in the eight months since the time of the crime?" If the lawyer knows that the victim picked the defendant out of a lineup shortly after the indictment came down—just two weeks after the crime—but that evidence was suppressed on the defense *Wade-Gilbert* motion (no counsel present), he's pushing the license pretty far. Having gotten the critical evidence suppressed, defense counsel should not argue that it does not exist.

But no court excluded the evidence of the eyewitness who put the defendant at the scene; the prosecutor just failed to produce it. It seems to me, therefore, fair and true to point out to the jury that the trial record is barren in that patch. And the lack of evidence due to failure of proof is indeed a valid ingredient of reasonable doubt. The secret knowledge of counsel should not impair his ability to comment on the gaps in the prosecution case.

The other option available exclusively to the defense is to contend contrary to personal belief. True (I maintain), the prosecutor is not ethically obliged to come to a conclusion on matters of credibility: whether the eyewitness's identification of the defendant is accurate, whether the alibi witness is telling the truth, whether the victim was in fact the first aggressor. In other words, whether the defendant is guilty. There are cases (I allow) where the prosecutor may simply say, "No opinion; that's what we have juries for." Other commentators, I should note, take a stricter view, enjoining the prosecutor never to bring to trial a defendant he would not himself vote to convict were he on the jury.

But we all agree that if the prosecutor believes that the defendant is innocent, he may not prosecute; if he believes that a prosecution witness is lying or wrong, he may not ask the jury to believe the witness, and (I, at least, would add) when he believes that a defense witness is truthful (on some peripheral point that does not cause the prosecutor to doubt the defendant's guilt), he may not try to make her look like a liar, even though perfectly legal means of impeachment are at hand.

The defense suffers no such constraints. Whether counsel chooses to arrive at a conclusion on issues that will be submitted to the jury is a matter of personal style. Some lawyers probably become convinced by their own efforts, and fight with a sense of personal conviction. Others doubtless maintain an attitude of general skepticism, committing themselves to no one's story. But whatever their inclination, whatever belief they may have achieved or succumbed to, the lawyers' performance and the ethical obligations behind it are unaffected. They owe an equally vigorous defense to the defendant they believe is guilty and the one they think is totally innocent.

To say it is owed may not be quite the same as to say it is given. I have little personal experience to consult, but it seems to me unlikely that a lawyer can go on for years manifesting total commitment to causes she believes to be false. Surely, when the client comes along whom the lawyer really thinks has been wrongly accused, the urgency of the defense must rise somewhat. Sincerity, I would think, inspires performance. But despite my inference from human nature (or my own), I am here to report that in the daily commerce of the courts—or at least what the jurors see of it—it is virtually impossible to separate by vigor the lawyers who believe in their clients' innocence from those who believe otherwise.

Arguing contrary to personal belief may mean you step up to the jury box after both sides have rested and, mustering all the earnest shows of deep inner conviction, proclaim, "Ladies and gentlemen, the prosecution case is full of holes" when your true feelings are, "I have rarely seen such an airtight case." Trial lawyers do it all the time. It's not even unethical because it would not be regarded as a statement of a personal knowledge or opinion. Both sides are commanded by the American Bar Associations Standards to refrain from expressing to the jury their own belief concerning guilt or innocence or the credibility of witnesses. To be sure, the injunction is a bit less strict for defense counsel, who may express such opinions where "warranted by the evidence." But in any case, defense comments on the holes in the prosecution case—even couched in personal terms—would be construed as an argument based on the evidence or (the asserted) lack of it. And that sort of argument, though insincere, is their job. Its effect on the notoriously low esteem in which the profession is held is no concern of theirs. Prosecutors, in contrast, must be wary not to exceed covert intimations of sincerity.

The special license accorded me, as defense counsel, to argue against my own belief also allows me to decide that, despite the fact that I have every reason to believe that what this prosecution witness has just told the jury is completely true, I have the means to make the witness look like a liar and I intend to use them. Even truthful and accurate witnesses can be effectively impeached. The damaging testimony of a police witness, let us suppose, accords closely with what my own client has informed me. But I have in hand a report written by the officer shortly after the event that makes no mention of several important facts in his testimony. Moreover, I have information that this officer had once boasted to an ex-girlfriend, "You should see me on the stand. I could be in the movies. I can make a jury believe white is black, round is straight, up is down." I think I would be breaking my ethical duty to my client to defend him "zealously" if I let this witness off unwounded by my impeachment.

The Code of Professional Responsibility (the "law" in most places governing what some insist is an oxymoron: legal ethics) commands zealous advocacy and describes zeal by telling us that the lawyer shall not intentionally "fail to seek the lawful objectives of his client through reasonably available means permitted by law." Acquittal—even of the guilty—is a "lawful objective," and impeachment—even of a truthful witness—by prior inconsistencies and disposition to lie are certainly "means permitted by law." I am neither concealing nor failing to reveal anything that I am required by law to reveal (not allowed), nor am I knowingly adducing false evidence or making a false statement of law or fact myself (also not allowed). Neither the Code nor the Model Rules say anything about making the probably truthful and accurate appear mistaken or fabricated. In fact, as I read those documents, they strongly suggest that that is exactly what the diligent lawyer is expected to do on behalf of his client.

The diligent lawyer for the defense, that is. The Bar Association Standards recognize a distinction in this regard. Standard 3–5.7(b) governing prosecutors provides:

> The prosecutor's belief that the witness is telling the truth does not preclude cross-examination, but may affect the method and scope of cross-examination. A prosecutor should not use the power of cross-examination to discredit or undermine a witness if the prosecutor knows the witness is testifying truthfully.

True, that "should" is hedged by "knows," but in this instance I would read it as: "has good reason to believe that . . . " The comparable provision governing defense lawyers, 4–7.6(b), reads as follows:

> Defense counsel's belief or knowledge that the witness is telling the truth does not preclude cross-examination.

Aside from the ambiguous alteration in the wording of the first sentence of the section applicable to prosecutors (poor drafting for a bunch of lawyers), the second sentence is missing altogether. The only thing a lawyer would conclude from this deletion is that defense counsel are at liberty to discredit even those witnesses they know to be truthful.

The distinction is also suggested by the advisory language of EC 7-13 of the Code of Professional Responsibility: "The responsibility of a public prosecutor differs from that of the usual advocate; his duty is to seek justice, not merely to convict." Falsely coloring evidence hardly seems to be seeking justice. The duty of defense counsel is energetically to seek acquittal by lawful means, which would seem to include the offer of helpful evidence that may be false and the impeachment of witnesses believed to be truthful. Counsel are enjoined by the Model Rules not to "falsify evidence" nor "offer evidence the lawyer *knows* to be false" (emphasis mine). But those ethical rules (insofar as they exert any pull on conduct) do not restrain the zealous defense lawyer from submitting evidence that she *thinks* is likely to be wrong, or arguing to the jury to believe it. Clearly, the sharply different license to distort puts a rhetorical weapon of major caliber in the hands of the defense only. Is it unfair?

My answer to this will be a reluctant "Yes and no." *No*, to the extent that the license to distort is founded on prerogatives themselves supportable by important social values, it is fair. *Yes*, insofar as the supposed basis is rotten, or the license exceeds the dictates of the underlying values, it is unfair. If my answer sounds tedious and grindingly academic, I apologize. But nothing is ever perfectly simple and nothing simple is ever perfectly true (not even this sentence). Perhaps my efforts to explain my answer will enliven it somewhat.

In our tradition, our proud tradition of controlled contention as the means of sorting out the confused traces of past events, it would be unthinkable to enlist defense counsel as another truth seeker. To free these lawyers of their total dedication to the interests of the client is to leave the government free of challenge. While the government's pursuit of a verdict reflecting the historic truth is a virtuous undertaking, it is also fraught with dangers of arrogance and oppression, to say nothing of error. At best, the prosecutor should be as receptive to and as diligent in the development of hypotheses of innocence as of guilt, while the court, in theory, is detached and impartial. But too many examples in history and other parts of our world today caution us that the prosecutor and the court, even with the best intentions, may join in a blind stampede to preconceived—and erroneous—judgment. It is in the vital interests not only of the defendant but of all who are interested in justice to establish a meaningful check on that proclivity. To accomplish this, defense counsel must be instructed to ignore the asserted objectives of the others, and to serve only as adverse counterweight. Perpetual challenge not only invigorates the truth seekers, it protects us all from the inherent temptations of power.

I'm not just saying this. These are good reasons, strong social policies animating the ethical imperatives laid on defense counsel: zealously, faithfully promote the interests contrary to the prosecutor's, heedless of personal feeling, oblivious to the nag of doubt, and obedient only to the limits of lawful means.

Up to a point, then, this specially commissioned challenger, this amoral privateer, serves a wholesome public purpose. And a certain amount of deception may well be within that useful ambit of tolerance. To wed the lawyer to the role, we must swallow an ethic that encourages the champion to keep his client's secrets and confidences, to express opposition he may not feel, to advance his client's cause though he secretly despises it. We cannot have him a committed advocate for the opposition and, at the same time, a judge of what causes are worthy. We cannot charge this player in the process to go forth and fight for the deserving few, let the rest hang. He cannot, he will not, we will not have him choosing his commitments by some occult power to recognize the righteous.

Frankly, I don't know how they do it. I don't think I could dedicate my professional life to the pursuit of undeserved breaks for the undeserving. It's hard to imagine taking pride in those cases when my efforts frustrated the demands of justice. Maybe they have a different notion of justice. But however they do it, I'm glad they are there, energetically, year in and year out, fighting for a contrary interpretation.

There are, of course, limits to our tolerance for unbridled opposition. The Code of Professional Responsibility suggests a few. We have already noted several of them, but let's run through them once more as a list of injunctions. A lawyer before a court shall not:

(1) take a position merely to "harass or maliciously injure another";
(2) knowingly advance a claim that is unwarranted by existing law

(with the broad exception that he may argue for the extension or reversal of existing law);

(3) conceal what he is required by law to reveal;

(4) knowingly use false or perjured evidence;

(5) knowingly make a false statement of law or fact;

(6) help create or preserve evidence he knows or should know is false;

(7) advise or help his client to do what he knows is illegal or fraudulent;

(8) state or allude to any matter that is either irrelevant or unsupported by admissible evidence;

(9) ask an irrelevant question intended to degrade a witness or someone else;

(10) assert personal knowledge of the facts in issue, except when testifying as a witness;

(11) state a personal opinion about the justness of a cause, the credibility of a witness, or the guilt of the accused (a large exception is tacked onto this one: counsel may argue based on her analysis of the evidence "for any position or conclusion").

In addition, the Code instructs that when counsel has received information that her client has perpetrated a fraud, and she cannot persuade the client to rectify it, she shall reveal it unless to do so would compromise the attorney-client privilege.

It's a pretty long list. But it requires the defense lawyer neither to disclose harmful data nor to confine her contentions to her sincere beliefs. Do either of these special entitlements exceed their social purposes? I believe both the advantages—to withhold and to distort—are unfair. Not unfair because the prosecution does not enjoy the same license, but because they needlessly undermine the value of a true verdict.

Commandment #3 in the catalogue above prohibits withholding

what the law requires counsel to disclose. Is there any good reason why "the law" should not require the disclosure of evidence found during defense investigation which strengthens the prosecution case? Just to pose that question will raise the hackles of the defense bar, but it deserves serious consideration.

Emotionally, I'm sure there is something in my suggestion that offends the basic cultural tenet that a defendant should not be made to cooperate in his own destruction. But this principle, important though it may be, has been confined, in criminal jurisprudence, to compelling the accused to divulge the present contents of his mind— conscious, cognitive revelations. He can be forced to assist in his own downfall by subpoena, enforced by the powers of contempt, commanding him to produce documents in his custody that might help convict him. He can also be compelled to stand in a lineup, to give his fingerprints, a voice or handwriting exemplar, a strand of hair for microscopic comparison, or a drop of blood for DNA analysis. He may even be held down physically while a blood sample is forcibly drawn for analysis of its alcohol content. Adverse evidence of all sorts may be taken from him against his will, save only evidence that consists of what he thinks or remembers but has not yet expressed.

So why should he not be required to name the secret witness who puts him at the scene of the crime? To reveal the expert who declined to testify in support of the defendant's story? Some would doubtless say that to require such disclosures jeopardizes the confidentiality of communications between the lawyer and his client. Trust, it is stoutly maintained, is the essence of effective legal representation, and insulation of all communications is indispensable to trust. To guarantee confidence and the constitutional right to effective representation, a privilege is universally recognized that cloaks professional communications with an impenetrable shield. The lawyer may have been steered to the disappointing witness by his client, may have approached the expert to try out a thesis based on what the client told him. To hand over these witnesses to the prosecutor might, indirectly, reveal the substance of the attorney's private consultations with the client. A breach in the ironclad privilege.

Related to this argument is the fear that the obligation to disclose negative results will discourage the defendant's quest for helpful evidence. Weakly associated with the defendant's constitutional right to call witnesses, the pursuit of possible sources of exculpatory evidence is, in its own right, extremely important in an adversary system where the government cannot be entirely trusted to follow defense trails with quite the same enthusiasm as it shows for leads to supportive evidence. Having to cough up what you wish you had never discovered, the claim is, chills the healthy impetus to independent defense investigations. In this, the defense bar would insist, no comparison may be had with the government's position; prosecutors should rejoice to uncover evidence of innocence.

There is, I admit, much merit in these arguments. But ultimately, I am unpersuaded. For starters, the lawyer's efforts to assemble a case may be related only by the most tenuous line of inference to anything the client told him. But even if he is following up on something he was told by his client, to disclose the product of an investigation inspired by a client's tip does not invade the confidence of the communication. Let's get realistic. To divulge the name of a witness who says the defendant was present at the scene does not reveal what the client told his lawyer, even if the lawyer was steered to the witness by the client. Disclosing what she learned as a result of a communication from the client is not the same as disclosing the communication— though the product may contain hints of the source.

The attorney-client privilege does not—and ought not—protect all such hints. The law in many places, for example, requires counsel to come forward before trial and serve the prosecutor with notice that he intends to rely on the defense of alibi—that the defendant was elsewhere at the time of the crime—and to furnish the identity of the alibi witness. Surely, such notice carries the broadest hint of what was discussed at the private conferences between lawyer and client. Yet no one, as far as I know, claims that such notice violates the privilege. So too, defendants are required to disclose other products of privileged communications—the reports of experts, for example, or (in California, at least) the names of favorable witnesses. These items carry the same risks of compromising the privilege, yet they are not invalid on those grounds. The conclusion is plain: the privilege does not extend to the elaborated results of shielded communication.

Nor am I impressed with the claim that the investigative ardor of the defense counsel will be dampened by a requirement that he disclose his adverse discoveries. Investigation is a risky business. One might say the risk is less for the prosecutor, who has an obligation only to justice and therefore little to fear from surprising discoveries. But in fact, the location of a witness who contradicts what the prosecutor earnestly believes to be the plausible scenario, which she plans to submit to the jury, is not a pleasant discovery. Do we worry that because she is obliged to turn over such a witness to the defense, she will be deterred from pursuing investigations beyond the bare bones of her case? Perhaps we should, but we do not. Though far less imbued with public interest, civil cases too should have the benefit of exhausting pretrial investigations. Both sides in civil litigation are saddled with extensive discovery obligations, yet they continue to investigate thoroughly. There is really no choice. Whichever side you're on, civil or criminal, if you are going to try a case, you have to chase leads down every alley.

I certainly do not mean to say that civilside investigators—or prosecutors, for that matter—do not adopt evasive tactics. "Listen well, but don't write it down," is a basic precept of interviewing. "Don't let your prospective expert send you a written opinion until you talk to her and make sure it will be helpful." We don't want any of these damaging documents in the files our opponents will be browsing through.

Not that attorney's files are totally vulnerable to the raids of discoverers. For half a century, at least, since the Supreme Court decided a civil case called *Hickman v. Taylor* in 1947, we have had an exemption from discovery of lawyers' notes prepared in anticipation of trial and reflecting the lawyer's thoughts about the case. The "work product doctrine," as we noted back in Chapter 3, is the litigating lawyer's friend, and hundreds of articles have been written in the professional and learned journals on its meaning and scope. In some law firms, I hear, every piece of paper generated by the litigation department bears the words: "The following is attorney's work product and therefore to be treated as highly confidential material" or something to like effect. But the invocation doesn't always work.

What makes the subject so intriguing is that the doctrine, or exemption, or quasi-privilege (even the Supreme Court cannot decide exactly what to call "work product") is not all-inclusive; there are still things a lawyer can write down that are discoverable. Among them may be a summary of what a prospective witness tells the lawyer or investigator—unadorned by comments and reactions of the lawyer. So if criminal defense counsel should be required to disclose adverse evidence that their investigation has turned up, I suppose we should expect that they—like those now bound to reveal such material—will have to learn how to conceal whatever is unprotected by the work product doctrine. But notwithstanding such evasive tactics, there seems little reason not to bind the defense counsel to the same obligations as other parties to litigation.

It may well be, as I suspect, that the fervor with which counsel pursue leads is directly proportional to their confidence in the client's cause. In this frame of mind, it is difficult to believe that the ethical license to ignore the unfavorable data discovered by those optimistic enough to dig it out weighs significantly in the diligence equation. Nor does it compromise loyalty or independence to demand that whatever either counsel discovers bearing on the issue should be made available to the fact finder.

So my conclusion is: curiosity is not so quickly cooled. Others pursue their investigations energetically despite the prospect of damaging their own cases. I see no reason why we should expect less from defense counsel in criminal cases, lawyers who are expressly urged to zeal by the Code of Professional Responsibility. And if they are deterred from their pursuits by the possibility of a shot through the foot, I do not see any reason to award them bulletproof boots at the expense of a fully realized trial.

The sincerity factor is more troublesome. I certainly do not want to impose on the defense, any more than the prosecution, the obligation to come to a conclusion either on credibility or on the ultimate issue of guilt. And I want the defense lawyer to go ahead and defend the person who wants a trial though he has confided his guilt to his lawyer. He is entitled to put the government to its proof, even if guilty in fact, and to have the competent assistance of counsel in doing so. So to me it is perfectly fair to allow defense counsel the advantage of contending contrary to well-founded personal belief.

The hard part of the question is how far this license allows counsel consciously to distort the evidence, to try to make the true appear false and the false appear true. Let's start with another look at Commandment #6 in my catalogue of prohibitions: the lawyer shall not help create or preserve evidence he knows or should know is false. I took that from DR 7-102 (A)(6) of the Code of Professional Responsibility, which actually provides: "In his representation of a client, a lawyer shall not . . . participate in the creation or preservation of evidence when he knows or it is obvious that the evidence is false."

I suspect that the provision, with its curious language—"creation or preservation"—is directed principally at suborning perjury and fabricating evidence. But is there any reason we can't read it to include presenting a witness who will give testimony the lawyer has good reason to think is false? Or creating the false impression that a truthful witness is lying? It's a stretch, but obviously harmonious with the tenor of the provision. Moreover, this reading draws some support from the Code, which notes in commentary (EC 7–26): "A lawyer should . . . present any admissible evidence his client desires to have presented unless he knows, or from facts within his knowledge should know, that such testimony or evidence is false, fraudulent, or perjured."

License to distort does not follow logically from the prerogative to contend contrary to belief. The lawyer may surely interpret facts in evidence in the light most favorable to the defendant—though the lawyer does not believe the client deserves such a favorable construction. The lawyer may emphasize weaknesses in the prosecution proof, or call the credibility of its witnesses dubious, although—to an objective observer—the claims are far-fetched. But does that entitle counsel to put on the stand a witness who she believes will lie, or to introduce evidence of mendacity against a prosecution witness she believes is truthful?

This is beginning to get a bit murky, I fear (as these ethical questions often do). Let me try to put it in concrete form:

> Let's suppose that you have a client named Clyde who is accused of murder. He tells you that he is a member of a street gang known as the Alpha Warriors. One night, he, along with two cohorts, were in the Keep Out Club when they encountered a group of four or five young men from the rival Beta Beasts organization. One of the Betas, a young man named Mort, came up to Clyde, he tells you, and accused him of messing with his Beta girlfriend. The argument grew until, outnumbered, your client thought it wise to retreat. In the

parking lot outside, standing alone, Clyde was approached by three of his antagonists. He tells you that he never saw a weapon of any kind in the hands of any of them, but he was afraid for his life because the Betas had a very tough reputation. To run would be cowardly, so he stood his ground and drew a snap-blade knife. Holding the knife in front of his body, he warned the menacing group to come no closer. Shouting insults, they rushed him and, Clyde says, to protect himself from serious injury or death, he stabbed Mort through the heart. At the preliminary hearing some days later, you learn that Police Officer Badge, one of the first on the scene, reported that he had found a loaded pistol stuck in a holster strapped to the middle of Mort's back.

You eventually convey to Clyde what you learned from Badge and discuss with him the defense of self-defense, explaining that it will be very difficult to mount since, if you put Clyde on the stand—and only if you do—the jury will learn that he was convicted five years before of a shakedown scam in which, pretending to be a police officer, he solicited "donations" from local merchants. It will therefore be crucial, you advise Clyde, to learn what the other witnesses at the scene recall.

A week later, you interview Bonnie, one of Clyde's companions on the night of the murder. Bonnie tells you that as Mort emerged from the club with his buddies and passed Bonnie headed toward Clyde, Bonnie saw him reach behind his back and draw a gun, which he brandished as he approached Clyde. When you ask, Bonnie admits that she has visited Clyde in jail since you spoke to him. At your next visit to your client, Clyde tells you that he now remembers seeing a gun in his victim's hand. The third Alpha, who has been locked up on an unrelated minor charge and hasn't spoken to either Clyde or Bonnie, tells you that he does not recall seeing any weapon in the hands of the deceased or any other Beta immediately before the stabbing.

You also learn that the prosecution will call Buddy, a Beta who was at Mort's side from his first encounter with Clyde in the Keep Out until his violent death less than an hour later. He will testify that although the deceased might have been carrying "heat," he never drew nor displayed the weapon. On your request, you receive a copy of Buddy's criminal record, which is extensive. It will be admissible if offered on the issue of Buddy's credibility.

The questions are whether you can (1) discredit Buddy by introducing his record on the perfectly legal (though somewhat dubious) theory that because he was previously convicted of unrelated crimes, he is not worthy of belief as a witness in the case against Clyde; and (2) put Bonnie on the stand to furnish the vital evidence for the self-defense defense despite the fact that you entertain the strongest suspicion that the tale was cooked up between your client and his girlfriend following your explanation to Clyde of the elements of that defense.

My problem is this: I do not believe that any good social purpose allows you to put Bonnie on the stand. Your own client's first story, the police report of a holstered weapon, and the fresh story of the third Alpha all give you good reason to believe that Bonnie's testimony is purposefully fabricated. That to me is close enough to the knowing use of perjured evidence to be prohibited without affront to your duty of zealous advocacy. And I see very little difference between putting Bonnie on to lie and attempting to paint Buddy as a liar when he tells the truth. Followed, of course, by an argument urging the jury not to take the word of a vengeful, convicted criminal like Buddy.

But if I say the two are alike, and the prohibition against using perjured testimony also prohibits impeachment of a truthful witness, where does that leave the argument to the jury urging them to misconstrue the evidence? I don't want to end up advising you not to stand up there in front of your jury and "interpret" the evidence in a way that would support the insupportable defense. Under this extension I would have to decree that you can't argue to the jury, for example: "It was dark. The deceased had a loaded gun in his belt, everyone agrees to that. The two young men were in a deadly confrontation. Don't you think it is likely that, at some point, the deceased took out that gun and threatened Clyde with it? Does it stand to reason that he would face Clyde's knife in that parking lot, his adrenaline pumping, without once reaching for the weapon he knew was in his belt? You heard the evidence of the deceased's henchman, Buddy, that no gun was drawn. But can you believe that? Obviously Buddy was trying to help convict my client, an Alpha, for the murder of his friend and fellow Beta."

I am loath to go that far. You are, by some construction, "interpreting" evidence in a manner favorable to your client, which you are allowed—nay, encouraged—to do. If I do not allow such argument, am I not reversing myself and holding that you may not contend contrary to personal belief? I don't want to do that.

So I am left with one of those hateful creatures, a logical anomaly. I can prohibit you from calling Bonnie on the ground that you have good reason to think that her testimony will be fabricated, but I must allow you to impeach Buddy and tell the jury to disbelieve him though you have the identical good reason to believe that he is telling the truth.

There is, I believe, no satisfactory release from this ethical dilemma. Impeachment of a truthful witness seems to lie close on one side to prohibited use of false evidence and on the other to permitted contention contrary to belief. Perhaps the best way out—and one must be found—is to console ourselves by noting that the impeachment of Buddy does not entail the creation or preservation of false evidence as such, but only the unwarranted inference to mendacity from admissible evidence on the issue of credibility. No section of the Code proscribes unwarranted inferences. Indeed, there may be good reason deliberately to avoid setting counsel the task of distinguishing the warranted from the unwarranted inference. Perhaps it is better to say simply: if the evidence is true (Buddy was convicted of these other crimes), and the inference is allowed by law (impeachment by prior conviction is expressly allowed by the rules of evidence), adversary zeal *requires* the attack on credibility. And that vapid suggestion of 4-7.6(b) of the Bar Association Standards to the effect that defense counsel's belief that he is impeaching a truthful witness "should, if possible, be taken into consideration" in conducting the cross-examination must be ignored as the meaningless nod to virtue that it is.

If this sort of consolation works for you, cling to it. It works admirably for the whole corps of practicing defense lawyers. I don't like it. It seems the kind of "legalistic" excuse for avoiding common decency that gives the profession a bad name. But I find it difficult to defend any other conclusion without calling the entire adversary structure of American criminal justice into question.

10

JURY IRRATIONALITY AND ITS INSULATION

Arousing the Unimpeachable Impulse

EVERYONE HAS STORIES ABOUT juries that went haywire. Most of them
are cases where the jury—in apparent disregard of powerful evidence
of guilt, off on some frolic and detour of their own—returned a
verdict of acquittal. Many of these travesties are high-visibility trials,
dramatized into pop culture by the ever-prurient media. Engraved on
the public mind is a passion murderer with some sort of contrived
rough-sex story, a killer cop with a transparently phony resisting-
arrest defense; a celebrity ex-husband with a variable defense and a
stacked jury, the public assassin of an incendiary Jewish leader, a
major racketeer hiding behind clever counsel; a big-time swindler
with an honest face, a weeping family, and an opulent defense—
people who, too often, seem to be able to empanel twelve good
suckers and true. To these well-publicized outrages, any judge or trial
lawyer regularly stationed in the criminal courts can add a dozen less
prominent examples of irrational acquittals.

The irrational verdicts for the defendant, however, are not the only variety. Not as noticeable, jury verdicts for the prosecution may be just as far afield. In the privacy of the jury room, the verdict of conviction may be cast not of the evidence of guilt but of bias, false assumption, sympathy with the victim, and plain old vengeful blame. Although we know these false convictions are out there, we find it harder to call examples to mind.

Certainly, if we go back over the history of major criminal trials, we can come up with a few outrageous convictions, cases in which the horrified public seemed to know more than the jury, to understand that an innocent martyr had suffered the atrocity of a false verdict of guilt. The "Scottsboro boys" probably come first to mind. But that was little more than an old-fashioned southern courtroom lynching. And the case is now sixty-five years old. Others (also drawn from ancient history), like Alger Hiss, Hurricane Carter, and the Rosenbergs, are fading from the literature of outrage. There are surely clearer and more current examples, but it is surprisingly hard to name them.

Perhaps one reason that irrational convictions seem relatively rare is that the reading public is more likely to agree with a verdict of conviction than a verdict of acquittal. The "evidence" received by the "jury of the whole"—the news-fed general public—is more likely to support a judgment of guilty than the evidence that the sworn "jury of twelve" receives in court. That's just the way the media work. The verdict of the jury of twelve that fails to accord with the verdict of the jury of the whole, therefore, is more likely to be a verdict of acquittal than a verdict of conviction. So, as members of the jury of the whole, we are most likely to feel the anguish of frustrated expectations—and remember it long and bitterly—when we think that the verdict of the jury of twelve released a guilty person.

There may be another reason—aside from the good feeling we get from convicting any likely culprit for every brutal or venal crime, and the disappointment we feel at having our most likely candidate escape. Our curious insensitivity may be due, in part, to the fact that for every defendant tried, some responsible agency has attested that there is at least some good reason to believe him guilty. He wouldn't be on trial at all if a grand jury or judge hadn't found evidence from which a reasonable petit jury could find guilt beyond a reasonable doubt. So the conviction—however irrational in fact—always appears to have an adequate foundation in the prosecution's proof. The verdict of guilt never seems to be one of those pure flights of fancy that describes so many irrational acquittals.

In addition to the verdicts of both sorts founded on whim, misunderstanding, or bias, verdicts may be wrong because the juries were corrupted by a variety of pollutants: bribery or intimidation (internal or external), exposure to unauthorized data or opinion, or the concealed disqualification of a juror. If the verdict that emerges from a fouled jury, whatever it may be, satisfies the beholders that justice was done, such contentment must be chalked up to ignorance or coincidence. A verdict produced by a corrupted or unqualified jury offends justice as surely as one founded on caprice.

The surprising thing is that these rotten verdicts are, for the most part, immune from challenge. An ancient, universal rule insists that jury verdicts are unimpeachable by either side for irrationality, or for most varieties of misconduct or disqualification.

Of course, if a verdict of guilt is supported by thin air, if a judge finds that no rational jury could have read such wisps as proof of guilt beyond a reasonable doubt, the verdict may be set aside (though my wife was recently reversed for doing just that). That is a sort of impeachment for irrationality, I suppose. But if the evidence could conceivably support the verdict, and jurors voted on wholly irrational considerations, gross misunderstandings of the evidence or the court's instructions, or in heedless disregard of the law, the evidence, and the ordinary canons of reason, we don't want to hear about it.

The governing maxim is clear and unequivocal: a juror will not be heard in court to impeach the verdict of his own jury. Even if all twelve execute affidavits swearing that the only reason they acquitted the defendant was that they thought police officers were required to lie under oath in order to win a promotion, the court will not receive them. Even if a juror recounts that she voted to convict only because she had a dream in which the victim appeared to her and told her the defendant had murdered him, courts will reject the report out of hand. The jurors, once they are freed of the court's control, enjoy their Constitution-given right to recount their experiences. But even if a juror holds a widely reported press conference, relating in detail all the false assumptions, misunderstood instructions, and faulty reasoning that lay behind the jury's verdict, no court will allow an attack on the verdict to be launched on that revelation.

That means no motion may be made by either side, even on the strongest supporting proof, that requires inquiry into the factors considered dispositive by the jury. In 1912, for example, the Supreme Court rejected affidavits from a lawyer based on conversations with jurors revealing that the jury, divided between conviction and acquittal of all four defendants, had compromised by convicting two and acquitting two. Jurors, the Court reminded us, will not be heard on matters that "essentially inhere in the verdict itself."

It's a deeply troubling rule. Although enacted into law by Congress and many state legislatures, although reaffirmed by the Supreme Court on several occasions and repeatedly by lesser tribunals in manifold applications and variations, it has distressed scholars. And for good reason. Our willful blindness concerning the true basis of a jury verdict speaks a dark distrust of the institution we profess to admire as the cornerstone of the American system of justice: the jury. It seems yet another example of the law's preference for the smooth, formal surface over the crude, messy substance beneath. Professor Albert Alschuler (whom we have already met), said as much when he wrote: "The refusal of courts to allow jurors to 'impeach' their verdicts by confessing misconduct illustrates once more our failure to hold jurors to ordinary standards of responsibility."

Thus prosecutors cannot impeach for irrationality, corruption, or anything, period, and defendants may not impeach for internal errors of any sort. Net result is that interests of finality, willful ignorance, and juror unaccountability triumph over the interests of a conscientious verdict by a qualified jury according to the law and the evidence.

How does this affect the balance of advantages? Insofar as most verdicts are convictions (by a factor of 3 or 4 to 1), the insulation of verdicts against anything but improper external influence gives the prosecution a great advantage. All those grievous errors of careless or willful misunderstanding, of coercive persuasion, of specious argument, and spurious debate—the deeply flawed process that generated the conviction—are sealed forever in the black box of the jury room. Even appeals cannot reach the derelictions hidden here, since appellate courts consider only errors on the record, and the impeachment rule prohibits making a record of this sort of malfeasance.

So the defense suffers a grievous impediment. But insofar as most appeals to irrationality are by the defense, and most of the irrational verdicts seem to be verdicts of acquittal, the helplessness of the prosecutor to go behind the verdict and cancel it for impropriety is a significant disadvantage to the prosecution.

So both sides have advantages and disadvantages. Wherever there is a foul verdict, the disadvantaged party suffers an unfair barrier to setting things right. Contemplating the evident injustice of insulation, one is tempted simply to conclude that verdicts should be vulnerable to proof of serious dereliction in their formation, that parties should not be disabled from demonstrating that the jury was not legitimately constituted, was corrupted, or failed to perform according to their oaths.

But, of course, it's not that simple. If it were, unimpeachability might be wrong but it would not be deeply troubling. What wrings the gut is that, much as we want our juries to judge the facts carefully and dispassionately and to apply a fair understanding of legal principles to those facts, we also want them to engage in their discussions vigorously and candidly, without fear of later challenge for faulty memory of the evidence, misunderstanding of the judge's instructions, or poor reasoning. We want to spare them, emerging from their labors groggy and exhausted, from the visits of disappointed lawyers probing for flaws with which to trash their product. And yes, we believe in finality. In the economy of court business, we can appreciate the urgent need to get on to the next case, to accept what's done as done—or at least to confine challenges to the appeals, writs, and other regular procedures along the line.

In addition to these worthy goals, some have suspected that the real reason we shield the jury room deliberations from the light of the courtroom is that our firm faith demands resolute ignorance. Glanville Williams, a venerable critic, once ventured that secrecy of jury deliberations was necessary to "preserve public confidence in a system which more intimate knowledge might destroy." Even the Supreme Court recently commented, in the voice of Justice O'Connor, "It is not at all clear . . . that the [jury] system could survive . . . efforts to perfect it."

Our determined deafness to tales of juror irrationality (and worse) is clearly dedicated to the preservation of verdicts as such. We are willing enough to hear of juror misbehavior or pollution when it comes to light before the verdict has been returned. Let a bailiff report that when he went in to fetch the jury, one of the jurors asked him to explain to another that the reason the defendant had not testified was probably that he had a criminal record. The judge will react immediately. Let a juror send a note to the judge complaining that a fellow juror had been boasting of his connections to the mob and making veiled threats about their likely response to the outcome; the court will evince a lively interest. Or let a juror report to the judge that one of the other jurors had confided that she was psychic and was picking up "astral radiations" to assist in evaluating the evidence; there will be a hearty judicial response.

Usually, the judge first calls the juror into chambers in the silent presence of counsel, to get the details firsthand. He may then call other jurors to try to learn how far the transgression polluted the rest of the panel. Finally, the judge will either let it pass with a warning and reprimand (if appropriate), or discharge the offending juror or jurors and replace them with alternates (if any are standing by), or (if no alternate remains, or in egregious cases) discharge the entire jury, declare a mistrial, and begin again.

The point is that without a verdict, the rule against juror impeachment of their own verdict is, by its own terms, inoperative. Or another way of looking at it might be that before the jury work has come to term as a verdict, the court remains in control, and neither party has a stake in resisting corrective measures. Once the verdict pops from the jury's womb, it must be respected as a live delivery. All the demands of "finality" are brought to bear on its preservation. And the jury, now discharged from court control, are to be released from further obligations of accountability.

Still, apart from this metaphor, it is not immediately apparent why the return of the verdict so dramatically alters the vulnerability of the jury process. Has our concern with the fair and dispassionate quality of the jury's performance suddenly evaporated? Are we no longer troubled by a verdict produced by a biased, fearful, self-interested, or heedless jury? Should the same virus that, if detected during trial or even during deliberations, would require remedial action be ignored if discovered after the verdict is in? If we are concerned with encouraging free interchange and a rather loosely structured decision process, unthreatened by judicial intervention, if we are concerned that jurors not undermine one another's earnest good faith, our indulgence of the tattletale during but not after verdict seems rather arbitrary.

Most courts and scholars believe that the current rule against jury self-impeachment began with a little old English case written in 1785 by the revered Lord Mansfield, a case in which two jurors confessed that the jury had arrived at its verdict by "tossing up"—probably a coin toss. Nearly all legal historians believe that that case, called *Vaise v. Delaval,* dramatically rewrote the common law, which, until then, had received, without qualm, affidavits from jurors attesting to defects in the process by which the jury had decided on their verdict.

A young scholar named Mark Commack has come up with an earlier case (1753) in which the loser tried to show that the jury, unable to agree unanimously, had decided—contrary to law—to abide by the vote of the majority. The court refused the application on the grounds that, having acquiesced in the verdict, jurors would not be heard to deny it. In another case from 1770, also found by Commack, Lord Mansfield himself notes that an affidavit from a juror describing what he thought or intended by his vote can never be read in court.

But whether the rule traces its lineage to *Vaise* or beyond, it has been a fixture of Anglo-American law for at least two centuries. Citing *Vaise,* courts have steadfastly refused to go behind the formal verdict returned to examine the minds of individual jurors or their reconstruction of the common enterprise. Perhaps the most dramatic example of the reluctance of courts to consider even the clearest evidence of juror incompetence occurred following the trial of a flashy petty gangster named John Dioguardi ("Johnny Dio" to the press) in New York. After the verdict, a juror wrote him a long letter confiding, among other things, that "I have eyes and ears that I can see things before it happen. I can tell you about other and what they are thinking and doing. . . . [My eyes] are only partly open. . . . Unfortunate, a curse was put on them some years ago." The court saw no reason to overturn the verdict of conviction.

The most recent, most authoritative, and most amusing judicial rededication to the see-no-evil, hear-no-evil attitude toward jury work came down from the Supreme Court in 1987. Titled *Tanner v. United States,* the case was one of those conspiratorial commercial fraud and corruption cases that our national government loves to bring. And rightly so; it's a good thing from time to time to remind our capitalist engines that they too are subject to law. But even the briefest recital of the facts of the case here would bring tears of boredom to all but the most stalwart industrialists. Not a case we would call jury entertainment. And this jury apparently sized up the chore they faced and took appropriate action. According to an affidavit submitted by one of the jurors after the verdict, several of the jurors customarily fortified themselves with alcoholic beverages at lunch, causing them to nap through the afternoon's testimony. The trial judge refused to hear any more about it.

Things got more interesting when counsel filed a second motion for a new trial including the sworn statement of a second juror, who had paid the lawyer an unsolicited visit to inform him that it felt like "the jury was on one big party." Seven jurors, he said in a sworn interview, usually drank liquor during the lunch recess, and four, including himself, shared one, two, or even three pitchers of beer during various recesses. Three jurors smoked marijuana regularly during the trial, and two used cocaine several times. The trial judge again turned a deaf ear, declining to order a hearing to develop these allegations.

What's going on here? the defendant protested. I have a constitutional right (under the Sixth Amendment) to a trial by jury and that means a competent jury, not a bunch of drunks and druggies. Well, yes, the Supreme Court answered, but we have a rule in this country, a respectable rule of long standing, that a juror will not be heard to impeach his own verdict. The conviction was affirmed.

Firm as this prohibition is, it is not absolute. The rule against self-impeachment allows that a juror may testify about "extraneous prejudicial information" or improper "outside influence." Still, courts don't always apply the "extraneous influence" exception strictly. The internal-external line is not always clear. Some judges, for example, think that extraneous influences can be exerted inside the jury room. One federal court received a juror affidavit, granted a hearing, and overturned a conviction based upon the recital that the jury foreman and two other jurors who knew the defendant told stories during jury deliberation of the defendant's prior misconduct. The Court of Appeals for the Second Circuit upheld the decision and the Supreme Court refused to review it. Such external improprieties are exemplified in the case of *Parker v. Gladden* in the Supreme Court in 1966, where an Elizabethan-tongued bailiff (as Justice Harlan, dissenting, dubbed him) reportedly said to jurors during deliberation, "Oh, that wicked fellow, he is guilty." He also told a juror not to worry, if their guilty verdict was erroneous, the Supreme Court would correct it. Correct it they did; the conviction was reversed for extraneous influence.

Of course, "externality," the Court was quick to point out in *Tanner,* was not to be taken literally. Whether a juror reads a forbidden newspaper on one side or the other of the jury room threshold is obviously of no significance. But the competence and comprehension of a juror was always thought to be "internal" and thus beyond the stretch of inquiry. "However severe their effect and improper their use," the Court wrote, upholding the trial judge's resolute indifference in *Tanner,* "drugs or alcohol voluntarily ingested by a juror seems no more an 'outside influence' than a virus, poorly prepared food, or a lack of sleep."

This benign view commanded only a bare majority of the Court. Four justices, led by Thurgood Marshall, dissented. "In directing district courts to ignore sworn allegations that jurors engaged in gross and debilitating misconduct," the minority scolded, "this Court denigrates the precious right to a competent jury." Besides, just as a matter of common sense, the dissenters wrote, drugs and alcohol are "outside influences" in that they do not relate to the processes of internal debate and decision.

Tanner was largely based on a provision of the Federal Rules of Evidence, Rule 606(b). Derived—it is said—from Lord Mansfield's decision in *Vaise,* the law provides that a juror is incompetent to testify to anything said or done during the jury's deliberations, or to any possible mental or emotional influence on a juror's vote on the verdict. Preserving Lord Mansfield's distinction, Rule 606(b) allows evidence of improper external influences, rejecting only the juror's recital of her or her fellow jurors' mental processes in arriving at a verdict, and anything occurring during the jury's debate that might have affected them.

But one of the startling things about *Tanner* is the Court's imperious disregard for the basic tenor of the rule they purported to apply. Rule 606(b) does not speak to reports of jurors regarding events before deliberations began, whenever they may be rendered. The juror is incompetent, the rule provides, to "testify as to any matter or statement occurring during the course of the jury's deliberations." Pretty clear, I would say. Yet, in blissful disdain for its terms, the Supreme Court applied Rule 606(b) in *Tanner* to exclude evidence of misconduct prior to deliberation, reported after verdict. Other courts probably have done the same. Why? Maybe because if it is fair to apply the principle to postverdict accounts of deliberative misconduct, it is as fair to apply it to postverdict accounts of internal juror transgressions prior to the commencement of formal deliberations.

But whatever its shortcomings in logic, social policy, or the application of statutory language, however the line of authority may waver before or since, the *Tanner* decision speaks eloquently of the prevailing preference for juror security and verdict finality over competence and fidelity in the performance of the task. Is this preference wise? Should we—not only in the interests of fairness, but for the sake of integrity of the jury system—allow some shift in the allowances and prohibitions?

To me, the rule against impeachment seems fair enough as far as it protects the individual thought processes and the collective deliberations of the jury and shields the former jurors from lawyers poking around in the debris of debate to find some mistaken premise or freighted pellet of jury room rhetoric. I'm with those who believe that, not only for the peace of mind of erstwhile jurors but for the general faith—our peace of mind—these matters should be insulated from the judicial probe. And if the defense benefits disproportionately from the forbearance, it's a price I'll willingly pay. I gladly acknowledge—and share with other lawyers and judges, I suspect— the belief that some things are better left unsaid.

It is also fair, I think, to refuse to insulate verdicts against subsequent examination for judgment-bending influences other than earnest disputation. Reports from jurors or others—the source, I would insist, contrary to Lord Mansfield, matters little—disclosing bribes or threats, prejudicial exposure, or improper inducements should not go unexplored. And if established, external corruption should fatally undermine the ostensible verdict.

The dictates of fairness are more elusive when drawing the line between the most obviously protected irrationality and the most clearly exposable. On which side of the line should we locate threats and corrupt inducements offered by one juror to another? Where do fraudulently concealed disqualifications of a juror belong? The Supreme Court ruled that the fact that a juror had applied during a criminal trial for a position as investigator in the district attorney's office is not grounds for overturning a verdict of conviction; concealed bias (if that's what it was) bespeaks no infirmity in the verdict. Should that disqualification or the gross misbehavior of the jury in *Tanner* have been ignored? And how about that venerable intruder into rationality, the law of chance? Where does the coin toss in *Vaise* belong?

Another thing: does fairness require the distinction written into the Federal Rule between shielded irrationality occurring during deliberation and other infirmities that might have distorted the verdict but happened earlier during the trial?

But apart from these elements of unfairness—the false and blurred internal/external distinctions, and the senseless exaltation of the deliberative stage—an overarching source of unfairness infects the insulation rule: impeachment of corrupt jury verdicts is a prerogative of the defense only. Even for the most blatant external influence—say, the bribery of the jury—the prosecutor may not challenge the resulting verdict of acquittal. It's almost unbelievable: a defendant who buys his acquittal may never again be tried for that crime. He may be prosecuted for the bribery, of course, but not for the crime on which the bribed jury acquitted him. It's not much consolation. Punishment for jury corruption may be lighter than for the underlying crime, and, in any event, it is often difficult to pin the bribe on the defendant personally. And anyway, if he could bribe one jury . . .

The firm prohibition against setting aside the corrupt verdict of acquittal does not derive from the rule against jury impeachment of their own verdict—that rule, by its own terms, is party-neutral. Rather, acquittals are unimpeachable because setting aside the verdict leads to a second trial on the same charge in the same jurisdiction, and—as we have discovered—that would violate the vital essence of the precious proscription of double jeopardy.

I have already winced at the obligation to explore in these pages the perplexing puzzle of double jeopardy, and I do not confront it with any greater equanimity here. It should be enough to say again that the precept protecting criminal defendants from being placed repeatedly at risk of conviction is so strong that it gladly tolerates judgments founded on serious errors. And this precept is hardened considerably when the defendant has once triumphed over his prior jeopardy. Prior acquittal most definitively bars reprosecution. One hundred years ago, the Supreme Court said it as unequivocally as they could, and their words have lost none of their clout today: "The verdict of acquittal was final, and could not be reviewed, on error or otherwise, without putting him twice in jeopardy, and thereby violating the Constitution." All this we have noted before in connection with appeals.

As applied to verdict impeachment, the double-jeopardy principle, by design, introduces a substantial inequality. Apart from any systemic interest in finality of judgment, jury integrity, and free jury room discussion that limits also defense challenge, the prosecution is disabled from attacking a jury verdict on grounds that a defendant could employ to nullify a verdict against him—external influence. Is it a fair advantage? The answer to that question, I'm afraid, stands squarely on how you feel about the double-jeopardy principle.

Some regard the constitutional proscription of double jeopardy as one of the bulwarks against government oppression. Without it, they speculate, we (the innocent) would never be safe against government persecution. Prosecution would be followed by reprosecution until, resources depleted, we would succumb to unjust judgment. This notion was advanced by the Supreme Court in a 1978 decision called *United States v. Scott:* "The law attaches particular significance to an acquittal. To permit a second trial after an acquittal, however mistaken the acquittal may have been, would present an unacceptably high risk that the Government . . . might wear down the defendant so that, even though innocent, he may be found guilty."

Back in Chapter 8, in connection with a similar concern expressed by the Supreme Court in an earlier case, I wondered whether the policy of the double jeopardy clause was actually protection of the innocent. While there are surely instances where our government, local or national, persisted in prosecution after prosecution, undeterred by defeat, until they nailed their target, those selected for persistent prosecution are rarely innocent. I am thinking of the repeated efforts to imprison Jimmy Hoffa and John Gotti. Conveniently, these targets afforded the government the opportunity to prosecute them several times for different crimes; thus the government ran afoul of no injunction against multiple jeopardy. So, too, cases in which earlier judgments are either reversed or aborted by mistrial may be reprosecuted—and often are—by the unrelenting government. I'm sure someone can cite an example wherein the government, bent on some unworthy political agenda, has persisted in the prosecution of an innocent person, perhaps unto ultimate and unjust conviction. Mistakes happen, even vindictive prosecutions of the innocent, but I am convinced that, by and large, the government has better things to do than repeat failed efforts against the guiltless.

But I am not here to argue for the repeal of the double-jeopardy clause of the Fifth Amendment. Hardly. I insist only that the double-jeopardy principle postulates a first immersion *that counts*. "Jeopardy," to my way of thinking, entails the hazard of conviction on a well-founded charge, before a court with jurisdiction, by a competent, fairly drawn jury performing its task with reasonable fidelity to the basic obligations of its oath. The "verdict" of a bribed or intimidated jury, the "verdict" of a fraudulently constituted jury, the "verdict" of a drunk or stoned jury, I claim, is a nullity. To my mild surprise, I find I am not all alone in this claim. I can take some comfort in a case, arising in the gentle climes of Cook County, Illinois, that just received federal approval as these pages are about to be set in type.

Harry Aleman, a petty gangster and hit man for a bookmaking ring, was charged with murdering a man named Logan in 1972. With some adroit maneuvering and the assistance of a lawyer named Cooley, who knew the ropes, Aleman was acquitted at a bench trial before Judge Wilson, who had taken a bribe of only $10,000 for the favor. (Judge Wilson was outraged when he learned that the same amount had been tendered to a mere eyewitness to alter her identification testimony. The good judge smolders no longer. When, some twenty years later, he was found in a nursing home and subpoenaed in an investigation of the episode, he walked into his back yard and put a bullet through his head.)

Some fifteen years after Aleman's acquittal, the prosecutors obtained some evidence of the bribe (from Cooley, among others, who was then in a federal witness protection program). Aleman was indicted again in 1993 for the same murder (along with another hit that the state could only then pin on him). The trial judge permitted the state to prove that the prior verdict had been procured by corruption and, overriding the defendant's double-jeopardy claim, allowed the prosecution to go forward and convict Aleman of the Logan murder. The Appellate Court of Illinois approved, and when the case reached the federal courts, the Court of Appeals for the Seventh Circuit (in 1998) saw no reason to disturb the result. The state had successfully argued (much as I argue here) that "by bribing Judge Wilson, Aleman created a situation in which he was never in jeopardy at his first trial. The first trial, therefore, was a sham and the acquittal there rendered has no effect for double jeopardy purposes." Granted this all has the scent of estoppel: the defendant should not be allowed to profit from his own misdeed. But the idea that encourages me is there as well: even an acquittal does not bar retrial if the first judgment was rendered by an ostensible tribunal which, by its own misconduct, had forfeited the authority to render a judgment worthy of judicial respect.

Outright corruption is not the only sort of disqualifying misconduct in my book. A verdict founded on a gross and heedless disregard for the law and evidence I would also regard as inauthentic. These are not verdicts of acquittal worthy of the status of an unimpeachable judgment. A group that includes people who lied about their affiliations, who fraudulently concealed disqualifications, is not a jury empowered to return a legally significant resolution. A faux-jury reporting a specious conclusion is simply not an event of legal consequence, certainly not the rendition of a "prior verdict of acquittal" that activates the superprohibition of the double-jeopardy concept.

So I would say where either party can offer reports, from jurors or others, of purported discoveries from within or without the crenelated walls of the jury room that, if true, would disqualify the jury or fatally undermine its verdict, the judgment must be discarded. Whether acquittal or conviction, the jury's decision is equally and likewise flawed, and no judgment of the court can stand upon it. I would therefore entertain affidavits offering this sort of proof. I might put a time limit on them so that we are not required to disinter judgments that have lain undisturbed for years. But I would not care that jurors are subject to postverdict challenge, or that they—like everyone else—are accountable for gross deviations from their sworn duty. Of course, not every report of misfeasance would automatically cancel the work of the trial or the precious judgment it produced. Far from it. I would simply have the court receive such declarations and proceed to determine whether in the particular circumstances the verdict is fatally flawed.

Upon a determination that the misconduct was gross and the dispassion of the jury severely compromised, if the corrupting influence was deeply corrosive, if the concealed disqualification of the juror betokens pernicious bias or patent incompetence, the verdict, either way, along with the judgment founded on it, should be declared null and set aside. The case would then have to be mistried and, even without the understandably withheld consent of the defendant, the mistrial should be upheld as required by manifest necessity. A retrial thereafter does not offend the double-jeopardy principle and seems to me no more or less than the just dictates of fairness.

I know this proposal will do little to endear me to my friends on the bench. Judges are profoundly reluctant to meddle in the workings of their fragile juries, to reopen closed cases for earnest adversary reexamination. I am fully sympathetic. But do I actually invite a new and costly wave of postverdict motions, hearings, and court jamming? I think not. Defendants are already free to impeach convictions on several of these grounds, and the cases where a prosecutor will try to upset an acquittal on grounds of juror fraud or jury corruption are few indeed. But even if we must tie up a courtroom here and there and now and again to vindicate the authenticity of our jury verdicts, is the promotion of clean adjudication not worth the price?

Others will doubtless meet my radical views with the protest that I am now introducing a real advantage for the defense, an advantage far more potent than the supposed advantages I have identified so far. It is, they will argue, overwhelmingly the defendants who will rush in to overturn convictions based on hitherto inaccessible claims of impropriety. Cases in which the prosecutor may attack a verdict of acquittal for jury corruption are one per decade; every week will bring a defense attack on a conviction for alleged juror misunderstanding of the law, disregard of the evidence, or other impeachable offense. My only reply is that I am taking all lawyerlike precautions against insubstantial claims: I am wording my standards to make it clear that while juror reports can be heard and motions can be made, the verdict will withstand all but the most grievous juror derelictions. So the worst that will happen is that judges will have to dismiss summarily a few more frivolous motions. No sweat. And for those that survive, canceling flawed judgments, justice will have been served. The Great Ostrich will have momentarily withdrawn his bewigged head from the sand.

One other consideration must be met before propounding any restructuring of the vulnerability of verdicts: have I invited onto the placid stage of postverdict litigation a new—and unwelcome—drama known as The Revenge of the Spiteful Juror?

In addition to protecting verdicts from disappointed parties, the great and unstated virtue of the rule against verdict impeachment has always been that it puts a lid on complaints by the resentful erstwhile holdout. A juror convinced against his will is of the same opinion still, to paraphrase the old homily. And freed of the confines and group pressure that finally overcame his better judgment, the former juror may find himself looking for a way to scuttle the verdict of his peers, or at least have the last word. What better way than Uviller's Dandy Impeachment Gambit (acronym pronounced You Dig)? Just send a letter to the judge telling him of the undue pressure, personal incompetence, and frequent misbehavior of your recent adversaries, tell him of the inappropriate external considerations they relied upon, their errors and misunderstandings of fact and law, and—if all else fails—tell the judge about your own concealed disqualifications. At the very least, you will tie up the case in hearings and embarrass your former fellows who may be called on to defend themselves. And maybe you will win in the end by getting the verdict of the stubborn majority overturned. And as these scenarios are played out in courtrooms all over, the lesson to sitting and prospective jurors rings loud and clear: this job is even worse than we thought; our words that we believed were secret, shielded by some sort of privilege, can be thrown back in our teeth, and the ordeal of self-justification goes on and on. The effect? People are further discouraged from jury service, and, once locked in, are ever more reluctant to express their views freely and frankly.

I really do not think my modest proposal to expand verdict impeachment somewhat is a doomsday script. With no help from me, jurors today may fear an inquiry into a fellow juror's allegations of external influence or misbehavior. True, I would add a provision permitting inquiry into the alleged incompetence of a juror, but how often does the Johnny Dio situation arise? And when it does, even jurors must appreciate that a court should not ignore it. Under my proposal, individual understandings—or misunderstandings—of the facts or law, personal feelings, communications among jurors, all would remain insulated. In short, I cannot imagine that a limited expansion, necessary to assure that the verdict was valid and uncorrupted by gross incompetence or duress, would chill juror participation.

Having said all that, I must confess that, trying to think constructively, I have great difficulty coming to grips with the issues here. They are simply too many and too disparate. There are urgent needs and totally incompatible values in conflict. And in the 250 years and more that courts and lawmakers have grappled with them, I don't think they have come up with a plausible reconciliation. The diverse strands are entangled to the point where despair is the only rational option of anyone who would try to make sense of the skein.

Should the proscription on postverdict challenge address only thought processes? Or should conduct be included? How are we to distinguish among intemperate argument, sustained intimidation, and outright duress? Does the exclusion of impeaching evidence cover only the communications between jurors, or does it exclude communications with outsiders as well? Is it a shield for exchanges, thought processes, and compromises during deliberations only? Or does it cover any confidential exchange at any time during service? Is it best enforced as a rule of juror incompetence, barring the juror or former juror from giving evidence (as the Federal Rules have chosen to do)? Or is it better understood as a privilege behind which a juror may elect to secrete confidential jury communications? Perhaps it is simply a form of the flat-out rule that where there is a formal expression of a legally significant event, no testimony will be heard from any source to explain or contradict it. These and many other alternatives on a web of interlocking circumstances dance in the mind.

Yet I feel obliged to sort it out somehow. So perhaps I must seize the beast by the horns and propose a solution. Even Hercules would set some conditions for this labor. A coherent solution, it seems to me, is impossible in the framework of the present dogma, along with its variations and accretions. So my solution requires some fantasy. For openers, I imagine the repeal of Rule 606(b) of the Federal Rules of Evidence. It was a bad idea from the start and has been a disreputable player since. I also require some rethinking of the meaning of the double-jeopardy provision of the Constitution in the context of a deeply flawed verdict, which I will insist is an irreparable nullity, not the judgment of a court.

The guiding purposes of my freehand restructure are these. I want to protect former jurors from postverdict harassment. This can be accomplished (imperfectly) by forbidding lawyers from approaching jurors. But that's a limited proscription and hard to enforce. And even if it were criminal for any person to question a former juror about anything that transpired during the juror's service, I'm not sure the benefits would outweigh the harms. So I choose to provide that, when presented with claims of juror misconduct or irrationality, the court should entertain only the spontaneous, unsolicited reports of the former jurors. What I mean by "spontaneous and unsolicited" is dictated by the purpose of the provision: to shield former jurors against importuning representatives of the losing party. It does not mean that the reluctant answers of the juror to the importuning of a talk show host will not be heard in court. Or that a juror memoir, published in a magazine, may be read by the judge only on the beach. It does mean that when a lawyer puts before the court the recital of a former juror undermining the verdict, that information must have come to the lawyer's attention in the first instance without any solicitation from any person involved in the defense or prosecution, or friends, relatives, associates, or agents.

Moreover, if these jurors are having trouble sleeping at night, I don't think it's too much to require that they notify someone of their misgivings within a relatively short span of time. As to more serious juror derelictions, I would allow the defense to pursue them and accord them a more generous time in which to do so. But I would restrict challenge on these grounds to the defense. I would open challenge to both sides only in the most grievous flaws in authenticity. These are the defects of such gravity that, in effect, they deprive the court of jurisdiction to enter a judgment based on the infected verdict. I address only those claims brought after the verdict—or the putative verdict—has been entered, but I make no distinction between the predeliberative events and those occurring during deliberation, and none between impediments of internal and external origin.

So, in sum, if left perfectly free to enact my preferences, I would probably end up with something like the following:

I. Parties, lawyers, and their emissaries are prohibited from approaching jurors to solicit statements concerning the foundations of their verdict or possible misbehavior in the course of their service. A spontaneous statement, however, unsolicited by parties, their attorneys, family, or representatives, from a juror to the court, or to any other person, made prior to or subsequent to the discharge of the jury, will be received and considered on the question of whether the jury should be permitted to continue or whether any verdict reported by it should be permitted to stand. Therefore:

A. Within thirty days after a verdict, a spontaneous statement will be received from any former juror setting forth any substantial defect in a juror's impartiality, mental competence, veracity concerning qualifications for service, or the process by which the verdict was arrived at; or improper external exposure, conduct, contact, corruption, or intimidation during service; or detailing any improper in formation conveyed to a juror, consideration offered or tendered to any juror, or intimidation of any juror that might have influenced that juror's vote.

B. Upon a determination by the court that the matters therein reported, if sustained, would fatally undermine the validity of the verdict, the court shall direct that a hearing be had thereon. After due consideration, the court shall determine whether the reported conduct, events, or circumstances so severely impaired the capacity of any juror or jurors to perform according to the obligations of their oaths that the interests of justice require the nullification of the verdict.

C. In like manner, within thirty days of verdict, any such statement will be received from any nonjuror reporting the above.

II. With respect to all other statements by or concerning juror qualification, competence, corruption, deliberative error, or other matter affecting the validity of the verdict, the following rules shall govern:

A. Neither defense nor prosecution may show by evidence solicited or sought to disturb a verdict any of the following:

1. individual understandings or misunderstandings of the law, the trial evidence, or the consequences of a verdict;

2. communications between jurors relating to the evidence, the law, or the reasoning of a juror concerning the verdict;

3. mental reservations concerning the vote ultimately cast;

4. manner of expression, hostility, affinity, or other aspect of a juror's motivation or attitude toward other jurors, parties, or any other individuals connected to the trial.

B. The defendant may show by evidence sought or solicited to set aside a verdict of conviction (on a motion made within one year of verdict) any of the following:

1. misconduct by a juror or jurors amounting to serious impairment of attention or impartiality, such as intoxication, exposure to harmful outside views, contacts, or sources of information;

2. a verdict arrived at by chance.

C. Either the defense and the prosecution may show by evidence sought or solicited to set aside a verdict of acquittal or of conviction (on a motion made within one year of verdict) any of the following:

1. intimidation of a juror or jurors by physical force or the threat of it either inside or outside the jury room, by another juror or by a nonjuror;

2. corruption of the jury or a member thereof by tender or promise of money or some other thing of value;

3. withholding information or lying by a juror at the time of selection concerning some material fact that might have been grounds for a challenge for cause;

4. mental incompetence or gross misconduct that substantially impairs a juror's ability to perform responsibly.

Inscrutability is a false badge of rectitude. Finality is not the ultimate goal of justice. Let us not scruple to reject the evident failures of the jury process. Postverdict challenges in a variety of garb are and should be tolerated in the interests of authenticity. Yes, we should protect our devoted and valued servants against undue probes and annoyance. And we should assure them as best we can (and the assurance is leaky at best) that their conversations with their fellows will be treated as confidential. They should not have to fear public humiliation in postverdict litigation seeking to undermine their conscientious best judgment. But let us not exalt these interests to insulate injustice, to bury grievous fault in the critical phase of a trial. Ultimately, such willful blindness only contributes to the public scorn for the competence of ordinary jurors. Some sacrifice must be made in the effort to achieve minimal authenticity of verdicts. Allowing limited challenge may actually enhance earnest and conscientious jury deliberation. Every little bit helps in a system—flawed though it might be—that remains proud of its jury component.

11

SUMMARY

The Fair Tilt

IF ALL GOES WELL in the complex and chancy business of bringing a criminal case from suspicion to verdict, the adversaries will not be evenly endowed. If the defendant is guilty, the prosecution should have an overwhelmingly powerful case. If the charge is brought in error, the defense should have full and convincing means of showing the fallacies in the government's thesis. Since we do not know in any given case which paradigm applies, the trick is to devise a system where advantages are so distributed that the inequalities will inure to the benefit of the deserving party. It's a tall order.

The only method I can design to assess the just distribution of advantages requires that the feature in question be set into the function it serves, and the resulting enhancement appraised. In other words, does the particular empowerment make it easier to do something that the party empowered should do? Equal or unequal, are these prerogatives drawn and assigned in such a way as to keep the system in balance? A system in balance, I imagine, is one that functions efficiently, according to its purpose, with the least wobble and peripheral friction.

Having put it thus, I cannot avoid cobbling up a working model of what I consider the just process. What is just is derived from a set of basic, often unspoken, cultural conventions. These are the propositions that most thoughtful, detached members of a given society tacitly agree constitute the parameters of fairness. Does this sound painfully naive? Who are these thoughtful and detached paragons? you ask. And may we rest assured that paragons always agree, tacitly or not? Not being a philosopher, I am ill-equipped to defend this sort of relative absolutism. But I don't know how else to put it. Law in both its substance and process is, after all, an expression of what we think is right, a collection of aspirational conventions. It is surprisingly difficult, however, to tease them out of the tightly woven fabric of common experience and invisible assumption. And if and when any intrepid soul undertakes to expose and describe these essential strands, there is bound to be disagreement, mocking any claim to universal accord. Undeterred, I must trim sail and beat upwind to reach a conclusion.

Let me start by summarizing in an elegant progression the few propositions I rank as fundamental to fairness, and follow with some explanation of each and the honor or dishonor it receives in America's current system of criminal justice. Let there be no mistake, the term *fundamental fairness* has a well-trodden meaning to constitutional scholars. It means implicit in the constitutional concept of due process. And those many particular precepts governing the criminal process that cannot be read by ordinary mortals in the express language of the Constitution come to us by grace of the superior discernment of our Supreme Court, which is particularly well situated to read the hypertext of the document.

In my catalogue of fundamentals, I will surely include many in the conventional canon. Since I am already out on this doctrinal limb, I will also dub as basic some ideas that are frankly idiosyncratic. As I have argued (but have not yet persuaded the Authorities), I believe these propositions to be fully consistent with—if not actually dictated by—the principles of the Charter and, in many respects, the developed judicial wisdom of interpretation. So I have no apologies for including them in my catalogue, though some will surely raise an eyebrow at such interlopers on sacred ground.

Gratuitous inclusion will be matched by gratuitous exclusion. I make no pretense to inscribe every core tenet of fairness in this basic canon. For example, that (arguably) most fundamental axiom, *likes should be treated alike,* has no place here. As I stipulated at the outset, I am not here concerned with the subject of parity between defendants. Similarly situated defendants should surely be treated alike, but the tilt between players on the same end of the field is simply not my chosen topic. And I hold that prosecution and defense in a criminal case are, in critical respects, different from each other. The equality axiom, therefore, is simply not a note in the chord I have tried to sound with my thesis. So the following paradigm should be read as a personalized set of ethical imperatives specifically applicable between the parties to a criminal litigation.

The just prosecution begins with

1. a well-founded accusation,
   a. charging only offenses previously defined as such,
   b. brought in good faith,
   c. after thorough and detached investigation,
   d. subject to disposition by freely negotiated settlement;

the case proceeds to trial, where

2. it should be pursued vigorously and supported with all available evidence;

thereafter

3. the prosecution evidence should be exposed to skilled and vigorous contention by
   a. evidence,
   b. impeachment, and
   c. argument;

until

4. it either fails or is sustained by the appropriately burdened party;

the verdict based on the evidence

5. should be found by a detached, attentive, and fair-minded fact finder;

and it should thereafter

6. be subject to limited review and affirmance or reversal within the constraint of a justly imposed prohibition on repeated jeopardy.

1. The Well-Founded Accusation

No one should be brought to trial on less than the evidence that it would take to persuade a reasonably prudent person that, unless satisfactorily explained or credibly contradicted, an inference of guilt is warranted. Of course that does not mean that guilt must be certain beyond plausible doubt. That is the standard for conviction. It doesn't even mean that responsibility is more likely than not. That is the civil standard. For criminal accusation the gate is simply that there is sufficient evidence from which a sane juror might conclude the person was guilty. Probable cause, we call it. The Supreme Court, in a 1994 case called *Albright v. Oliver,* declined the invitation to inscribe the right to be prosecuted only on probable cause among the basic entitlements known as "substantive due process," the basic catalogue of fair-trial entitlements. I'm sort of sorry they didn't do so. It certainly seems to me like the essence of fairness. But the Court's reluctance doesn't mean that there is no such right. They made it clear that they merely preferred to lodge that right elsewhere in the Constitution.

In our tradition, we must begin any list of the fundamental tenets with the so-called principle of legality, or *nulla poena* (sometimes *nulla crimen*) *sine lege,* as it is phrased in the familiar Latin maxim. No punishment except according to law. In a liberal democracy such as ours, individual dignity begins with the assurance that our freedom will not be arbitrarily curtailed by the government. The cause for suspending the liberty of a fellow human creature must be the considered choice of fellow citizens that certain clearly defined conduct deserves imprisonment. And this democratically decreed criminality must be published in advance of the conduct in question so that the actor can consider the consequences before engaging in the proscribed conduct. We lawyers seem to be among the last to believe in free will. Without choice, there is no sin; without choice, there is no crime. That is the moral predicate of criminal law. Secret edicts, ex post facto laws, or expeditious or vindictive restraints are the marks of tyranny—that is the essence of the justly revered principle of legality.

Under my breath, I want to add that the criminal laws must themselves be fair, that conduct penalized must be truly offensive, that the punishment decreed must be commensurate with the gravity of the offense, etc. But I hesitate to do so. First, these notions are no part of the venerable principle of legality. But more to the point, I have no litmus for essential fairness of a law or for the proportionality of punishment. To be sure, the Eighth Amendment to our Constitution says punishments shall not be cruel or unusual, but the content of the concept of cruelty is left to the generations to decide and revise eternally. So, too, such important issues as whether assisting a suicide should be criminal cannot be resolved, I fear, by resort to some principle of eternal fairness, but must be grappled with by the democratic process. Is using—or even selling—marijuana "truly offensive"? Should larceny be punished more severely than assault? Is it a crime to attempt to commit a crime that is impossible to complete? I know of no basic tenet of fairness that can resolve any of these old and current controversies, so the issue probably does not belong here among the basic tenets.

It should go without saying that the accusation brought by a public prosecutor should serve only public interests. Private antagonism, political or other, should be banished from the prosecutor's discretionary control board; personal gain or the service of private interests has no place in these decisions. In a word, selective or vindictive prosecution is inconsistent with the authority we have delegated to public officers to choose their targets and name their crimes. The decision to charge should be founded exclusively on careful and thorough investigation, including scrutiny of any leads inconsistent with the hypothesis of culpability. So far, as I read it, the fairness count of our system is high. I hear the rustle of dissent already; even to this point, other scorekeepers will arrive at a different rating, I am sure.

The investigation should also be enabled by a set of tools for prying evidence from reluctant witnesses and digging it out of shadowy, private spaces. I believe covert spying—like electronic searches—should be allowed only on court authorization, though courts have not yet seen the analogy. Once authorized, however, participatory espionage can go as far as the boundaries of entrapment allow. Searches of private places, documents, and conversations by law enforcement people (with court permission) is entirely fair and should (with the help of electronics) be made easier.

When it comes to interrogation of the suspect, I favor a short opportunity for conversation, untrammeled by warnings or advisories of any sort. Thereafter, I would have interrogation conducted in open court, repeatedly if necessary, with the important proviso that the failure of the suspect to respond—like a demonstrably false response—could be taken as a basis for the inference that he was concealing guilty knowledge. It would not be unfair, I think, to reconfigure the shape of investigatory license to emphasize the importance of evidence gathering without infringing on important basic rights of security in person and private spaces, and personal sovereignty over cognitive material.

No critical summary of the American criminal justice system can ignore the overwhelming proportion of the docket disposed of by negotiated guilty pleas. The target of much abuse, plea bargaining—in one form or another—is the mainstay of the process. Professor Stephen Schulhofer, a longtime critic of the prevailing system of resolution, has put it bluntly: "Plea bargaining is a disaster. It can be, and should be, abolished."

It is certainly true that defendants, facing serious and strongly supported charges, are not altogether free-minded when they consider the offer of a reduced charge or sentence in exchange for capitulation. But it is difficult to see their disadvantaged position as an unfair liability. A favorable settlement, induced by the hazardous position in which the evidence places the culprit, can hardly be called an unfairly coerced disposition. I have written about plea bargaining at some length in *Virtual Justice,* and I must resist the temptation to be drawn into debate with Schulhofer (and his battalions). I must simply repeat that although I have misgivings about certain features of the system, I do not regard plea bargaining as oppressive, and find little basis for Schulhofer's preference for the fast, virtually uncontested trial favored in a few jurisdictions like Philadelphia and the Bronx. While dissatisfied in some ways with the bargains they have struck, the majority of defendants who plead guilty do receive some benefit in exchange for their acceptance of culpability. I find it hard to regard them as victims of an unfair process. And court dockets remain crowded with those who choose to put the government to its proof, including—we must assume—a goodly proportion of the wrongly accused, along with those charged on weak evidence.

Nor can it be said that a prosecutor, burdened by the press of the caseload, seeking the cooperation of smaller fish against the larger, or possibly looking at a file that sags with problems of proof, is unfairly cheapening crime by offering a reduction in the penalty decreed by the legislature. Not every case is the most aggravated example of its genre, not every sentence should be the max. It is hardly my task to lay down a set of guidelines for fair negotiations or a schedule of fair discounts. Let me just say that if the prosecutor has fairly charged a supportable crime, the docket is not unduly stressed, and the parties negotiate in good faith, the market can probably be trusted to deliver an acceptable level of justice.

2. Fully Empowered and Vigorously Pursued Prosecution

For a very long part of our history—and, to a certain extent, to this day in other legal systems of common ancestry—criminal charges were brought by the victim or the victim's family. The injury effected by criminal conduct was to a private person who sought to vindicate it by resort to law. In America we broke with this tradition and cut a sharp divide between public and private law. Criminal behavior, which may at the same time amount to a private injury, offends public laws, and public offenses are delegated to public officers to pursue.

In this English colony, we began to replace private prosecution with public responsibility some hundred and thirty years before nationhood. By the middle to latter half of the nineteenth century (as police forces were beginning to appear here as in England), private prosecution was being outlawed altogether in the American states.

Today, private prosecution is generally—though not entirely—disallowed in the United States.

We occasionally see criminal cases followed by civil suits on behalf of the injured party or the victim's family. It is easy to mistake this for a second, private, prosecution, albeit under the reduced standard of proof associated with civil suits: proof by a preponderance of the evidence rather than beyond a reasonable doubt. But what might appear to the ordinary observer as double jeopardy by civil lawsuit is clearly tolerable—indeed, perfectly just—to the lawyer. Accountability under the criminal laws does nothing to redress the injury suffered by the victim and in no way precludes a legal remedy for the private wrong. And "jeopardy" means risk of punishment, not of rendering compensation for damage.

With that possible confusion out of the way, we return to Basic Tenet Number 2. Having delegated to our public prosecutors our ancient prerogative to seek legal vengeance, we demand in exchange a vigorous champion. That means not only a lawyer committed to the energetic development of each case, but one who is prepared justly to claim the confidence of jurors, judges, and the public at large. What that takes is hard to say, but we surely know when it is missing. The curious footnote to this important characteristic of a fair system is that the government's advocate, while exhibiting every show of virtue and confidence to the jury, must take special care to say nothing that might be read as a personal endorsement of the prosecution case or the credibility of the witnesses on whom it relies. That is regarded—with some warrant—as an unfair thumb on the scales.

In addition to energy and unbiased aim, our prosecutor must have access to all probative evidence. Except in the egregious case where "punishing" the prosecution for the grievous transgressions of its law enforcement agent may be appropriate, I do not think the virtue of the court—or the integrity of the system—is enhanced by the partial blinding of the fact finder. Exclusions for constitutional transgressions have doubtless served well in the three decades or so in which they controlled state and federal criminal prosecutions. Police agencies are more professional, more sensitive to the constraints on power required by the dignitary rights of their targets. With this accomplished, I think the time has come to relax these rules from automatic to discretionary, to allow judges to assess whether the interests of justice would be better served by admission or exclusion in a particular case. Fairness to the prosecution dictates, I think, a case-by-case analysis with appropriate weight for the necessitous conditions of the necessitous case.

I have already indicated my preferences for control of investigations into private spaces and conversations, and into the mind of a suspect. Where the investigation is within lawful bounds, the product must be admissible in court. I have growing doubts over the wisdom of converting the trial forum into the mindless enforcement mechanism of such constraints as we deem appropriate on the police-led investigation of a crime. I do not, however, by relegating the matter to sound discretion, mean to consign it to the outer reaches of unenforced legal homilies.

Here is an unavoidable crunch point in the modeling of fairness. As a society, we have decided there are social and personal values more important than the conviction of the guilty, and these may impede the acquisition of evidence of guilt. The easy example is torture. For centuries (particularly in Continental countries) and to this day in many parts of the world, torture was a normal feature of interrogation. If we are worried about unreliable confessions procured by torture, we might easily have a rule that precludes the use in evidence of statements obtained by torture unless corroborated by other evidence. After all, torture does produce some true renditions. But obviously, unreliability is not the only reason we abjure the use of torture in criminal investigations.

Another fairly easy example is our refusal to allow the jury to hear evidence that has been acquired by a groundless intrusion into a private place—say the DEA does a sudden, unannounced midnight sweep of a neighborhood, breaking forcefully into every residence and turning it upside down looking for drugs. Any contraband thus recovered would be excluded though clearly reliable evidence of criminal possession. There are things more important than probative reliability. Government agents arbitrarily intruding on basic personal rights of security with no overriding justification offend values more important than those offended by the criminal behavior proved by the intrusion.

So the easy cases make the point. There are some constraints more highly valued than the free pursuit of the guilty. And insofar as the government's investigation imperils these values without redeeming justification, fairness demands that courts reject the resulting evidence. To this extent, both for its deterrent effect and its symbolic value, most thoughtful Americans today accept evidentiary exclusion as the appropriate response of a just system.

The difficulty comes in trying to identify those redeeming justifications, the factors that, in a particular situation, render rejection of the gain contrary to the broad interest of justice. Degrees of tolerance vary, the balance between competing objectives swings with the beholder.

The Constitution recognizes these flexible and controversial standards by enjoining police searches and seizures, for example, only when they are "unreasonable." Investigation by interrogation has less flexibility, though it is clear that only those self-inculpatory statements that have been "compelled" by the government are excluded. The term has received a generous reading from the Court. And the negative inference from refusal to give an account of oneself has been prohibited under the "right of silence." I am not convinced this is good—or sound—jurisprudence.

Personally, I tend to view truth-defeating exclusions with misgiving. I have said that if I could, I would revise the American exclusionary rule to allow courts, on a case-by-case basis, to make a careful evaluation of degrees of necessity and invasion and exclude where the interests of justice demand. I have also submitted a radical redesign of the interrogation process, substituting open judicial examination for delayed or protracted police questioning, with a logical inference allowed from a suspect's refusal to cooperate.

So I conclude that when it comes to full and vigorous prosecutorial pursuit at trial, our system is not performing as it should. I do not think I cut back on any vital values when I argue that fairness demands greater access to probative evidence and a better chance that all verdicts will be based on a more complete picture. As to virtue, and the use of the adjudicatory forum to instruct law enforcement agents in the demands of the Bill of Rights, I say little (and know little) other than, let's not overdo it at this point in our maturation as a law-respecting government. Cops are always in need of instruction, granted. They need to know, if nothing else, that someone is watching. But just how much instruction they actually receive from the courts today is questionable. Too many courts, too many finely wrought opinions, to many thinly sliced situations, major transmission problems. We would do far better with a cleanly articulated statute for the acquisition of evidence of all sorts, though it left some room for discretion in its application on a case-by-case basis.

3. Subject to Vigorous Contention

Our adversary model contemplates, above all, a full and well-endowed challenge to the prosecution case, mounted by the singly dedicated Champion of the Contrary View. While scorn and derision doubtless have a place in the arsenal of the defense, there is nothing like evidence to contradict the prosecution theory. Here the defense is severely disabled, by license and—often—by resources.

The matter of disparity in resources—the simple matter of having the people and the time to pursue leads, to analyze tactical positions, and to plot strategy—is problematic. I have suggested that the balance of forces is not so grossly or universally skewed as might at first appear. Many defendants have considerably greater resources than the prosecutor. Even those—certainly the vast majority—who have virtually none can command a basic crew of counsel, investigator, and expert and send the bill to the state. I have further ventured that, again contrary to popular perception, legal skill—which is a big item in the resource department—seems to be more or less randomly distributed among government prosecutors, high-fee lawyers, contract defense lawyers, and the ordinary bar available for assignment.

By coincidence, as I write this, I have just been retained as an expert in an indigent defense case, a noncapital homicide tried in a small New England city. The defendant is represented by assigned counsel (whom I have not yet met) but whose papers I have read. I can attest that this lawyer is doing an excellent job with an extremely subtle legal contention. It's thorough, it's creative, it's well presented. I have worked with the gold-plated criminal bar on occasion, and I am confident that no defendant could pay for a better defense. My fee is considerably lower than I would normally charge; I'm sure the lawyer's is too. But neither of us would decline to take the assignment at whatever rates the state is paying.

Apart from resources, there is the evident imbalance in legal license. The defense boasts nothing comparable to the government's authority to pry evidence from the uncooperative, to go into private spaces—legally—look around and take what they need. It's a comparative disadvantage of major proportions, no doubt about it. The disparity is not, however, unfair. It is not unfair because it is the product—the necessary product—of the differing roles of prosecution and defense. The affirmative obligations of the state, as the surrogate for the injured (as well as for the rest of us law abiders who have been indirectly offended), to bring the responsible predators and malefactors to justice demands that they be given the authority to pursue evidence. The defensive position, while often fortified by counteroffensive, is essentially responsive. Investigatory license is reduced by the reduction of responsibility for initiation.

This will surely not satisfy those who argue that it is not enough to assert that the government's one-sided access to evidence serves its unilateral responsibility to make the case. A purpose enjoying equal functional importance, the argument would run, is the defendant's capacity to make a case to contradict the government's. There is considerable merit to this argument. In an adversary system of controlled contention like ours—wholly apart from considerations of a level playing field—the common interest is best served by enabling the contending parties to produce before the neutral fact finder the most complete substantiation for their opposed positions that diligent investigation can turn up. It is false, in some light, to rest content on the thesis of a single burdened party when, as a practical matter, defense is not always a passive, responsive position.

While the Constitution does not expressly recognize a defense right to adduce evidence in court, there is a strong suggestion of it in the Sixth Amendment, which grants the defendant the right "to have compulsory process for obtaining witnesses in his favor." By the late eighteenth century, the right of the defense to introduce proof was also implicit in the Fifth Amendment's guarantee of due process of law. But important as it is, the right to prove exculpatory or mitigating facts is readily—and often severely—curtailed.

In 1992, James Allen Egelhoff was camping and collecting mushrooms in the Yaak region of northwestern Montana. He met and befriended two people, Roberta Pavola and John Christenson, who were doing the same. On Sunday, July 12, the three sold mushrooms they had gathered and spent the rest of the day drinking and partying in and around the town of Troy. The trio left a party sometime after 9 P.M., bought some beer at 9:20, and continued drinking. At about midnight, sheriffs responding to reports of a drunken driver, made a grisly discovery. They found Christenson's station wagon stuck in a ditch. In the front seat were Pavola and Christenson, each dead of a single gunshot wound to the head. In the rear Egelhoff was sprawled, shouting obscenities. An hour later, his blood-alcohol level was measured at 0.36 percent, more than twice the level of intoxication that would render the average person visibly dysfunctional. On the floor near the brake pedal was Egelhoff's revolver with two spent cartridges. Egelhoff had gunshot residue on his hands.

At his trial for murder—"deliberate homicide," as Montana calls it—defendant was allowed to allude to his intoxication (his defense was that the murders must have been the work of a stranger because he, the defendant, had been too drunk to point a gun). But the jury was instructed, in accordance with Montana law, that they could not consider the defendant's drunkenness on the issue of his state of mind. State of mind was a critical issue. The law of the Montana specifies that a person is guilty of deliberate homicide only when he kills another with the purpose of effecting death, or consciously aware that his conduct will cause that result. The jury convicted, Egelhoff got eighty-four years.

The Supreme Court of Montana reversed. They reasoned that Egelhoff had a due-process right to have the jury consider all the evidence relevant to an element of the crime charged, as his mental impairment surely was. When the Supreme Court got the case in 1996, they divided 4–4, with Justice Ginsburg delivering the concurrence (on her own theory) that yielded a majority to reverse the high court of the State of Montana. In all, five separate opinions were filed. It's worth a brief digression to explore how the minority speaking for the Court, under the leadership of Justice Scalia, arrive at their conclusion that the state may limit defense access to vital evidence without offense to the due-process clause.

At the top, Justice Scalia notes that Egelhoff wisely declines to defend the opinion of the Montana Supreme Court that he is entitled by the due-process clause to present for jury consideration all relevant evidence on an element of the offense charged. The rules of evidence, for example, limit the right to introduce defense evidence just as they curtail the prosecution. Scalia reminds us that only a few years earlier, the Court had repeated their consistent approval of rules that preclude important defense evidence for failure to observe procedural rules. In that 1991 case, *Michigan v. Lucas,* the U.S. Supreme Court—again reversing the high state court—held that the Sixth Amendment was not necessarily offended when a state trial judge, in a rape prosecution, refused to allow the defendant to introduce evidence of a prior sexual relationship with the victim (as the state law allowed) because he had failed to give advance notice of his intention to do so (as the statute required).

Scalia goes on to note that states are largely free to set their own procedures, subject only to the concern of the due-process clause with the fundamentals. Historical practice is the primary guide to the fundamentals. Going back to the early days of British and American common law, he recites that voluntary intoxication was never considered an excuse and, according to some notable contemporary commentators, it was treated as an aggravating factor. Not only was drunkenness rejected as an excuse, the common law did not even recognize it as a factor going to the mental element of intention. In the nineteenth century, however, many courts allowed evidence of intoxication on the aggravating element of a specific intent to accomplish a particular object—the intent to kill, for example, in a prosecution for deliberate homicide. But this rule has never become so "deeply rooted as to be ranked as fundamental," and hence Montana's statute cannot be said to be contrary to due process. Justice Scalia concludes with some words suggesting approval of the rule that the defendant is entitled to claim no benefit from his own boozing.

The upshot is that even when it comes to introducing evidence at trial that might excuse, justify, or mitigate culpability, the defense enjoys no unrestricted license. Indeed, his access to proof may be sharply and devastatingly curtailed by local evidentiary and procedural rules. It is something of a jolt to discover that the Constitution tolerates the exclusion of evidence of innocence from the jury's consideration. And it is well to remember that an equal number of justices, signing on to Justice O'Connor's dissent, found a violation of due process in the removal "from the jury's consideration a category of evidence relevant to determination of a mental state where that mental state is an essential element of the offense that must be proved beyond a reasonable doubt." Justice Ginsburg, the vote that tipped the scale, did not see the issue as a due-process question at all but rather as part of the state's prerogative to define crimes—here as a crime committed by any person, drunk or sober.

This split, in effect, returns the question to us. Is it fair to limit defense proof for failure to give timely notice? Or because the state has chosen to align itself with those who do not regard voluntary intoxication as an excuse of any degree regardless of how it might impair cognitive capacity? Or shall we, in the search for fairness, be satisfied if the restriction does not transgress the outer limits we call due process? And if that is our litmus, is it true that neither of these restrictions offends the basic canons of fairness?

I find this a really hard call. You may well call it differently, but my inclination is to say that failure to give timely notice of intent to introduce evidence like an alibi (remember *Wardius v. Oregon?*) or prior sexual intimacy should not preclude such evidence in the absence of a showing of actual prejudice suffered by the prosecution. I don't know whether I would call the exclusion a violation of due process, but if that's what it takes to get the evidence admitted notwithstanding the omission, I'll go for it. But on the voluntary intoxication evidence, I find myself with Justice Scalia and his group. If on this controversial question, a state chooses to align itself with venerable jurisprudence and insist that, regardless of relevance, self-intoxication is neither excuse nor mitigation, I cannot see that the preclusion is repugnant to basic fairness.

So from the Court's recent deep and bitter division, we must conclude that the dictates of fairness in the matter of allowing trial proof by the defense are not clearly etched. And insofar as the law is law, it does not fully accord with the dictates of fairness—at least for some of us.

In addition to the matter of limits on the use of defense evidence already in hand, are there unfair disabilities in the defense powers of acquisition? There is certainly a vivid disparity between the devices available to the defense and the prosecution for prying evidence out of private enclaves and reluctant repositories. Yet it is difficult to imagine a defendant equipped with full powers of pretrial investigation enjoyed by the prosecution—search and eavesdrop warrants, custodial interrogation, immunity power, and the rest. How would it work? By what agencies would the process be executed, to what investigative panels would the data be produced? And even if we can dream up a regime in which the defendant is so armed, we would have to devise some parallel statutory constraints on defense delving and probing, since the Constitution restrains government power only. The excursion is entertaining, but a fantasy only, the harmless concoction of imagination playing in the never-never-land of The Clean Slate.

Rest assured, we are not about to witness the private forces of the defense, emboldened by public license, descending on the startled community to mine for fresh evidence. Here, in the territory we actually inhabit, the government remains the burdened party, and the only party empowered to gather evidence from uncooperative custodians. At the same time, the government remains the only party effectively constrained by law to protect the private interests of those who would decline assistance. Rather than indulge flights of fancy, we will continue to debate the entitlement of the defense to a secondhand share in the yield of the prosecutor's lode.

When it comes to secondhand information, the defense is accorded considerably broader rights of discovery than the prosecution. Most notably, the defendant has the right to learn anything the prosecution knows that might help the defense or undermine the credibility of the government's witnesses. This trick is not in the government's repertoire. Still, there are limits which some argue shut the defense out of the information it needs most—the identity of a supposed government informer, for example, or the expected testimony of a vital government witness.

There are also those who think discovery is too generous in that it enables the wily defense to construct a perjured story to fit within the cracks of the prosecution case. While I cannot adjudicate these conflicting claims, I have proposed a mild form of restriction to hold the defendant to a broad theory of defense adopted before learning of the details of the prosecution case. I have suggested that, instead of the customary "plea" in response to a charge, the defendant should be required to file an "answer" that would commit him to a position on the facts. But the idea is deeply flawed and probably would not work. The only "theory" the defense need maintain in our adversary regime is "not proved." And that position implies no commitment to any alternative factual scenario. Perhaps this dispute on the issue of defense discovery between the too-much and the not-enough factions can be simply disregarded as a standoff on the fields of fairness. That's my inclination.

In a more serious vein, I think it does make a difference in the ability of the defense to meet the prosecution case with proof, whether the defendant himself is preparing for trial in jail or on the street. No one could persuasively argue that the remedy is to have all accused malefactors and predators loose on the streets working, in their way, to improve their chances of acquittal. Perhaps with ankle bracelets and such high-tech replacements for the bail bond, we might hope for a somewhat improved release ratio. But to me these palliatives only thinly cover the rotten core of the current bail release system. I have suggested a general reformulation, modeled on the Federal Bail Reform Act. In state courts—home to the overwhelming bulk of criminal adjudication—we desperately need a radical overhaul of the whole bail system, from underlying assumptions to operational criteria. If nothing else, we should try to improve fairness by honestly acknowledging and effectuating the valid purposes of pretrial detention, while at the same time making certain that all who need not be held are released, regardless of their financial ability to meet the monetary security fixed by judicial whim.

In addition to defense by evidence, let us not slight the important tools of discrediting the prosecution and arguing freely from the gaps in the prosecution case. Here the defense enjoys a considerable advantage. But it's difficult terrain to navigate. The ethical imperatives are confused. While conscientious dedication to truth might impede counsel's devotion to her client's interests, she must resist the temptation (if any be detectable) to lend her forensic efforts to the advancement of a verdict consonant with historical events. She is not the prosecutor's investigator, she is not a juror. In all but the rare case of an innocent client, the defendant's lawyer must strive to make the true appear false and the false appear true. Wherever her client's interest requires, counsel must not allow the conscientious commands of sincerity or candor to deter impeachment of a prosecution witness or to dampen argument based on distortion of the evidence.

There are limits on defense counsel's tortuous affair with truth.

They seem to be centered on the knowing use of perjury. I don't believe they inhibit the ethical license to withhold harmful evidence or to argue contrary to sincere belief. As I have indicated, I have a lot of trouble with this idea, but I can find no principled way to resist the logic of it within our adversary system.

4. Sustained by the Burdened Party

The so-called presumption of innocence, which most Americans would rate among the essentials of a just design, expresses nothing but the obligation imposed upon the charging authority to establish guilt as alleged. Uncertainty, under this design, always accrues to the benefit of the defense. There is nothing unfair about this inequality; it epitomizes the American idea of justice. But there may be something to the point that it hardly compensates the defense for its disadvantages in other areas. Moreover, there is probably some truth in the observation that the legal presumption of innocence is at odds with the popular presumption that the smoke of a prosecution is itself some evidence of the fire of culpability.

Be that as it may, the essential presumption of innocence lays securely on the shoulders of the prosecution the risk of equivocal evidence. I have noted that despite the smoke = fire counterpresumption, juries do occasionally acquit people they believe are probably guilty because they think the burden was not met. So it is probably worth something in the list of advantages, even if not quite so much as its catalogue price. But there has been some slippage in the secure location of the burden. Only the core elements of the crime are the unshiftable burden of the prosecution; defenses may be assigned to the defendant to establish if claimed.

Relieving the prosecutor of the burden to prove the negative of these defenses surely reduces the advantage bestowed on the defense by the presumption of innocence. But of course it is not necessarily unfair on that account. Insofar as certain defenses are not the contradiction of a core element of the crime—as the defense of alibi might be—it is not unjust to place upon the defense the burden of persuasion regarding extraordinary facts peculiarly within his knowledge—such as insanity, self-defense, entrapment, or duress.

It really goes to one's conception of culpability. If guilt implies a sane person, acting in the exercise of free will, and without the urgent necessity of protecting himself or others from imminent harm, the government should retain the obligation of proving these constituents, along with the more conventional core elements of the crime. But if those features of human action may realistically be presumed in the ordinary case, the prosecution's burden might be confined to the establishment of the conduct defined as criminal, together with the culpable mental state. Increasingly, the latter seems to be the choice of fairness. And this election, incapable of spreading beyond a few special defenses, does not seem to me unjust. So in these limited circumstances, the prosecution shares—and rightfully shares—in the benefits of presumptions to carry them across the abyss of unconvincing evidence.

5. Verdicts Found by Qualified Fact Finders

We cannot, of course, call an accurate verdict an element of fundamental fairness much as we might like to. Truth is the irretrievably elusive factor in this business, and the best we can hope for is a process that maximizes the likelihood of an outcome that conforms reasonably closely to the historical facts. But that—the optimal process—is surely one of the fundamental things we have in mind when we call the system fair.

Proud of our English legal heritage, we have always assumed that the best fact finder would be a jury of lay people having neither knowledge nor inclination concerning the parties or the issues of the lawsuit. Carried away by enthusiasm for this old Brit invention, the Founders even ensconced the right to a jury trial in civil cases in the Seventh Amendment—one of only four of the many rights announced in the Bill of Rights that were never made binding on state courts. In criminal cases, the right to a jury is assured by the Sixth Amendment (which is binding on the states), but what is a "jury" empowered to return an operative verdict?

I have elsewhere wondered whether the method of selection of our juries, combined with the dubious capacity of jurors to discern the truth in the artificial setting of a courtroom, should undermine our confidence that juries can be trusted to return accurate verdicts. Though it is a favorite of mine, I do not rehearse this aria in these pages. Here I am concerned with the irrationality of verdicts insofar as they may be the product of improper influences on the jurors, concealed incapacity, misconduct, and gross misunderstanding of the case. And, specifically, I turn this concern to the examination of advantages accruing to the defense from the rule precluding postverdict inquiry into the rationality of the verdict. Even the narrow allowance for defense impeachment of an adverse verdict finds no counterpart on the prosecution side; the double-jeopardy clause bars a prosecution challenge to a verdict of acquittal though procured by outright corruption.

With some difficulty, I have arrived at a position that the integrity of verdicts is more important to the system than the interests of finality and juror protection that animate the anti-impeachment rule. I have even made so bold as to suggest that the iron grille of double jeopardy should yield to a prosecution challenge in the extreme situation where the purported verdict of acquittal was nullified by corruption, intimidation, or disqualification of a juror. It is only fair, I have argued, that the prosecution be allowed to retry a case where the "verdict of acquittal" was a sham.

6. Jeopardy and Review by Appeal

There is no constitutional right to appeal. The Founders, apparently, thought a fair trial was enough. Still, every American jurisdiction provides at least one level of review, and the Supreme Court has held that, once provided, access to appellate review may not be unfairly limited. And a good thing, too. Our criminal jurisprudence encourages an intense hunt for game as the appellate hawks comb the dense undergrowth of the vast trial record in search of points for appeal (stretching the imagination, along with the aerial vision, of the reading segment of the bar). And the error derby keeps our trial courts in line and generates what we call "law"—the opinions of our appellate courts. So one would have to say today that the right to have a superior court look over the rulings and other legal issues arising at trial is a fundamental aspect of the process.

Only the legal issues, however. The appellate court is not a second jury (at least in theory) that will review the facts. The one point that appellant cannot argue on the appeal (although it is frequently ill-concealed in the subtext) is that the defendant is, in fact, innocent.

This comes as a surprise to the uninitiated; one would think that true guilt or innocence would be a perpetual concern of the courts. Not so. The firm reply of a superior court when appellant hints that he is actually innocent is always, "The jury has spoken on that, and their voice is final." Well, not quite final. There are three or four extraordinary tapers that might reignite the ultimate issue normally extinguished by the verdict. Postjudgment motions may be made by the defense to the trial court to vacate the judgment. Many of these motions, once called by their ancient name, the writ of error *coram nobis,* are directed at basic flaws like the jurisdiction of the trial court over the matter, the credentials of the prosecutor, or the competence of defense counsel. But postjudgment motions also include a few things that might be seen as related to guilt. A judgment will be set aside, for example, on proof that the prosecutor knowingly introduced false or perjured evidence. Or that the defense has recently discovered evidence that, had it been known and introduced at trial, might have changed the verdict. Or that since the judgment, a vital prosecution witness has recanted her testimony, and the current version is more likely true than the testimonial version.

The other remedy for conviction of an innocent is executive clemency. Exercising one of the few prerogatives of absolute monarchs that survive into our era, the chief executive of the state or federal government has completely discretionary authority to grant a pardon, or to reduce the sentence ordered by the court and required by law. Of course, clemency is rarely granted; pardons are even more unusual, and pardons on the grounds of innocence are museum pieces.

The normal means for challenging a judgment of conviction is by appeal. As I say, on appeal, the verdict can be upset only if it was founded on an error of law. Errors committed by the trial judge (errors allowing improper adverse evidence or precluding lawful, helpful proof) as well as prejudicial excesses of the prosecutor (such as vouching for his witnesses' credibility) are reviewable—and a verdict procured thereby may be reversible. But only a verdict of conviction or a motion setting aside a verdict of conviction is reviewable.

Our old friend, the principle of double jeopardy, bestows on the defense not only protection against repeated efforts by the government to convict him, or to multiply punishments for a single transgression, but also against government efforts to procure a judgment free of serious error by setting aside a flawed acquittal. In effect, this protection bestows on the defense the unreviewable license to seek the first acquittal by any device that works. Again, this offends principles of fairness not because it is one-sided but because a well-founded premise is converted into an invitation to unjust manipulation.

I feel no cerebral dislocation in construing the first jeopardy as continuing through appeal to a final disposition of the case in a reversible error–free trial. That would allow appeals from acquittals and, upon reversal, retrial—all within a single jeopardy. After all, the barrier of double jeopardy is not insuperable. The defendant, by taking an appeal, forgoes his objection to a retrial, and mistrials requiring a fresh start may be granted on manifest necessity even without defense consent. The reversal of acquittals infected by reversible error would fit comfortably with these special cases of extended jeopardy. But it will never happen.

While awaiting the day that will never dawn (or "meanwhile," as we pragmatists like to say), we might wipe that East Coast smirk off our faces and take California seriously for once. California has, it appears, relaxed all traditional barriers to interlocutory appeals under the ancient writ by which an appellate court could, at any stage of the proceeding, order a trial court to do what it was required by law to do. They call it a writ of mandate; the more traditional jurisdictions probably still call it the writ of mandamus.

The astonishing thing about California practice is the tolerance for interrupting a trial in progress to avert an error in the bud. It gives the prosecutor a chance for a review of errors that he would otherwise have to swallow. It gives the defense a shot at averting errors that might be deemed subreversible. And apparently, not only are the interruptions tolerated at the trial level, but the appellate court will expeditiously instruct trial judges on all manner of trial rulings that might constitute errors of law—and that covers a wide range of mistakes.

CONCLUSION, IF ANY

AS WE CONCLUDE THIS trek through some of the exotic regions—along with the mundane—in the land of criminal law enforcement, we might wonder whether we have fully addressed the question with which we set out: Is the brand of justice we deliver fair to both sides? Fair enough to support pride? It is, I realize, rather late in these pages to ask, but have we at least settled on a working definition of what we mean by *fair*? At least, are we agreed that we do not mean what sports fans would consider fair—that is, an evenly matched contest? Playing on a level playing field?

I suppose one might say that, absent gross oppression, what is fair in the criminal justice system—as in life in general—is what is familiar. As we grow accustomed to the way we do things, we find it harder and harder to imagine doing them differently. And fairness is found in the satisfaction of seeing the process work again as experience has taught us to expect. By this logic, it is hardly surprising that—from our present vantage—our system looks agreeably fair. After all, things generally work out pretty much as expected. What more can you ask?

There's a good deal of weight to that notion. Whether it's the delivery of medical service, or a government of checks and balances, or the workings of the courts, many people would say that the way it is is pretty much the way it should be. But the obvious trouble with this fairness-as-familiarity thesis is that so many people see one aspect or another of our customary procedure as grievously unfair. So I fear that we cannot in good faith encourage contentment in the dubious by pointing to the general level of contentment among the contented.

I have tried to argue that fairness can be measured by the fit of form to function. Tedious as the project may be, each challenged item, every facet of the process in which one or the other party enjoys—or is said to enjoy—an advantage or suffer a disadvantage, must be examined in terms of the function it serves in the overall enterprise, and criticized according to how well or ill it serves that function.

Having adopted a method, I found myself trying to calibrate it. No gift of humility is required to see that this is a matter of judgment on which well-intentioned people might widely differ. Does a defendant enjoy an undue advantage in the license of counsel to distort or conceal on his behalf? Is the prosecution unfairly divesting itself of burdens to disprove defenses? Should the prosecution be entitled to pursue a case to a disposition free of serious error? Or is the notion of retrying a defendant, once acquitted, repugnant to basic canons of fairness? These and a host of other dilemmas bedevil any pretense of a definitive conclusion.

And, even where I think I perceive a remediable fault, I hesitate to prescribe a remedy. For me, any notion of reform suggested by the misfit feature must be appraised by some sort of reality gauge. You worry about the efficiency or the truth-seeking efficacy of the adversary system? You have qualms about the supposedly superior faculties of the jury to discern historical truth from the artificial data parade in the courtroom? You wonder whether the unbridled license of the news media to publish virtually anything—and as often and loud as they please—injects a subtle poison into the adjudicatory process? I'm with you, but fifty years ago, Justice Jackson sounded the right note of caution to the would-be reformers. Writing for the Supreme Court about the "archaic, paradoxical, and . . . compromise[d]" law of character evidence, "by which an irrational advantage to one side is offset by a poorly reasoned counterprivilege to the other," Jackson warned, "To pull one misshapen stone out of the grotesque structure is more likely simply to upset its present balance between adverse interests than to establish a rational edifice" (*Michelson v. United States* [1948]). With this caution firmly in mind, I have nevertheless pointed out a few misshapen stones that might be extracted from the adversary structure—and replaced by better-crafted masonry.

But despite my critical stance—to say nothing of an academic career of relentless flaw finding, I suppose that (to some extent) I too am prey to the fallacy of familiarity. For all in all, when day is done, I must say it seems to me that the American system for the delivery of criminal justice, while tilted in many respects, is not out of balance in that, in the main, it embodies a fair distribution of license and limits to the parties, an allocation that closely corresponds to their differing functions in the process. It is, in other words, tolerably fair.

My qualifiers in the preceding sentence indicate that I am far from sanguine that the system works as well as it might. Justice is a delicate business and justice in the criminal process is particularly fraught with hazards. But with some imagination and a dose of courage, we might attend to some of the faults that today impair the system. I am not optimistic that the major impediments to justice—the adversary mode of investigation and presentation, and reliance for resolution on the lay jury—will be, can be, fixed. But within the basic design of our inherited mode of adjudication, much can be done to construct a process that even more closely approximates the elusive dictates of fairness.

INDEX

absentia, trial of a defendant in, 167

accuracy of verdict, interest of prosecutor and defense counsel, 20

accusation, process of, 34

acquittal, false judgments of, 255

acquittal of the innocent, enhancing the likelihood of, 147

adaptive perjury, as argument against full defense discovery, 96; incidence of, 97

adverse counterweight, defense counsel as, 242

aggravating factors in culpability, 159

aggressive prosecution, the power of initiation as, 56

Agonistic parity, 16

Ake v. Oklahoma, 75; as Magna Carta of defense investigative entitlement, 80

Albright v. Oliver, 64, 282

allegations of indictment, contrasted with defense story, 40

Allen, Woody, 167

Alschuler, Professor Albert, 203, 258

ambush, trial by, 92

answer to charges, contrasted with plea, 40, 100

Apodaca v. Oregon, 145

appeals, by prosecution allowed, 223; by defense, 303

Armstrong, United States v., 51

arrest, street discretion in charging, 35

attorney-client privilege, as shielding leads, 246

autrefois acquit, as antecedent of double jeopardy, 221

Babcock, Barbara, 4

Bail, where wealth disparity counts, 166; why defendants are in jail in lieu of, 169; recognizance as alternative to, 170

Bail Reform Act of 1984, federal, 171, 177

"Balance of Advantage," 5, 21

Baldus Study, 24

Beale, Sara, 116
benefit of the doubt on matters of fact and of law, 234
Benton v. Maryland overruling *Palko v. Connecticut*, 227
Bissell, Nicholas, Jr., 171
Black, Justice Hugo, 75, 227, 230
Blockburger v. United States, 229
Brady doctrine, 91
Brady v. Maryland, 90
Brennan, Justice William, 5, 110, 228
burden of proof, unequal but fair, 9; *de facto*, 84; shifting, 149, 151; and the option of concealment, 237
burdens and presumptions as the solution to the rational quandary, 143
bureaucracy, a good word for, 71
Burger, Chief Justice Warren, 122

California, open and mutual discovery in, 107; "writ of mandate," 233
Cardozo, Justice Benjamin, 28, 81, 202, 226
Chambers v. Mississippi, 129
charging decisions, review of, 34; prosecutor's discretion in street arrests, 36; prosecutor-initiated cases, 36; adversary sharing of, 43; victim-initiated, 43; collegial sharing, 44
Code of Professional Responsibility, 240; EC 7–13, 241; 243; DR 7–102(A)(6), 249; EC 7–26, 250
Commack, Mark, 262
concealment and dissimulation: defense advantages, 236
"conduct that shocks the conscience," 29
conviction, false verdicts of, 256
crack cocaine, disproportionate prosecution of African-Americans for, 51
credence, empirical studies regarding, 141

death penalty, 57; quirky features of law in New York, 60

defense counsel, obligation to truth, 138
defenses, variety of, 158
"dignitary interest" as justification for exclusionary rule, 197
Dioguardi, John, 262
disclosure, by the defense, limited but obligatory, 106; expansion of, 237
discovery, 86; "open files," 93; reciprocal, 102
discretion, internal controls on prosecutors', 46; judicial review for abuse of, 46; unguided, the virtue of, 68; regulation of by rule making, 68; corruption of, 187; as legal lawlessness, 212
disparity of resources, Supreme Court's concern with, 75
Dixon, United States v., 229
double jeopardy, 145, 218; provision in the Fifth Amendment, 222; by impeachment of a verdict of acquittal, 267
Douglas, Justice William O., 91
dual-sovereignty rule as "exception" to double jeopardy, 227, 229
due process as fair trial, 4, 26

economic disparities, criminal justice as a manifestation of, 162
Egelhof, James Allen, 292
Eighth Amendment, U.S. Constitution, 179; meaning of excessive bail provision thereof, 180
elemental shuffle, limit upon, 153
elements defenses and sentence factors, distribution thereof, 153
entrapment, 48, 53; subjective and objective theories of, 54; as a check on charging discretion, 56
"Equal Justice under Law" as cruel hoax, 7; as requiring a level playing field for adversaries, 75
equal protection, selective prosecution as a question of, 50; for indigent defendants, 75

evidence, illegally acquired, defendants' control over, 191

executive clemency, 303

executive prerogative, advantage of, 33

expert assistance, defendants' entitlement to, 80

facts, prosecutors' advantage in digging for, 73; recitation of to support legal conclusion, 76

fairness as evenly matched combatants, 4; as symmetry and as experience, 8; in the hands of the parties, 16; as the product of "market" forces. 17; universal precepts of, 22; as familiarity, 305

false statements by lawyers, ethical constraints on, 41

Federal Rules of Criminal Procedure, Rule 26.2, 105; Rule 16, 105

Federal Rules of Evidence, Rule 410, 10; Rule 607, 133; Rule 606(b), 265, 274

Fifth Amendment, right of indictment by grand jury in, 62

financial resources, of defense and prosecution compared, 162

Frankfurter, Justice Felix, 26, 124

Fuhrman, Mark, as image of the racist cop, 114

Furman v. Georgia, 58

General Electric v. Joiner, 210

Gershman, Bennett, 5, 33, 42

Ginsburg, Justice Ruth Bader, 293

Goldkamp, John S., 173

Goldstein, Abraham, 5

"good faith exception" to exclusionary rule, 211

government as battalion of liars and incompetents, 118

Grady v. Corbin, 228

grand jury, investigation before, 37; prosecutor as counsel to, 38; as check on power of initiation, 60, 65

Green v. United States, 227

Gregg v. Georgia, 58

Griffin v. California, 202, 205

Griffin v. Illinois, 75

Hand, Judge Learned, 111

"harmless error," 124, 224

Harris, New York v., 98

"heat of passion," as mitigation, 150

Hickman v. Taylor, 248

Hinckley, John, 152, 158

house arrest, electronic monitors as enforcing, 171; as alternative to bail, 171

hung jury, presumption of innocence and, 144

immunity, 37; defense power to confer, 84

impeachment of verdict, by juror, impermissibility of, 257

impeachment use of excluded evidence, 98

indictment, 39; by grand jury, state right to, 62

inequality and unfairness, 18

initiation, as essential to role of prosecutor, 19

inquisitorial alternative to the adversary system, 61, 99

insanity, shift of burden of proof with regard to, 152

isometric freeze, product of excessive checking and balancing, 42

Izazaga, People v., 108

Jackson, Justice Robert, 307

Jencks rule of discovery, 90

Johnson v. Louisiana, 145

Johnson v. Oklahoma, 80

Joiner, General Electric v., 210

judicial selection, as a critical factor, 214

juge d'instruction, contrasted with grand jury, 60; American magistrate as, 63; 99

jury deliberations sealed, 258

jury misbehavior, before verdict, 260

jury predisposition, presumed shift in, 114; theories explaining, 116; empirical evidence of, 117

Kennedy, Randall, 23, 25

lawyering skills, random appearance of, 74; balance of, 163
legality, principle of, 213, 283
liberal democratic credo, the criminal trial as testing grounds of, 8
Lilburne, John, 203
Lucas, Michigan v., 294

magistrates' hearing as opportunity for bootleg discovery, 63
Magna Carta, as origin of due process, 26
"malice aforethought" as element of murder, 150
"manifest necessity," justification for unrequested mistrial by, 220
Mansfield, Lord, 262
Manual, Department of Justice, Chapter 27, 69
Mapp v. Ohio, 196
Marshall, Justice Thurgood, 76; 80, 88, 106, 264
Martin v. Ohio, 152
material elements of a crime, shift of burden regarding, 149; contained in "core definition" of, 153
McClesky v. Kemp, 24
McMillan, Dynel v. Pennsylvania, 153
metaphor, theater as, 2; sports as, 3
Mezzanatto, United States v., 10
Michelson v. United States, 307
Miranda rules, 200
mistrial, motion for, 217
Model Rules of Professional Conduct, Rule 3.4(e), 126, 241
Mulaney v. Wilbur, 149

National Commission on State Courts, study of effectiveness of counsel by, 165

natural law, 28
"nature and cause" of an accusation, to be disclosed to the accused, 94
nemo tenetur seipsum accusare, 203
news media as guardians of public values, 66
Nobles, United States v., 103
notice of alibi, as violation of attorney-client privilege, 246
nulla poena sine lege, 283

objection as means for preserving error for review, 124
O'Connor, Justice Sandra Day, 260, 295
orangutans, stipulated trial by, beyond the power of parties, 16

Palko v. Connecticut, 202, 226
Parker v. Gladden, 264
parties to criminal trial, unlike parties to civil action, 19
Patterson v. New York, 151
perjury, prosecution for as a means of keeping defendants honest, 99
"plain error," reviewable without objection, 124
Posner, Judge Richard, 134, 136
Powell, Justice Lewis, 24, 50, 104, 129
prescriptive alternatives to the exclusionary rule, 194
presumption in legal parlance, 142; and proof, 143; moral value of, 147
presumption of credence, prosecution entitled to, 138
presumption of guilt, 113, 140, 148
presumption of innocence, 119, 144; how it's working, 148
preventive detention, constitution hurdles to, 178
private prosecution, 43, 286
professional detachment, as inherited from English practice, 127
professional virtue, precious image of, 66

propensity, legitimate issue in entrapment only, 53

prosecutor, as counsel to grand jury, 38; superior investigative resources of, 74

"queen for a day," 14

racism, the persistent toxin of, 23

Rankin, Anne, 173

Reagan, Ronald, attempted assassination of, 152

reasonable doubts of eleven of twelve jurors, no acquittal on, 144

recognizance, release on, as alternative to bail, 170

Rehnquist, Justice William, 77, 179

resources for the development of evidence, defendants' deprivation of, 74, 82; adequate for major criminals, 82; indigents' access to, 83; those with modest assets are most deprived, 83; lack of as affecting outcome, 83

responsive role, advantages of, 32

reversible errors, 216

"right to silence," nowhere in the Constitution, 202

Rochin v. United States, 26, 55

Rothwax, Judge Harold, 97

Salerno, Anthony, 178

Scalia, Justice Antonin, 229, 294

Scott, Judge Thomas E., studies of effectiveness of bail reform by, 186

Scott, United States v., 268

Schulhofer, Stephen, 285

search and seizure, snarled law of, 197

selective prosecution, defense of, 48

self-defense, defense of, shift of burden of proof with regard to, 152

sentence disparities correlating with race, inevitable part of system, 24

Single, Eric W., 173

Sixth Amendment to Constitution, as ordnance of defense, 20; ingredients of,

94; proper scope of the right to counsel under, 207; trial by jury under, 263; right to adduce evidence under, 292

skepticism, healthy, contrasted with disposition to reject prosecution case, 119; and the presumption of credence, 139

social science, contribution of, 172

"Spiteful Juror, Revenge of the," 272

sports, as metaphor for criminal trials, 3

sports ethic, fairness as, 4

Stack v. Boyle, 178

standards, articulation of, for the charging choice, 67; as stimulus to contention, 68; benefits of, 70

Standards of Criminal Justice of the American Bar Association, Prosecution Function, Standard 3–5.7(b), 241; Defense Function, Standard 4–7.6(b), 241, 254

stare decisis, 199

subpoena, power of, to compel defense evidence, 84

Tanner v. United States, 263

Terry v. Ohio, 196

theater, criminal trial as, 2

Thomas, Justice Clarence, 10, 19

trial, prospect of as deterrent to reckless accusation, 64

truth, ethical obligation of defense counsel to respect, 97

Vaise v. Deleval, 262

verdicts, rotten, immune from challenge, 257

Vidmar, Neil, 116

Virtual Justice, 208, 285

"voucher rule," as bar to impeachment of parties' own witnesses, 129, applied against prosecutors, 136

vouching for the credibility of witnesses, by prosecutors, 120, 134; by defense counsel, 126

Waite, David Alan, 50
Waite v. United States, 50
waivability, 9
Wardius v. Oregon, 87, 295
Warren, Chief Justice Earl, 200
Wheeler, Gerald and Carol, 173
Williams, Glanville, 260

Williams v. Florida, 109
Winship, In re, 144, 150
work product, as exempt from discovery, 104, 248

Young, Billy, United States v., 122